MW00830777

Piracy and Policy in the Americas:

1775-1865

A Short History

Josh Milner

ISBN 978-1-62806-070-6

Library of Congress Control Number 2015949206

Published by Salt Water Media, LLC
29 Broad Street, Suite 104
Berlin, Maryland 21811
www.saltwatermedia.com

The images on the front cover are Sloop *Providence*, oil painting by W. Nowland Van Powell courtesy of the Naval History and Heritage Command; Walking the Plank by Howard Pyle; Captain David Porter courtesy of the Naval History and Heritage Command. The back cover image is *Kearsarge vs Alabama* by Currier & Ives, courtesy of the Library of Congress

Table of Contents

AUTHOR'S NOTE 7

GLOSSARY 9

CHAPTER ONE
American Revolutionary War Piracy 11
Tory Picaroons 67

CHAPTER TWO
The Quasi-War and French National Piracy 89
The Revenue Cutter Service 116
Toussaint Louverture 128
Thomas Truxtun 136
Birth of the U.S. Navy 145

CHAPTER THREE
Pax Britannica Piracy - The Deadliest Period: 1815-1835 ...
.... 153
Pirates and Their Prey 180
The Laffite Brothers 188
David Porter 201
Thomas Lord Cochrane 205

CHAPTER FOUR
American Civil War Piracy 219
Practical Piracy 258

BIBLIOGRAPHY 273

PAUL JONES ᴛʜᴇ PIRATE.

Paul Jones the Pirate

Author's Note

For the most part, this work presents a rather broad look at the last ninety years of piracy in the Americas, although some aspects and individuals are examined a bit more closely. As the policies of various nations have been responsible for both fostering piracy as well as initiating efforts to end it, issues of policy form a common thread throughout the work. As "simple" piracy had been the original topic which initiated the research for this work, much of the corresponding policies unearthed in the process were not only quite surprising, but in themselves did much to shape the course of the writing. While policy issues are generally boring fare, much of the items found here should prove to be much more interesting. Hopefully, it should prove to be informative.

I would like to sincerely thank all the authors listed in the bibliography, for this work simply would not exist had it not been for their previous efforts. Books and writings from the finest historians pertaining to the subjects of policy and piracy have been used in an effort to paint the proper picture. I hope they don't mind. Of course, I would also like to recognize the men who literally wrote these pages years ago by actually living the events; such as the young men of the nascent United States Navy, Marine Corps, Revenue Cutter Service and Continental Navy, Army and Marines. I would also like to thank the U.S. Navy and Coast Guard for providing so many fine pictures and art work on their websites, which I urge anyone interested in American naval history to investigate. I suppose, for better or worse, there is more than one pirate who should also be recognized … for without the influence of their various, nefarious deeds, no research would have been started.

The *Mystic Whaler*, a fine example of schooners of the period.

Glossary

Adjudicate - Judgment of the prize court or Court of Admiralty; the vessel is either released or awarded to whoever seized it.

Ballast - Heavy items, such as stones or lead, placed low in a ship's hold for stability.

Barge - A large boat with oars and perhaps a small sail, much like a galley.

Battery - A fortified gun-emplacement.

Brig - A square-rigged vessel with two masts.

Cartel - Group of ships carrying prisoners for exchange.

Consort - One ship paired with another, often a smaller vessel or "tender."

League - Three nautical miles.

Leeward - Downwind, or against the wind.

Picaroon - A shore-based pirate, generally using small boats, galleys and barges.

Prize court - Courts which review the legality of captured enemy vessels.

Ship - A vessel with three masts -- foremast, mainmast and mizzenmast.

Sloop-of-war - Smaller warships, such as armed sloops, schooners and brigs.

Specie - Gold and silver, sometimes coined.

Strike - To surrender the ship by lowering the colors (flag).

Tender - Generally a small vessel acting as a supply ship for a larger one, also used to perform routine duties.

Windward -- Upwind, or with the wind in your favor.

Captain Kidd in New York Harbor
by Jean Leon Gerome Ferris — Library of Congress

Revolution Era Map of the American Colonies —
U. S. National Archives

Chapter One

American Revolutionary War Piracy

As much as they ever bore freedom, revolutions and civil wars were notorious breeding grounds for piracy. For many of these actions, the piratical aspects are inescapable and obvious. However, mainly due to nationalistic tendencies, a great many acts of out-right piracy have been transformed into a seemingly patriotic endeavor -- either at the time of incident, or by subsequent generations years after the event's passing. Often, both sides engaged in revolutionary struggles have branded their enemy's actions as piracy, which in many cases is correct for both belligerents. In these respects, the American Revolution is no different.

The roots of the American Revolution took hold with the ending of the French and Indian War in 1763, which removed any French threat from North American soil. However, the war had been incredibly expensive for Britain, who now looked to her American colonies for revenue to help cover the cost. For Britain, American taxes -- many of which had been on the books for years, but never really enforced -- did not seem extravagant, especially as the North American colonies had directly benefited from British protection. It would be the issue of taxation -- specifically relating to shipping duties -- which would spark violent American action years prior to the events at Lexington and Concord.

Robert Harvey makes an apt notation in *A Few Bloody Noses*;

> "The importance of the American

colonies' thriving trade in piracy and smuggling cannot be overstated. Raiding Spanish ships was estimated to bring 100,000 pounds a year to New York alone; the prize money of a single cargo could range from 50,000 to 200,000 pounds. At least one million pounds a year flowed into North America from piracy compared with 40,000 pounds a year taken in British tax revenues from the colonies."[1]

Undoubtedly, the profits from smuggling far surpassed that of piracy in the pre-revolutionary American colonies. The triangle trade -- rum from New England distillers traded for African slaves, who were then traded for sugar or molasses in the West Indies, completing the transaction and providing the ingredient for the rum distillers -- not only made untold fortunes, but was the primary target of Britain's Sugar Act of

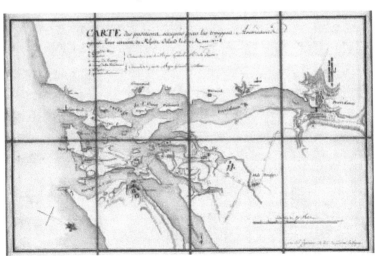

**Naraganset Bay, Rhode Island —
U. S. National Archives**

1 Robert Harvey, *A Few Bloody Noses: The Realities and Mythologies of the American Revolution.* (New York: Overlook Press, 2001), 22.

1764. At the time, five-sixths of Rhode Island's rum production was fueled by smuggled molasses. While the later Tea Act would receive most of the historic acclaim, it was the Sugar Act which caused the first British casualties.[2]

Tarring and Feathering a Boston Excise Collector U.S. National Archives

Shortly thereafter, the British sent a handful of Royal Navy vessels to the American colonies in order to suppress smuggling, enforce the taxes on trade and bolster the few vessels used in collecting customs. Immediately following the arrival of such ships, many coastal towns would nearly riot in response, such as the incident in 1765 which involved a boat from HMS *Maidstone* dragged into town at Newport, Rhode Island and then burnt in defiance at the *Maidstone*'s attempt to impress local sailors. In 1769, the revenue sloop *Liberty* would reap the wrath of Newport after firing upon a boat fleeing from customs agents. Later, when the captain and crew of *Liberty* were ashore, locals slipped down to the docks, cast-off the sloop and grounded her by cutting down her sails, hacking holes in the hull and setting her adrift. Shortly after *Liberty* ran aground, another group of men set her aflame. In April, 1771 a customs agent was severely beaten on the waterfront after having made the mistake of inspecting a vessel at night. The actions of June 9, 1772 would exceed all others. The *Gaspee*, a small sloop-of-war, had been sent to patrol the

---

2   William G. McLoughlin, *Rhode Island: A History.* (New York: W.W. Norton, 1978, 1986), 85.

Capture and Burning of H.M. Revenue Schooner *Gaspee*

waters off Newport and was relatively active in pursuing smugglers. However, having chased a fleeing sloop through shoal water, *Gaspee* grounded on a sandbank. That night, boatloads of Newport men -- led by molasses smuggler John Brown and slave ship captain Abraham Whipple, an experienced privateer from the French and Indian War -- boarded *Gaspee*, overwhelmed her sleeping crew and shot her commander in the groin. Lt. Dudingston would later recover from his injuries, but *Gaspee* was burnt to the waterline.[3] As the destruction of one of the King's vessels and the shooting of one of his officers were crimes punishable by death, it is remarkable that the wrath of King George would not be unleashed until Boston hosted its infamous "Tea Party" eighteen months later -- which he referred to as "violent and outrageous proceedings," although the only item harmed was a cargo of expensive tea.[4]

Boston Tea Party, 1773, lithograph by Sarony and Major

---

3   Ibid, 90-91.
4   Benson Bobrick, *Angel in the Whirlwind: The Triumph of the American Revolution.* (New York: Penguin, 1998), 91.

Boston Harbor from Constitution Wharf
U.S. Naval Academy Museum

The Legalities of War

In response to Boston's "Tea Party," Parliament passed four acts, collectively called the Coercive Acts, which dissolved the Massachusetts assembly and, perhaps more importantly, included the Boston Port Act. The Port Act was in all actuality a blockade of Boston, with Admiral Samuel Graves arriving as commander of the North American Station in order to see to its implementation, having twenty-seven warships on station by the summer of 1775.[5] Blockades had always been one of the legal determinates in bestowing belligerent status on those suffering the blockade; as it was an internationally recognized

---

5   John A. Tilley, *The British Navy and the American Revolution.* (University of South Carolina Press, 1987), 3. Graves arrived in Boston aboard the 50-gun *Preston* on June 30, 1774, summer of 1775 fleet total, 49.

Boston Defenses, 1775 - U.S. National Archives

formal act of war -- providing it is recognized by a foreign power. This action alone gave justification to Continental forces, especially naval forces -- although in 1774 the colonies had not yet chosen to unite in war and had only begun to heed the call for a Continental Congress. Not surprisingly, it would be Rhode Island who first called for such a gathering.[6]

The sovereign rights of states, meaning nations, provide an interesting aspect in this area. State sovereignty issues would form the basis for the "states' rights" argument which has raged in one form or another throughout the course of American history, sometimes with disastrous effect. According to this view, the states -- although in 1774 the colonies had not yet declared themselves as such -- held that they were each independent "nations" who happened to be united against a common enemy, with ultimate participation resting on them and not the Continental Congress.[7] Both the states

6   William G. McLoughlin, *Rhode Island: A History.* (New York: W.W. Norton, 1978, 1986), 84.

7   Carol Berkin, *A Brilliant Solution: Inventing the American*

and their self-proclaimed sovereignty would result from the Declaration of Independence and subsequent writing of new state constitutions as mandated by the Continental Congress.[8] In itself, this last aspect is a bit of a conundrum. Such sovereignty was not touted in 1774, however, and Massachusetts would not use the legal openings made by the Boston Port Act to commission either a state or private navy until weeks after the Battle of Bunker (Breed's) Hill in June, 1775. Not surprisingly, Rhode Island would commission the revolution's first American warships, leading Massachusetts by mere weeks. However, "Rogue's Island" -- as the state would soon come to be called -- did not commission the vessel under their self-proscribed authority, nor that of the Continental Congress.

The First Commissioned Ships

In many respects, confusion and uncertainty reigned during the early stages of the American Revolution, as it would for the majority of the eight-year conflict. The degree of confusion and uncertainty becomes obvious when the war's early naval history is reviewed.

As mentioned, Rhode Island would commission the first American vessel, on June 12, 1775 -- five days prior to the Battle of Bunker Hill, although nearly two full months after the engagements at Lexington and Concord. The frigate HMS *Rose* had been sent to Newport by Admiral Graves in autumn, 1774 to "be a severe Checque to the prodigious smuggling

---

Constitution. (New York: Harcourt, 2003), 14-19.

8   Pauline Maier, *American Scripture*. (New York: Knopf, 1997), 163, excepting for the Virginia and New Jersey state constitutions which were written prior to July, 1776 and conformed to the new mandate.

carrying on there with Impunity."[9] After suffering from the effectiveness of this frigate for nearly a year, along with threats from the Royal Navy during the summer of 1775 which promised to bombard Newport if provisions were not supplied,[10] the Rhode Island General Assembly ordered the Committee of Safety to "charter two suitable vessels ... to protect the trade of this colony."[11] The sloop *Katy* was the first vessel chosen for commission, with *Washington* becoming her consort.

Commodore Abraham Whipple by Edward Savage

Not surprisingly, the two leaders of the *Gaspee* affair would be involved, as *Katy* was owned by John Brown and Abraham Whipple was appointed captain. *Katy* was very lightly armed with six four-pounders, some swivel guns and was wholly inadequate to perform her intended function; namely, to harass the frigate *Rose*. While *Katy* would later be re-christened *Providence* and become John Paul Jones' first command, her initial commission was not attributed to Rhode Island authority, but that of "His Majesty's Name George the Third."[12]

9   James L. Nelson, *George Washington's Secret Navy*. (New York: McGraw-Hill, 2008), 58.

10   William G. McLoughlin, *Rhode Island: A History*. (New York: W.W. Norton, 1978, 1986), 93.

11   James L. Nelson, *George Washington's Secret Navy*. (New York: McGraw-Hill, 2008), 58.

12   Ibid, 59.

While it seems quite absurd for Rhode Island to commission a warship in King George's name in order to engage His Majesty's vessels, nothing can better illustrate the mindset of many Americans prior to 1776. To put it simply, many people thought that the events which led to armed conflict were due to the workings of "ministerial forces" and were not blamed on King George III. It was as though all of these events had played out not only without the King's knowledge, but that he would somehow side with the American perspective if he truly knew what was happening. Of course, a hope for reconciliation among some colonists bolstered this belief.[13] This attitude led to tenuous uncertainty in many areas of the early war effort, especially concerning naval operations. It was one thing to arm and defend one's home and hearth against menacing "ministerial forces," but it was quite another to create a navy or issue letters of marque and reprisal against British shipping. Moreover, the opposing view of revolution is called treason, which was an issue that took many Americans some time in rationalizing. After all, the Continental Congress had drafted and dispatched the "Olive Branch Petition" to the King in July, 1775. Commissioning naval forces was considered to be an offensive action and would be much harder to justify. Eventually, King George III would make his position clear when he addressed Parliament in late October, 1775. He placed blame for the colonial turmoil solely on the Americans, involved in a "desperate conspiracy" enacted "for the sole purpose of establishing an independent Empire." After a rather long rant, the King said it was time "to put a speedy end to these disorders by the most decisive exertions."[14] Reprints of

---

13   Scott Liell, *46 Pages: Thomas Paine, Common Sense, and the Turning Point to Independence*. (Philadelphia: Running Press, 2003), 14-15, 84-85.

14   Pauline Maier, *American Scripture*. (New York: Knopf, 1997), 25.

the speech would infuriate Americans and corroborate Thomas Paine's position in his pamphlet *Common Sense*, which not only justified the reasons for independence, but debunked the theory that King George III was somehow separated from the actions of his ministers.

Unlike Rhode Island, Massachusetts would commission their first warships under their own authority. The events surrounding the appropriation of these vessels, however, compare nicely with the *Gaspee* incident. In June, 1775 the small logging town of Machias (located in today's Maine), was forced by near-starvation to broker a deal with Loyalist Ichabod Jones, a frequent supplier for the British in Boston. Jones blew the deal by infuriating the townspeople, who promptly captured his loaded lumber vessels, *Polly* and *Unity*. The chase continued, with *Unity* and the local *Fallmouth Packet* running down the small Royal Navy sloop *Margaretta*, capturing her and killing her commander, Midshipman Moore. Jeremiah O'Brien had been among the leadership involved in capturing *Margaretta* and was given command in July when the Massachusetts Provincial Congress condemned the three vessels and then commissioned *Polly* as a warship, armed with the miniscule *Margaretta*'s guns. The vessel was commissioned specifically for the protection of Machias. As a result, Admiral Graves dispatched the armed schooner *Diligent* to the area, promising the governor of Nova Scotia that "the Pirate will soon reap the Reward for his Perfidy." That would not be the case, as *Diligent* and her consort, the shallop *Tatamagouche*, were seized without a fight after their officers had ignorantly come ashore at Machias.[15]

It would seem reasonable that after Rhode Island and Massachusetts commissioned warships -- embryonic state

15   James L. Nelson, *George Washington's Secret Navy*. (New York: McGraw-Hill, 2008), 35.

navies, actually -- such actions would inspire more commissions. However, that did not happen, mostly due to a last attempt at colonial reconciliation with Britain and a Continental Congress still unsure about commissioning either a navy, privateers, or even suggesting that other colonies fit-out their own vessels. The arguments against a navy were heated, long-lasting and even claimed that such a creation would "corrupt the morals of our Seamen. It would make them selfish, piratical, mercenary, bent wholly upon plunder..."[16] By late in 1775, the political environment would change once more and not only crystallize the need for commissioned ships, but release a virtual flood of them. In the meantime, no other commissions were authorized, although one man would decide to offer his own.

General Washington's Fleet

"Appeal to Heaven Flag" flown by Washington's schooners

When George Washington arrived at Cambridge to command the various militias which formed the Continental Army in the summer of 1775, he faced a multitude of problems. Washington was not pleased by the behavior and undisciplined manner of the New England militias and was particularly unhappy with how they elected their officers. Many historians often link this

---

16   Ibid, 112.

behavior to the age-old pirate practice of electing their officers and captains, with some historians even going so far as to attribute the far-reaching democratic habits of the Yankees to years of seaborne conditioning -- an interesting but over-simplified theory. As displeased as Washington often was with these men, however, they would not prove to be his biggest problem.[17]

Gunpowder would be Washington's chief concern, especially when he learned exactly how lean the supply had become, a mere thirty-six barrels. Black powder readily absorbs moisture, which ruins it, so an army's store of gunpowder would continue to decrease over time even if no weapons had been fired. While the New England militias did have a "Wild West" habit of discharging their muskets for no reason, it was not the cause of the powder shortage. There simply wasn't enough. However, Washington did circulate orders regarding such wastes of powder. "It is with indignation and shame the General observes, that notwithstanding the repeated orders which have been given to prevent the firing of guns in and about camp, it is daily and hourly practiced." Supplies were so low that if the British decided to attack, the Continentals wouldn't have enough powder to fire more than a volley or two, at the very best.[18]

After contacting congress and nearly everyone else with demands for more powder -- although careful not to reveal exactly how low supplies were, lest the British find out -- Washington decided to take matters into his own hands. At first, congress directed him to petition Rhode Island to send one of their vessels to Bermuda, who was not only sympathetic to the plight of the colonies, but also dependent upon

---

17   Ibid, 45 refers to election of officers and the corresponding pirate/privateer practice, 43 Washington arrived in Cambridge on July 2.
18   Ibid, 56 gunpowder supply, 57 gunpowder waste and quote.

their provisions. Bermuda had already let it be known that they would "allow" the Americans to take the British supply of gunpowder on the island, they just had to come and get it. However, by the time Abraham Whipple arrived, the powder had been removed by the Royal Navy. After reviewing his commission from the Continental Congress and finding it to be rather ambiguous in some areas -- as the general wording of the document allowed a far-ranging latitude -- Washington reluctantly decided to arm and commission a schooner in order to procure gunpowder from British ships supplying munitions to Boston's "ministerial forces." *Hannah* was fit-out and sailed by late August, 1775. Washington realized he was over-stepping his bounds, as naval commissions must originate from a legislative body such as the Continental Congress, so he kept the entire enterprise as quiet as he could. Author James L. Nelson bluntly sums up the legality of Washington's actions; "It was a decision he did not actually have the authority to make."[19] Considering the ineptitude of his commanders

Columbus, one of the original Continental Navy ships, 24 guns

---

19   Ibid, 84.

and the fact that his "fleet" would quickly grow to six vessels, he did a remarkable job of keeping congress in the dark.[20]

In effect, Washington's squadron of schooners "birthed" the Continental Navy, although they were manned by men from the Continental Army, listed as "privates" and not sailors. While the remaining vessels would technically be later absorbed into the Continental Navy on November 30, 1775, there was no actual navy at the time of Washington's commissioning, nor did he have the power to commission anything. As James L. Nelson notes, "A true American navy could only come from the Continental Congress." Such action was piratical, as Washington himself knew and is the reason why he kept the whole matter quiet, hoping that when he revealed the existence of his fleet, it would be during an explanation of how he managed to capture a British munitions ship full of gunpowder. Under such circumstances, his illegal commissions would probably be overlooked. Congress would overlook the legal aspects of this fleet anyway, but it wouldn't be until November that John Manly in the schooner *Lee* captured the munitions ship *Nancy*, loaded with a bounty of gunpowder, artillery and various military supplies.[21]

October 13, 1775 is considered by many to be the actual birth of the Continental Navy, when congress ordered two vessels to "cruise east" in the hope of seizing British supply ships. Letters of marque and reprisal were authorized in November and expanded in March, 1776 to allow for the seizure of any British vessel. Massachusetts and Rhode Island responded to the Continental legislation almost immediately

---

20   Ibid, 59-61details Bermuda powder and Whipple's run, 84 *Hannah*, 85 Continental Congress' commission for George Washington, 78 his reluctance to commission "privateers."

21   Ibid, 157 details congressional approval of Washington's schooners on November 30, 1775, 213 covers Manly and *Nancy*, taken November 29. Nelson quote on 328.

and offered a flurry of their own state commissions, especially after March, 1776 when the expansion of legal prizes made the effort and investment a much more profitable venture. Rhode Island would launch sixty-five privateers between May and December of 1776.[22] Throughout the war, American privateers would carry a hodge-podge of Continental and state commissions. More substantial efforts to establish the Continental Navy would come at the end of October, when funding for the purchase and conversion of merchant vessels was appropriated, along with a provision to build thirteen frigates. A rash of related acts would follow the next month, not the least of which was the creation of the Marine Corps on November 10.

However, to Washington's great dismay, congress would be extremely slow in establishing prize courts for the adjudication of captured vessels and eventually passed most of the responsibility onto the states. The prize court problem would be responsible for a few mutinies, as unpaid soldiers felt they were being cheated. The importance of prize courts cannot be understated, as noted by James L. Nelson, "prize courts were as crucial to the system as ships and guns." Serious problems developed right from the start, as *Hannah*'s crew mutinied soon after bringing their first prize into port, for which they received no prize money. The vessel was a re-captured American prize taken by the Royal Navy, which happened to belong to a member of congress. Discrepancies in prize payments would hinder the Continental Navy throughout the war, as privateers were afforded the full value of captured vessels, while Continental captures only garnered half, and originally only a third.[23] Legal proceedings concerning re-

---

22   William G. McLoughlin, *Rhode Island: A History.* (New York: W.W. Norton, 1978, 1986), 96.

23   James L. Nelson, *George Washington's Secret Navy.* (New York:

captured American vessels and wrongly captured American shipping would smolder in the court system for years -- right along with many of the regular prize disputes. On the advice of John Paul Jones, congress finally raised share values to two-thirds of a vessel's worth, in an effort to encourage enlistment in the Continental Navy and not civilian privateers.[24]

The British

**Viscount Howe —
Library of Congress**

While arguments can be made that the Boston Port Act constituted enough of a blockade to afford legal belligerent status to the American colonies, it is clear that the Prohibitory Act of 1776 most certainly was a blockade.[25] Regardless, the Capture Act of December 22, 1775 proclaimed the colonies to be in a state of rebellion, prohibited trade with the colonies and allowed for the seizure and condemnation of American shipping.[26] While indecision and confusion abounded on both sides, it is surprising that Britain was still indecisive after

McGraw-Hill, 2008), 262, note on October 13 "birth" and November 10 Marine Corps legislation, calling for two battalions, 97-98 *Hannah* mutiny, Nelson quote on 184.

24   Robert H. Patton, *Patriot Pirates*. (New York: Random House, 2008), 78.

25   John A. Tilley, *The British Navy and the American Revolution*. (University of South Carolina Press, 1987), 82, 102.

26   David Syrett, *The Royal Navy in European Waters during the American Revolutionary War*. (University of South Carolina Press: 1998), 4.

receiving of Declaration of Independence -- but they were. General Howe continued to offer impossible negotiations for peace even as he chased Washington across Long Island and New York later that summer. Such examples suit the war, for the English people themselves were of divided opinions concerning the rebellion and especially how to handle it. Under such a mindset, it is not surprising that the government responded slowly in the way of naval preparedness, for much of the ships sent to America were nearly tethered to the British army, as their role in supporting the troops far outweighed that concerning a few rogue American vessels.[27] Since many felt the rebellion would be quickly squashed, and with an eye on the cost of war, Britain built only nine new frigates from 1775 to 1778, the vessel historically built to run-down enemy privateers and warships of equal or lesser strength. Such was the case during the early stages of the French and Indian War, as forty-two frigates were ordered from 1755 to 1757. Due to such poor preparations, hinged on the hopes for a limited conflict, the Royal Navy was stretched thin and in no position to cope with the virtual flood of privateers released by the Americans once they decided to do so. The effects of frigates on privateer activity becomes clear when the last three years of the war are examined, during which time the Royal Navy was augmented by roughly sixty new frigates and reaped a terrible toll on American shipping. However, during the early years, it was the poorly equipped rebels who held the advantage.[28] In the first two years of the war, rebel cruisers cleared over 700 British vessels in American prize courts alone.[29] The amount of prizes sold in Europe and the West Indies during this time

---

27   Ibid, 2.

28   Ibid, 3.

29   James M. Volo, *Blue Water Patriots: The American Revolution Afloat.* (New York : Rowman & Littlefield, 2006), 46.

probably comprise a vast fortune, although due to the sheer piracy involved in such sales actual prize totals can only be imagined.

While trying to settle the rebellion cheaply, the British did send a few of their smaller home-water vessels to America in 1775, along with activating a variety of 50-gun warships. Larger warships were much less effective in running down swift privateers, and while a few 50-gunners did make captures, it is doubtful that the cost of maintaining these ships was any less than building more sloops, brigs and schooners would have been. From June to December, 1775, the North American Squadron captured sixty-eight rebel vessels, most of them merchants and smuggler. In conjunction with these actions, the British took a firm stance against America's fledgling seaborne activities and decided to punish port towns as a lesson to the colonies; "lay waste burn and destroy such Seaport Towns as are accessible to his Majesty's Ships." While the bombardment and burning of Charles Town was done in an effort to flush rebel snipers from the area prior to the attack on Bunker Hill, the real punitive effort would focus on Falmouth, today's Portland, Maine on October 19, 1775. Arriving the day before, the British were nice enough to warn the inhabitants to leave before unleashing a day-long barrage from their ships with red-hot shot and combustibles, making sure to completely eradicate the town by sending ashore boat crews who torched the few structures left standing. Of course, this action did not have the desired effect of cowing the Americans. Instead, the attack strengthened the rebellious resolve of the colonies, especially in other port towns along the coast, as batteries and forts were quickly constructed to defend against such abject lessons.[30] The Royal Navy was

30   James L. Nelson, *George Washington's Secret Navy*. (New York: McGraw-Hill, 2008), 146. The burning of Norfolk was not "hatched" in

quick to realize their mistake with such punitive action and made no other efforts to repeat the Falmouth episode.[31] However, many more communities would burn, but only Norfolk, Virginia would face a similar bombardment on January 1, 1776.[32]

Instead, the British looked to legal means of persuading American seamen to stay at home -- the Pirate Act of 1777. This act called for all Americans captured on privateers and Continental Navy ships to be imprisoned with no recourse other than escape, death or joining the Royal Navy. Not only was due process denied these captured sailors, but no one charged with "Piracy upon the ships and goods of His Majesty's subjects" was to be exchanged for British prisoners of war. No seamen would be exchanged until 1779, and only then because the battle of Saratoga had provided the Americans with roughly 5,000 prisoners for use as leverage. Additionally, the torn British populace was not warm to the Pirate Act, which some called "shocking to humanity" and "unconstitutional" for the five years it was enforced.[33]

Since the Royal Navy mostly concentrated their efforts along the coast of North America and the Caribbean, many American privateers decided to hunt the practically unguarded European waters. In this regard, the British completely underestimated the ability of the rebels to carry the commerce war to their shores, but would soon see their mistake. By the

---

the same way as the punitive Falmouth expedition was, it did not originate from the Royal Navy, but more from Lord Dunmore.

31   John A. Tilley, *The British Navy and the American Revolution.* (University of South Carolina Press, 1987), 59-60 Falmouth, 46-48 50-gun warships.

32   Benson Bobrick, *Angel in the Whirlwind: The Triumph of the American Revolution.* (New York: Penguin, 1998), 183.

33   Robert H. Patton, *Patriot Pirates.* (New York: Random House, 2008), 34, quotes on 142.

summer of 1776, rebel ships began to be sighted, with the *Rover* being perhaps the first to cruise there. Many would follow, as the Americans thought that they might be able to lure some of the blockading ships away to Europe, although the larger possibility of widening the war and taking easy prizes undoubtedly held more sway. Historian David Syrett notes the effects of rebel privateer activity up to early 1777; "From Gibraltar to the North Sea, American raiders appeared to be running wild, capturing British merchant ships at will..."[34] France was generally happy to purchase captured British goods and vessels, even though such action was piratical both for France and the rebels who sold items there. However, France saw a golden opportunity to weaken their age-old enemy and was impressed by the number of early American prizes. Such sales were piratical and Britain vehemently protested, but other than lip-service and occasionally jailing someone for a short span, France had little qualms in providing a market for pirated vessels and wares and often supplied substantial numbers of crewmen for the ships. According to Syrett, "Commanders of American cruisers found it was generally possible to dispose of prizes, obtain supplies, refit their vessels, and recruit seamen in French ports."[35] Benjamin Franklin, the American envoy sent to France in the hopes of attaining a treaty, not only saw the possibility of drawing France into the war through American privateers, but warmly suggested that these captains use French ports and encouraged all available French assistance. Prior to the battle of Saratoga, which was responsible for the eventual Franco-American treaties of 1778, a dummy corporation under the name of Roderique

---

34   David Syrett, *The Royal Navy in European Waters during the American Revolutionary War.* (University of South Carolina Press: 1998), *Rover* note on 6, quote on 10.
35   Ibid, 6.

Hortalez & Company was created in order to funnel French and Spanish financing to the rebels.[36]

The potential of war with France kept the British from enforcing the blockade as strictly as they would have liked, as they did not wish to provoke France by seizing a great number of their vessels. Even so, some neutral shipping was seized. Indeed, many British merchants hired French shipping to carry their goods, as it kept them safe from rebel capture. Oddly, even after the Pirate Act and the legislation prohibiting the shipment of military supplies to the colonies, American smugglers were treated quite differently than those captured on warships. Thomas Truxtun would lose two vessels while making Caribbean smuggling runs to Dutch St. Eustastius, but would spend little time in a holding cell. Truxtun's first captured vessel, *Charming Polly*, was seized by the British before any law was enacted which enabled them to do so, in a sort of "preventive piracy" action.[37]

Legalized piracy in the form of British legislation and Orders-in-Council had long been that nation's hallmark and would play a role in widening the war after France joined the fight in 1778. While French military and monetary aid to the rebels was of no small consequence, their entrance into the war placed the colonial rebellion into a much lower priority for the British. An Admiralty dispatch to Lord Howe on March 22, 1778 leaves no room for doubt, as it stated; _____ "... the object of the War being now

36   Robert H. Patton, *Patriot Pirates*. (New York: Random House, 2008), 49-53.

37   Eugene S. Ferguson, *Truxton of the Constellation: The Life of Commodore Thomas Truxton, U.S. Navy, 1755-1822*. (Baltimore: Johns Hopkins University Press, 2000), 20-21 *Charming Polly* in 1775, caught again with *Andrew Caldwell* in 1778 on 33, released both times. *Polly's* capture happened before entering St. Eustatius with a legal cargo, not after having loaded military stores, which were the only captures permitted at that date.

changed, and the Contest in America being a secondary consideration, the principal object must be the distressing France and defending and securing His Majesty's own possessions against Hostile Attempts."[38]

Not only did America become the "back burner" of British interest practically overnight, but most of the ships in the North American Squadron were almost immediately sent to bolster the attack on the Caribbean island of St. Lucia. Additionally, as General Howe's army in Philadelphia was now at risk of being bottled-up, should the French send a naval force to the Delaware River, Howe was ordered to abandon the city. Moreover, twenty frigates were ordered back to Europe to protect the home waters.[39]

Admiral Rodney by Sir Joshua Reynolds — Library of Congress

1778 proved to be a pivotal year. The British blockade of the American coast, which up until this time had drawn little international complaint, was drastically changed by the British, who seized any ships carrying either goods bound for the rebels or those carrying French cargo. Britain would make an enemy out of one of their longest standing allies, Holland, whose merchant fleet -- the world's second largest -- dealt heavily in carrying naval stores to

38   John A. Tilley, *The British Navy and the American Revolution.* (University of South Carolina Press, 1987), 121.
39   Ibid, 121.

France. While the sale of munitions to the Americans from Dutch colonies such as St. Eustatius was a profitable venture, along with the related purchase of pirated wares and vessels, such profits paled in comparison to the money Holland made by selling naval stores to France. For the past hundred years, naval stores -- spars, rope, lumber, turpentine, tar, etc. -- were not considered contraband of war, which was explicitly stated in the 1674 treaty between Holland and Britain. However, the British now declared such stores to be contraband and authorized even merchants under convoy protection to be stopped, searched and seized. At the time, there was no legal basis for a foreign ship to comply with such searches, but the British cared little about it. In order to appease the Baltic and Nordic nations which manufactured these supplies, Parliament passed legislation in autumn, 1778 which stated that all confiscated naval stores would be purchased by Britain. Such stores were needed by the Royal Navy as well, since the rebelling American colonies had long been their supplier. However, Russia's Catherine II initiated the League of Armed Neutrality as a result of British seizures, although this was really just a ploy on her part to gain some sort of international prominence. The League was more of a joke than anything else, as not only did it agree that naval stores were contraband, but did not help defend fellow member Holland when Britain declared war on them.[40] While naval stores truly were the reason for the widening of the war by Britain, they used the excuse that a draft treaty between Holland and America, captured at sea in 1780, was the real reason for the fight -- along with the fact that the Dutch did not join them in war

---

40   David Syrett, *The Royal Navy in European Waters during the American Revolutionary War.* (University of South Carolina Press: 1998), 97-100, profits from naval stores 102, League of Armed Neutrality, 119-126.

against France, which their previous treaties stipulated. The war against Holland would see Admiral Rodney capture St. Eustatius in early 1781, spending three months there while acting as a self-appointed "prize court." The result of Rodney's money-hunger allowed the French fleet under de Grasse to arrive off Virginia, enabling the victory at Yorktown which was ultimately responsible for American independence.[41]

**Surrender at Yorktown —
U. S. National Archives**

One interesting note concerns Spain, who France finally convinced to join the war in June, 1779. Spain really wanted only one thing, the return of Gibraltar from the British, who had conquered "the rock" seventy-five years earlier during the War of the Spanish Succession. Spain provided one of the war's many ironies, for they really wanted no part of it and were persuaded by France, who nearly promised them Gibraltar. Since France could not deliver on this "promise,"

---

41   Alexander DeConde, *A History of American Foreign Policy.* (New York: Scribner's, 1963), 31-32. Also, John A. Tilley, *The British Navy and the American Revolution.* (University of South Carolina Press, 1987), 237-239 describes Rodney in St. Eustatius.

the war dragged on while a diplomatic return of Gibraltar was sought, which was an exercise in futility since Britain would not part with it.[42]

Spain did not share France's sympathy for the American cause, even though they "invested" in the dummy corporation which funneled supplies to the rebels early in the war and refused to deliver American diplomat Arthur Lee over to Britain in autumn, 1776. The British claimed Lee was a pirate, as he arrived in Spain aboard a rebel privateer.[43] However, at no time was Spain comfortable with the idea of colonial rebellion, lest it infect their colonies. As a result, they would neither meet with diplomat John Jay, nor recognize American independence until after signing the treaty which ended the war in 1783. While they didn't mind an effort to weaken their age-old enemy England by investing in American trouble-makers and bringing hefty profits to Spanish ports by means of captured goods and vessels, their feelings for the Americans were not very warm. Because of this, they immediately ended their past policy of allowing British colonial goods to travel freely down the Mississippi River. As Spain happened to own both sides of the river in the West Florida - Louisiana region, they simply refused to let American vessels flow past Spanish territory and out to sea. This pertained to all such rivers, not just the Mississippi. To say this created much strife is a massive understatement, for it did much to feed piracy along the Gulf Shore long after the Spanish "opened" the river by instituting a system of permits and tolls in 1788.[44] Indeed,

---

42   David Syrett, *The Royal Navy in European Waters during the American Revolutionary War.* (University of South Carolina Press: 1998), 69.

43   Robert H. Patton, *Patriot Pirates.* (New York: Random House, 2008), 56.

44   Alexander DeConde, *A History of American Foreign Policy.* (New York: Scribner's, 1963), 27-29, 48-51.

the very same issue concerning navigation of the Mississippi would underlay much of the reasoning for Andrew Jackson's unauthorized thrust into West Florida in 1818, thirty years later.[45]

Piracy

Many Americans were prepared to go to any lengths in order to win independence, regardless of what rules had to be bent or broken. Such is the case with George Washington, whose need for gunpowder was so dire that it pushed him to commission armed vessels in an effort to procure the precious powder, even when he knew perfectly well that he did not possess the legal authority to do so. It is said that necessity is the mother of all invention, which Washington well illustrates. The efforts of Benjamin Franklin during his time in France form a close parallel, for he did all he could to foster the commissioning and out-fitting of privateers and Continental vessels in Europe, along with making every effort to suggest that American privateer captains use French ports to dispose of prizes while convincing many willing French officials to unofficially

Benjamin Franklin in Paris

45   Daniel Walker Howe, *What Hath God Wrought: The Transformation of America, 1815-1848.* (New York: Oxford, 2007), 76, 97-98. There were many factors involved in Spanish - American strife in the Gulf, including free black and Indian "maroons" who raided across the border. It was also a widely-known fact that Spain had long been a supplier of arms and munitions to the local tribes.

sanction the piratical process. *General Mifflin, Tyrannicide, Rising States, Freedom, Montgomery* and many other privateers heeded Franklin's call and sold scores of prizes in French ports in 1777.[46] Of course, many other Americans -- both patriot and Loyalist -- where drawn to the sea simply because the war provided an excellent opportunity to make money from legalized robbery and didn't often care when lines were crossed. Numerous British colonies would be quick to outfit their own illegal privateers -- both prior to the availability of official British letters of marque and reprisal in 1777 and long afterwards. For some, war can be quite profitable.

**Esek Hopkins
by John Chester Buttre —
U. S. National Archives**

Esek Hopkins, who historian John A. Tilley refers to as "a slightly piratical Rhode Island sea captain," became the first and only Continental Commodore of the war, at least in official rank. Due to the work of his brother Stephen, the Continental Congress appointed Esek Hopkins to lead the freshly-converted merchantmen which comprised the first batch of Continental Navy vessels.[47] His little squadron plundered Nassau in March, 1776 and made off with over eighty pieces of artillery and powder greatly needed by Washington's army, although much of Nassau's powder had been sent off in a sloop during the

---

46   Robert H. Patton, *Patriot Pirates*. (New York: Random House, 2008), 158, 163.
47   John A. Tilley, *The British Navy and the American Revolution*. (University of South Carolina Press, 1987), 92.

night. However, the following month the Continental squadron would get tore-up by the frigate *Glasgow* off Block Island while returning to Rhode Island. Esek Hopkins was then bottled-up in Providence for quite some time as a result. This would be one of the reasons for Hopkins' suspension in March, 1777 and subsequent dismissal from Continental service in 1778 -- for by all rights, his squadron should have captured *Glasgow* instead of being shattered by the lone frigate. Other factors were involved, however, such as the arbitrary manner in which he dispensed his artillery. Coincidently, Hopkins' old friend John Brown happened to be heavily involved in privateers and would cast artillery specifically for them, but not for the Continentals.[48] However, it is only fair to mention how Hopkins was hampered in recruiting Continental sailors due to the attraction of joining one of the state's many privateers, along with a litany of local corruption and favoritism which handcuffed Hopkins even further.[49]

The problems suffered by George Washington do much to reveal the piratical picture. Four of his original six commanders would be dismissed from service, for reasons falling generally under the categories of disobeying direct orders, exceeding their commissions, seizing friendly shipping, the wanton plundering of vessels, ransacking towns and taking captives.[50] Initially, Washington's captains were only allowed to target ships supplying the "ministerial army," which would mostly be the case until the Continental Congress authorized

---

48   Robert H. Patton, *Patriot Pirates*. (New York: Random House, 2008), 90.

49   Samuel Eliot Morison, *John Paul Jones: A Sailor's Biography*. (New York: Little, Brown and Co., 1959), 97.

50   James L. Nelson, *George Washington's Secret Navy*. (New York: McGraw-Hill, 2008), 238 Moylan quote, "...General was Much Surprised at the Rapacity of the Crews in stripping the Prizes of every little Thing they could lay their hands upon."

the capture of any British vessel in March, 1776. With the exception of John Manley, however, these men generally did as they pleased. When ordered to cruise the mouth of the St. Lawrence in order to intercept two brigs carrying military supplies bound for Canada, Captains Broughton and Selman disregarded the order, seized a variety of vessels -- most of which were later released when found to be patriot-owned -- and teamed together to plunder Charlotte Town, Nova Scotia, taking two men prisoner -- one of them being Acting Governor Callbeck.[51] Early and continued raiding of Canadian shores would brand American privateers as pirates in both the written Canadian history and in actual fact. Privateers would raid Nova Scotia time and again, laying the foundation for the rumor that Samuel Hall of the *Mary Jane* might have actually buried treasure before being captured by the Royal Navy. One of the bloodiest privateer-on-privateer engagements of the war occurred between the *Resolution* from Liverpool, commanded by a displaced Loyalist who surrendered to the American privateer *Viper* after a ninety minute fight which left fifty-one men dead.[52] Needless to say, Washington was less than pleased when Broughton and Selman presented their captives, which were promptly ordered to be released. Both men were soon basically fired, with the option of returning to their militia units rejected, although Broughton would later obtain a commission and fight on land.[53]

Sion Martindale suffered grandiose plans from the very beginning, as he squandered time, money and unnecessary armaments in fitting-out the schooner *Washington* for service.

51   Ibid, 88 initial orders to captains, 161-162, 174, 194.
52   Harold Horwood and Ed Butts, *Bandits and Privateers: Canada in the Age of Gunpowder*. (Halifax: Doubleday, 1988), 37-39 Hall and treasure, 48 *Viper* victory.
53   James L. Nelson, *George Washington's Secret Navy*. (New York: McGraw-Hill, 2008), 238-241.

Certainly, no time was saved by insisting that the vessel be re-masted and rigged as a brig, nor in the weeks wasted in procuring enough cannon to satisfy Martindale. The *Washington* would be the most heavily-armed vessel in the General's fleet, carrying 6 six-pounders, 4 four-pounders, ten swivel guns and a compliment of seventy-five men. A large compliment of swivel or pivot guns would set the standard for most American ships, as they were excellent for close action. The crew would continue the pattern established with the mutinous *Hannah*, as they nearly mutinied after taking their first prize, a very small vessel "of little value." However, the seamen became sated by winter clothing, as Martindale's preparations had delayed the vessel's launch until late November and the men were miserable cruising the cold sea. *Washington*'s second cruise would see her captured by HMS *Fowey*(20). For all his gun-related delays, Martindale would be captured without firing a shot and then shipped to England with his crew for trial and imprisonment, charged with "Acts of Rebellion and High Treason Committed on the High Seas." The biggest irony involves the *Washington* herself. After Martindale spent so much time and money fitting her for cruising, the British did not find her seaworthy and refused to take her into service. Admiral Graves had hoped to use the captured *Washington* as a "wolf in sheep's clothing" in order to dupe other American vessels, with Graves' highest hope being to ambush other schooners from Washington's fleet.[54]

For all of George Washington's qualities, his reservoir of patience must have been unfathomable. Even so, it did not take long for his temper to flare because of the actions of his "sailors" -- mostly privates taken from ranks of the Massachusetts militia, many nearly against their will. The

54   Ibid, 222-225, quote on prize 222, "wolf in sheep's clothing," 253, treason charge on 247.

particular regiment these men came from is noteworthy, for it was almost entirely composed of unemployed sailors and men from the waterfront. In need of money, they decided to join the local militia. While many of these men proved troublesome, greedy, disrespectful and prone to drunkenness, the 14th Continental Regiment served well throughout the war and performed such other notable feats as ferrying the army across the Delaware River on Christmas, 1776 after having performed a virtual Dunkirk-like evacuation of the same troops from Long Island that summer.[55] Many of these men would crew the fire ships, gunboats, galleys and shore batteries which engaged a British sortie up the Hudson River led by Captain Hyde Parker and Captain James Wallace in the hated frigate *Rose* during the summer of 1776. So intense was the action that both Wallace and Parker were knighted for it.[56]

Phoenix and *Rose* on Hudson, 1776 —
U. S. National Archives

---

55   Ibid, 81-82. When many of the unemployed sailors joined the army at Cambridge, the general feeling at Marblehead was "good riddance!"
56   John A. Tilley, *The British Navy and the American Revolution.* (University of South Carolina Press, 1987), 84 describes the action of the Hudson.

Regardless of the unit's future exploits, however, Washington became heated over "our rascally privateers-men."[57]

"The plague, trouble, and vexation I have had with the crews of all the armed vessels is inexpressible. I do believe there is not on earth a more disorderly set."[58]

Of those who would serve as a Washington captain, not all were terrible. William Coit was fearless and engaged several vessels of the Royal Navy, but like many others, he wasn't very picky in distinguishing friend from foe when choosing prizes. John Manley was exceptional, however, bagging the first major prize of the war and continued to perform a very impressive service and account for a large portion of the squadron's thirty-eight legal prizes.[59] He would later be captured three times, escape twice from prison and also see extensive service commanding privateers. Those who sailed under Manley generally proved to be a more contented bunch, mostly for the simple fact he regularly took legitimate prizes. While a lack of prize courts held-up the payment of shares, the men were still getting paid wages and also got to loot whatever ships they did capture. The non-payment of prize shares was a serious complaint, especially for those of Washington's fleet, who waited nearly a year for payment on the initial catch of vessels. Such delinquency also affected the worth of shares as most of the cargo had long disappeared. Historically, whether the ship was pirate, privateer or a state-owned vessel, a happy crew was one which took prizes, even if they were just a string of small ones. In this respect, the young Horatio Nelson -- the future victor of Trafalgar and undoubtedly Britain's best-loved

57   James L. Nelson, *George Washington's Secret Navy*. (New York: McGraw-Hill, 2008), 201, Washington quoted.

58   Robert H. Patton, *Patriot Pirates*. (New York: Random House, 2008), 34.

59   Ibid, 329. 38 of roughly 55 captures were judged "good prizes."

admiral -- offers a good example. Lieutenant Nelson gained his first command fighting against rebels while stationed at Jamaica in 1777. His very first command was a captured American vessel, which became the tender *Little Lucy*, working in consort with HMS *Lowestoffe*. By the end of 1778, he had some 400 pounds in prize money coming to him. However, his luck would change when promoted to master and commander and given the *Badger*, a captured American brig. While *Badger* was well-armed with 12 four-pounders and two half-pound swivels, she was in a very worn condition and was condemned shortly after Nelson's service aboard her ended. As a result, no prizes were taken by Nelson with the *Badger*. The closest he came was to chase a privateer until the wind died-out, forcing him to watch the vessel escape under the use of her oars, which *Badger* did not have. As a consequence, the crew soon became unruly and desertion became common for the duration of the six-month cruise, with twenty-one of brig's ninety men running off, including a midshipman. Nelson, never known to be a tyrant, was forced to order a number of floggings.[60]

One cannot mention Washington's fleet without including a note on James Mugford, who wasn't commissioned to command at all, but as acting sailing master, took the *Franklin* out to sea when the vessel was between commanders. *Franklin* was also quite low on crewmen, which had been sent to serve aboard other vessels in the "fleet," so Mugford first rounded-up a crew of sailors. Nearly as soon as the schooner left port, she fell in with the store ship *Hope*, one of many ships which would be captured as she sailed for Boston, completely unaware that the British had already evacuated the city. *Hope* provided a bonanza for the Continentals, as she was loaded

---

60   John Sugden, *Nelson: A Dream of Glory, 1758-1797*. (New York: Henry Holt, 2004), 116-137.

with 1,000 carbines, bayonets and related articles, along with a staggering 1,500 barrels of gunpowder. Mugford tried to run *Hope* directly into Boston and grounded her on a bank. Looking to capitalize on the situation, during the night of May 19, 1776 boat crews from HMS *Renown* and *Experiment* attacked *Franklin* as she stood anchored near the stranded *Hope*. The Americans were vastly outnumbered but amazingly tenacious, repelling all attempts to board and even capsizing one of the boats, which drowned a lieutenant. However, just before the British fled, James Mugford became the only American fatality, "run through with a lance while he was cutting off the hands of the Pirates as they were attempting to board him."[61]

Captain Gustavus Conyngham
Naval History and Heritage
Command

For the most part, many American privateers and Continental Navy vessels practiced much of the same sorts of piracy, such as selling prize vessels in the ports of France and Spain. More privateers -- especially those with questionable commissions -- would use the Caribbean markets of St. Eustatius, Cuba, St. Thomas and Martinique to sell captured prize goods with a much larger frequency than would ships of the Continental Navy.[62] Three of the

61   James L. Nelson, *George Washington's Secret Navy*. (New York: McGraw-Hill, 2008), 318-319, quote on 319.
62   Robert H. Patton, *Patriot Pirates*. (New York: Random House, 2008), 16.

commanders responsible for capturing most of the Continental Navy's prizes, Lambert Wickes, John Paul Jones and Gustavus Conyngham, would all sell vessels in Europe long before the Franco-American treaties. Wickes sold many prizes quite cheaply in Nantes, France to quickly get rid of them and was quite productive. Wickes' luck would not last long, for he drowned when the *Reprisal* sank in a storm in 1777, as did all but one man aboard.[63]

John Paul Jones would be commissioned a lieutenant in the Continental Navy due to a well-placed connection he met while taking refuge in America for having killed a man. According to a letter Benjamin Franklin received from Jones -- originally John Paul, with Jones being added as a later alias -- he had been forced to run-through a "mutineer" while in port at Tobago. It is rather doubtful that the sailor was truly mutinous, for earlier in the letter Jones freely admits not having paid the crew. He wished to purchase additional cargo to clear a larger profit on his return voyage and simply wanted the crew to wait for their wages -- probably not the first of such tales given to the dead "mutineer." Jones began his service as First Lieutenant aboard the flagship *Alfred*, initially refusing to command sloop-of-war *Providence* and another smaller vessel, which he felt beneath him. Jones would later relent and perform excellent service while commanding *Providence*, briefly with *Alfred* and would

Sloop Providence
Naval History and Heritage Museum

63   Ibid, 163, 167.

excel with *Ranger*, which he cruised about the English Isles picking prizes and panicking the coast. It would be aboard the converted French merchantman *Bonhomme Richard* where Jones achieved real fame by taking the frigate HMS *Serapis* in April, 1779 and reputedly retorted to the question of surrender with -- "I have not yet begun to fight!" Whether he said exactly that or not, Jones certainly did not strike and captured *Serapis* in a bloody boarding action which accounted for roughly 150 casualties on each ship. Most notably, it is one of the few engagements when the victor lost his ship, as *Bonhomme Richard* -- so named in honor of Benjamin Franklin and his famous *Poor Richard's Almanac* -- sank two days after the battle ended. It was Jones' last real command, as he mostly spent the remainder of the war overseeing the construction of *America*, the only 74-gun ship-of-the-line built in America during the war, which was given to France.[64]

Perhaps the most notable Continental Navy commander was Pierre Landais, as he was undoubtedly the worst in Continental service. Having served some years in the French Navy and receiving the rank of captain, Landais resigned his commission in 1775. He soon met American envoy Silas Deane, who had Landais command a supply ship to America in 1777 and sent with him a letter of recommendation to the Continental Congress.[65] Congress made him a captain in the Continental Navy and gave him command of the frigate *Alliance*, building in Salisbury. *Alliance* and Landais would deliver John Adams to France, who had nothing nice to say

64   Samuel Eliot Morison, *John Paul Jones: A Sailor's Biography*. (New York: Little, Brown and Co., 1959), 23-25 "mutineer" incident, 39 commissioned Lt. 39, 238-235 *Serapis* fight, 327-330 *America* 74-gun liner.
65   Robert H. Patton, *Patriot Pirates*. (New York: Random House, 2008), 54. Doesn't specifically mention this instance -- Morison covers that -- but does cover Deane's policy of offering officer commissions to Europeans, an Arthur Lee initiative.

about Landais. "He is bewildered - an absent bewildered man - an embarrassed mind." Adams' assessment would prove astute, for while serving in Jones' squadron of French ships in 1779, Landais would not heed any orders and often rant and rave, cursing up a storm upon the arrival of even a mere suggestion from Jones. When *Bonhomme Richard* was grappling *Serapis*, Landais neither attempted to fight the smaller *Countess of Scarborough* or help with *Serapis*. Instead, he sailed about aimlessly and fired several broadsides into *Bonhomme Richard*. Landais is later reputed to have flatly stated that he desired to sink Jones and then take *Serapis* for himself. As wild as this seems, it is most likely true, for it appears that Landais was actually insane. Upon making port in Holland, Landais was immediately dispatched to see Franklin, who either fired him or accepted his resignation. Some months later, as Jones was fitting *Alliance* for a cruise to America with supplies, Landais happened into the same port. Instead of boarding ship to Philadephia as a passenger to plead his case before congress, Arthur Lee gave him the idea that he should raise a ruckus with the French government and simply take *Alliance* for himself. With Jones busy chasing the ladies of Paris, this was easily accomplished. Landais' journey to Philadelphia would be re-routed to Boston, as that is where the majority of the un-paid sailors hailed from -- but not before Landais was relieved of command. Apparently, he had a habit of issuing threats and becoming enraged and even brandished a knife at Arthur Lee for taking the first piece of pork at dinner. Lee would be amongst those who gave testimony to congress, which quickly dismissed Landais from service. However, in 1810 the practiced schemer would be paid by the United States government for past-due prize shares on vessels that Denmark had long-since cleared.[66]

66   Samuel Eliot Morison, *John Paul Jones: A Sailor's Biography.* (New

Captain Gustavus Conyngham was an extremely prolific Continental commander, but in all fairness, there were barely any rules that he did not break on a regular basis. Commissioned in France as a captain in the Continental Navy by Benjamin Franklin in March, 1777, Conyngham was given command of a converted mail packet, armed with 4 four-pounders and rechristened *Surprise*. The ownership of the vessel was at least half in private hands -- if not a higher proportion, in all actuality -- which would not only prove troublesome when it came time for prize pay-outs, as a Continental ship received a lesser share than did a privateer, but also regarding the legality of the vessel itself. Even for colonial privateers, launching from a home port was a long-established mark of credence, to say nothing of a state-owned warship. Moreover, all commissions came from the Continental Congress, so unless Franklin had Conyngham's papers already in hand, he was stretching his authority at least as much as Washington had with his "fleet." Conyngham would do his utmost best to stretch the situation even further.

With the close of the French and Indian (Seven Years') War, there were many provisions stipulated in the treaty, one of these being that Dunkirk was not to be fortified against attack and that France wouldn't harbor enemy privateers. This was specifically because Dunkirk was the closest point from England and the stipulation was needed in order to safeguard the town from becoming the perfect base for enemy privateers or pirates. A British commissioner lived in Dunkirk to ensure that the treaty was followed. As a result, when Conyngham almost immediately took several prizes off the English coast and sailed them into Dunkirk, it is not surprising that there

York: Little, Brown and Co., 1959), 189 -190, John Adams quote on 190, 259 sees Franklin, 235 and 238 fires on Jones, 235 wish to sink Jones, 293 Lee's idea to take *Alliance*, 300-301 grant of $4,000.

was a tremendous political uproar. Of course, this was exactly what Franklin wanted -- a large political problem that could launch Britain and France at war with one another overnight. During the summer of 1777, Lord Germain stated;

> "We lately had so many privateers upon our coasts and such encouragements given them by France, that I was apprehensive a few weeks ago that we should have been obliged to have declared War."[67]

While that did not happen, France was quick to jail Conygham. However, he was soon let out, as it was only a few months later he boarded the *Greyhound* under the alias Richard Allen. Within a short time, his true identity was "revealed" and the ship was rechristened *Revenge*, of fourteen guns, twenty-two swivels and a crew mostly comprised of French sailors. The American diplomat William Hodge was briefly jailed by France as a result, as he had largely backed the enterprise, but his incarceration would also be brief.[68] Conyngham went on to rack-up an impressive sixty-plus captures in eighteen months while sailing the Atlantic and Caribbean.[69]

William Hodge came to France in 1777 from the French island of Martinique, in the Caribbean's Leeward Island chain. He had been assisting William Bingham, sent by congress in mid-1776 to create a network for smuggling military supplies. Bingham arrived aboard the *Reprisal*, with Lambert Wickes

67   David Syrett, *The Royal Navy in European Waters during the American Revolutionary War.* (University of South Carolina Press: 1998), 10.

68   Robert H. Patton, *Patriot Pirates.* (New York: Random House, 2008), 173, 178. Also, David Syrett, *The Royal Navy in European Waters during the American Revolutionary War.* (University of South Carolina Press: 1998), 6-10.

69   Benson Bobrick, *Angel in the Whirlwind: The Triumph of the American Revolution.* (New York: Penguin, 1998), 383.

PAUL JONES the PIRATE.

**Paul Jones the Pirate —
Library of Congress**

engaging HMS *Shark* even as Bingham was being rowed to shore. *Shark* withdrew when the French fort opened fire in order to enforce neutrality rights and respect for the marine league. Nearly as soon as he landed, Bingham began offering illegal privateer commissions, watering-down the "regulations" so that only one American had to be included in the crew. By the end of 1776, American privateers -- or those with rebel commissions -- captured 250 ships in the West Indies. Six months later, the Royal Navy counted eighty-two British vessels lying in the harbor of Saint Pierre.[70]

The actions of William Bingham would be copied across the Caribbean. The British island of Antigua was extremely vigorous, offering illegal letters of marque and reprisal against American vessels in late 1776, mostly in a self-proclaimed effort of defense against the depredations of rebel privateers. The truly notable ingredient is that Admiral Young was briefly jailed on the island for seizing such local pirate craft, but was freed after posting bond. British Grenada, St. Kitts, Nevis and the Bahamas would follow suite by enabling such pirates; while on Martinique, St. Thomas and St. Eustatius illegal rebel commissions could be easily obtained, along with available ships and business partners willing to back practically any adventurous smuggler or pirate.[71] The success of colonial

70   Robert H. Patton, *Patriot Pirates*. (New York: Random House, 2008), 70-73.
71   Ibid, 144-148.

New Providence Raid
Naval History and Heritage Command

British privateers would prove considerable, especially in the strategically-located Bahamas, which by May, 1782 recorded 127 American ships "Captured and Libeled in the Court of Vice-Admiralty in New Providence."[72] When Britain finally offered letters of marque and reprisal in 1777, New York Loyalists commissioned one hundred privateers almost immediately. Over 1,000 privateers would sail from ports in Britain and the West Indies, with more being added after the war expanded to provide French targets in 1778.[73]

Plundering was a love shared by nearly all combatants involved during the American Revolution. Hessian soldiers were reputed to be the worst of all looters, undoubtedly

---

72   Michael Craton, *A History of the Bahamas*. (San Salvador Press, 1999, first printed 1962), 143-144. The Bahamas' Acting Governor John Gambier floated along many illegal letters of marque and reprisal in the 1778 time frame.

73   Robert H. Patton, *Patriot Pirates*. (New York: Random House, 2008), 107.

second only to seafaring Americans.[74] Even from the start, Washington was not only shocked at the out-right theft committed by American sailors who ransacked nearly every ship they stopped at sea, but realized he was powerless to prevent it. "[The] General was Much Surprised at the Rapacity of the Crews in stripping the Prizes of every little Thing they could lay their hands upon."[75] The silver set looted from Mrs. Selkirk by the boat crews of *Ranger* in 1778 was something Captain John Paul Jones was not only powerless to stop, but was actually fortunate to experience because the men were satisfied merely with the silver.[76] In general, looting and plundering was endemic during the war for nearly all involved. To some degree it is understandable, especially as many Continental sailors and soldiers often went months or years between paychecks. Often, the payment was in extremely depreciated Continental currency, with a large number of soldiers receiving no payment at all until long after the war ended. The issue of divided loyalties muddied the waters further. As roughly one third of the population was Tory or Loyalist -- with another third patriot -- mere opportunity often gave such theft an even uglier face, as untold numbers of people were branded "Tory" in order to have their property confiscated according to the various state laws. This is where the term "lynch law" derives, due to patriot colonel and "judge" William Lynch, who imposed fines and jail terms upon suspected Loyalists as he saw fit.[77] Indeed, such tactics would account for the worst

---

74   John A. Tilley, *The British Navy and the American Revolution.* (University of South Carolina Press, 1987), 109.

75   James L. Nelson, *George Washington's Secret Navy.* (New York: McGraw-Hill, 2008), 238.

76   Samuel Eliot Morison, *John Paul Jones: A Sailor's Biography.* (New York: Little, Brown and Co., 1959), 143-146.

77   Benson Bobrick, *Angel in the Whirlwind: The Triumph of the American Revolution.* (New York: Penguin, 1998), currency issues and non-

piracies found during the war, centered around the Chesa-peake Bay -- Delaware River region. Aside from the number of homes and towns ransacked and burnt, perhaps the best illustration of out-right plundering can be seen after the fall of Charleston to the British in 1780. The British Army and Navy would vehemently fight over the spoils of Charleston for the duration of the war.[78]

Ransoming captives was neither legal nor condoned, al-though to capture an enemy by practically any means necessary was pretty much fair game for both sides. One such example concerns the capture of British General Richard Prescott from his quarters on Aquidneck Island by Major William Barton, who spirited away his captive in a whaleboat equipped with muffled oars. Prescott was then later exchanged for captured Continental General Charles Lee.[79] During the Selkirk raid, Jones had come to capture the Earl of Selkirk, but settled for the silver to appease his crew and actually returned the Selkirk silver after the war. Of course, to ransom people for money was unacceptable -- although Jones came quite close to threatening the port of Leith with destruction if a ransom was not paid -- but that neither came to pass, nor would it have been by any means legal. The same can't be said for many privateers, who regularly ransacked towns and ransomed sev-eral under the threat of burning them. Noah Stoddard and *Scammel* provide a good example, for with the help of other privateers they raided and ransomed Lunenberg, Nova Scotia for a 1,000 pound note toward the end of the war.[80]

---

payment 473-476, "lynch law" on 323.

78   John A. Tilley, *The British Navy and the American Revolution*. (University of South Carolina Press, 1987), 187.

79   William G. McLoughlin, *Rhode Island: A History*. (New York: W.W. Norton, 1978, 1986), 96-97.

80   Harold Horwood and Ed Butts, *Bandits and Privateers: Canada in the Age of Gunpowder*. (Halifax: Doubleday, 1988), 43-45.

However, until outlawed by Parliament in 1782, it was perfectly legal to ransom a prize vessel back to its owner. Britain hadn't minded the practice, as it helped clear the docket at the courts of Admiralty -- but this is the precise reason why the practice was abolished. With no prize court, anyone could literally capture anything and simply hold it for ransom. The practice of ransoming ships had long been a pirate favorite and would continue to be for years to come, a habit especially loved by the Laffite brothers some thirty years later. Many American privateers engaged in ransoming vessels, as did some Continental captains, including John Paul Jones at least once and Gustavus Conyngham on a variety of occasions.[81] Throughout the war, Loyalist fishermen along the New Jersey coast were regularly forced to pay ransom to local patriots in order to keep their vessels.[82] By contrast, Admiral Howe issued orders which exempted similar patriot vessels from capture, to the distress of the First Lord of the Admiralty Sandwich. While some local patriot craft were captured, Howe's order was mostly complied with.[83]

The British held nearly every form of American warfare in low regard, such as targeting officers, taking cover, utilizing guerrilla and ambush tactics … the list is almost endless. Certainly, much credit was also given to the rebels for their courage and audacity, especially at sea, but such actions did not change the general opinion of the British military. One particular habit of privateer crewmen was especially loathsome to the British -- that of using "combustibles" to booby-trap abandoned vessels. Considering the technology of

81   Robert H. Patton, *Patriot Pirates*. (New York: Random House, 2008), 173, legalities of ransoming prizes on 178.
82   James M. Volo, *Blue Water Patriots: The American Revolution Afloat*. (New York : Rowman & Littlefield, 2006), 202.
83   John A. Tilley, *The British Navy and the American Revolution*. (University of South Carolina Press, 1987), 103-104.

the time -- which began and ended with black powder in this instance -- it is amazing that such a ploy worked more than once, although this limitation suggests the rate at which the practice must have occurred. However, such "combustibles" caused a considerable number of British casualties, with eleven sailors being killed in an explosion shortly after boarding the grounded privateer *Nancy*.[84] Continental Captain Lambert Wickes often used the device.[85] Of course, explosives are indiscriminate killers, as can be seen with James Anderson, who ran the American ship *Morris* aground off Cape Henlopen, rigged the military supplies to explode and was killed in the ensuing blast.[86]

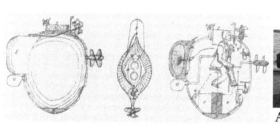

American Turtle
—
Naval History and Heritage Command

Bushnell's American Turtle — Library of Congress

On this note -- surely full of legal haze -- the exploits of David Bushnell cannot be ignored. An intrepid inventor, Bushnell designed and constructed the submarine *American Turtle*, a one-man submersible propelled by a hand crank. *Turtle* was a truly remarkable invention and was put to the

84   James M. Volo, *Blue Water Patriots: The American Revolution Afloat.* (New York : Rowman & Littlefield, 2006), 110 privateer *Nancy*.
85   Robert H. Patton, *Patriot Pirates.* (New York: Random House, 2008), 66.
86   Michael Morgan, *Pirates and Patriots: Tales of the Delaware Coast.* (New York: Algora: 2005), 36.

test when the British fleet entered New York harbor in the summer of 1776. Piloted by Ezra Lee, on the night of September 6, Lee successfully brought *Turtle* under the stern of Admiral Howe's flagship, HMS *Eagle*. On top of *Turtle* was an auger-like device with a timed explosive charge attached to it, but the screw failed to find purchase as either iron fastenings or the copper sheathing kept the auger from boring into wood. After repeated efforts, Lee finally drew the attention of British sentries and swiftly retreated after releasing the explosives, which detonated harmlessly. The Royal Navy was quite agitated over the incident and doubled their night patrols, but were undoubtedly pleased when they discovered the *Turtle* after taking New York and promptly scuttled the world's first combat submarine. Of course, had *Turtle* been successful in her efforts, there is little doubt that the British would have deemed such action as treacherous piracy. The following year, Bushnell designed a series of powder kegs timed to explode and sent them down the Delaware River in an effort to destroy the British fleet. The attempt proved wholly ineffectual, although after witnessing a keg explode, the Royal Navy unleashed their longest sustained bombardment of the war, clearly winning the "Battle of the Kegs."[87]

Cost of Victory

The American Revolution was not a pretty conflict. While victory at Yorktown in October, 1781 brought much of the war on the continent to a halt -- excepting operations on the

---

87   James M. Volo, *Blue Water Patriots: The American Revolution Afloat*. (New York : Rowman & Littlefield, 2006), 197-198. Also, Benson Bobrick, *Angel in the Whirlwind: The Triumph of the American Revolution*. (New York: Penguin, 1998), 310 for length of action.

Yorktown Harbor
Library of Congress

frontier and sporadic skirmishes -- the battle at sea would rage for all eight years of the war. Historian Charles Royster notes;
> "The most recent and most conservative analysis of military mortality in the Revolutionary War finds this war to be second only to the Civil War in its proportion of deaths to population."[88]

While Royster was generally referring to battle-related deaths, which by itself is quite a statement, it should be acknowledged that the American populace faced similar ordeals as did the armed forces. Disease, depravation, starvation, horrendous crimes and uprooted or dissected families were tales shared in many areas of the freshly-independent states,

---

88   Charles Royster, *A Revolutionary People at War: The Continental Army and American Character, 1775-1783*. Published by the Institute of Early American History and Culture. (University of North Carolina Press, 1980). Excerpted from *Major Problems in American Military History*. (New York: Houghton Mifflin, 1999), 83.

although the region along the Atlantic coast undoubtedly paid the greatest price. Port-towns of the New England coast suffered dearly for independence. While the Continental Navy lost a total of 832 men in combat, it was the privateer crews who paid a much greater price, as they seemingly wagered their lives against the potential profits to be had from commerce raiding. The Boston privateer *Speedwell* of fourteen guns and ninety men was sunk by a British frigate, leaving just a sole survivor. HMS *Brune* sank a twelve-gun privateer with a single broadside, although most of the crew was saved from destruction.[89] Certainly, vessels of the Continental Navy share similar tales, but simply can't match the privateers in the number of such incidents. In Essex County, Massachusetts, the town of Newburyport lost twenty-two privateer vessels and 1,000 men. Salem lost nearly twenty privateers, while Gloucester lost every letter of marque vessel launched from her harbor, all twenty-four. The population of adult males in most New England coastal towns was halved by the war. One of every three women in Marblehead was left widowed. Considering that only ten percent of all captured privateers sailed from Essex County, these numbers loom large indeed.[90]

The Continental Congress lists 1,697 commissioned privateers during the war -- 301 ships, 541 brigs, 751 schooners or sloops and 104 boats and galleys. By contrast, there were only forty-seven vessels of the Continental Navy and various combined state navies which saw service during the war. The privateers captured or destroyed sixteen vessels of the Royal Navy and took countless prizes, with estimates of 2,000 to 2,200 being not uncommon.[91] The Continental

89   Robert H. Patton, *Patriot Pirates*. (New York: Random House, 2008), 21.
90   Ibid, 111.
91   James M. Volo, *Blue Water Patriots: The American Revolution Afloat*. (New York : Rowman & Littlefield, 2006), 44-47.

Navy captured or destroyed a dozen Royal Navy warships and accounted for 198 prizes.[92] The total worth of these prizes is arguable, as some historians estimate the value at ten million pounds, while others put the figure at two or three million pounds per year of the war.[93] Regardless, two facts are clear; the first being that the actions of American vessels certainly managed to put a much larger strain on the British economy and political atmosphere while simultaneously creating a wealth of propaganda for the divided populace to discuss. Secondly, but just as importantly, the prizes captured by American cruisers were often much more valuable than the dollar-figure attributed them, for quite a few ships were seized carrying military stores and supplies that simply could not have been duplicated by other American efforts, especially in the early, crucial years of the war. Certainly, the smugglers and blockade runners should also get some credit in this area, for while hauling military stores often came secondary to luxury goods -- which was the historic wartime standard -- smuggled supplies that managed to reach American ports proved crucial. Of course, the privateers also brought in actual gold and silver from aboard their prizes, which was desperately needed as a medium of exchange, as the paper "Continentals" were so worthless many people would not accept them.[94]

The price American seaman paid for their efforts was high

---

92   Robert H. Patton, *Patriot Pirates*. (New York: Random House, 2008), 215.

93   Robert Harvey, *A Few Bloody Noses: The Realities and Mythologies of the American Revolution*. (New York: Overlook Press, 2001), on 320, Harvey estimates at least 10 million pounds.

94   Benson Bobrick, *Angel in the Whirlwind: The Triumph of the American Revolution*. (New York: Penguin, 1998), 234. Many who reenlisted in the Continental Army in late 1776 demanded a bounty and refused to accept Continental currency. As a result -- as he would often do -- George Washington paid the bounty from his own pocket. The problem of accepting "Continentals" would only grow much worse.

indeed, although like prize totals and values, the numbers fluctuate. It is estimated that between 8,500 to 12,000 Americans died in British captivity during the war. While the number is probably closer to the latter than the former, the majority of these deaths were most certainly suffered by American sailors. Due to the period's often vague record-keeping and the fact that many sailors served aboard both privateers as well as Continental vessels, the estimates range from between 60,000 to 70,000 seamen having sailed from American ports aboard some sort of warship.[95]

Certainly, some of those who died in captivity were not sailors, but as ground troops were generally more readily exchanged than captured seamen -- thanks to the Pirate Act -- a vast percentage of imprisoned sailors died. Americans captured in European water generally found their way to English prisons, while patriots captured by the New York of Halifax Squadrons invariably found their way to confinement in America -- probably aboard the prison ship *Jersey* in New York harbor. Of the New York Squad-

Prison Ship *Jersey*
Library of Congress

---

95   James M. Volo, *Blue Water Patriots: The American Revolution Afloat.* (New York : Rowman & Littlefield, 2006), 47 estimates at least 11,000 dead. Also, Charles Royster, *A Revolutionary People at War: The Continental Army and American Character, 1775-1783.* Excerpted from *Major Problems in American Military History.* (New York: Houghton Mifflin, 1999), 87 estimate of 8,000 dying aboard *Jersey.* Additionally, Harold Horwood and Ed Butts, *Bandits and Privateers: Canada in the Age of Gunpowder.* (Halifax: Doubleday, 1988), cite historian D.W. Knox's estimate of some 70,000 American seamen having sailed.

ron, young Horatio Nelson noted in late 1782; "Money is the great object here. Nothing else is attended to."[96] While Nelson's statement was relating to the lust for prizes, it does much to sum-up the state of mind for many New Yorkers.

As far as actual incarceration is concerned, the comparison of internment in England to being held in the colonies presents a stark contrast. In little more than five years, only one hundred men died in England's Mill and Fortin prisons.[97] Certainly, there was no luxury to be had, but the provisions were sufficient, as was shelter. Doctors came to the prison every day and for the sick there was a hospital. There were sutlers on hand, who sold tobacco, bread and various food items along with other small necessities. Many prisoners constructed model ships and sold them to local townsfolk who often visited the prisons. Indeed, some of the finest examples of model ships have been built by prisoners of war, with many skilled French prisoners having used the bones of their rations in construction. Such pastimes still live-on, for perhaps the best matchstick-modeling can be found in America's prison systems. Additionally, Benjamin Franklin did his very best

Bone Model by French POWs U.S. Naval Academy Museum

to provide each prisoner with one shilling a week, and even though some weeks were missed, this shilling undoubtedly helped to feed and care for many prisoners. Most of this money came from a collective effort, but it is certain that the

---

96   John Sugden, *Nelson: A Dream of Glory, 1758-1797.* (New York: Henry Holt, 2004), 216.

97   Robert H. Patton, *Patriot Pirates.* (New York: Random House, 2008), 99.

good doctor put forth many of his own shillings.[98] To further the effort at exchanging prisoners, Franklin offered bounties for captured British sailors, although no European exchanges would occur until 1779. Early in the war, only while the Howe brothers commanded were some prisoners exchanged in America.[99]

Andrew Sherburne sailed aboard Continental vessels as well as privateers, getting his start with the Continentals aboard *Ranger* in 1779 at the age of thirteen. His autobiographical account is often used by historians, and while he wrote this memoir late in life, Sherburne provides an excellent example of the average sailor for many reasons. The fact that he was just a boy also illustrates the mostly forgotten fact that boys of all ages played a large role aboard rebel ships. While most children were initially "powder monkeys" as Sherburne had started out, more and more children would fill the role of common sailor as the war progressed and vast quantities of able-bodied men were locked away in British prisons. Sherburne mentions sailing with thirty boys on a late-war cruise, a number which comprised a third of all hands. When captured, boys -- regardless of age -- were treated no differently by the British. The young sailor was captured three times, with each event providing excellent general examples. Initially, Sherburne was captured at the fall of Charleston in 1780 when *Ranger* became trapped in port by the British fleet. Most of the crew manned shore batteries and were later paroled after capture, as Sherburne was. He was next captured aboard a fishing shallop off Newfoundland in May, 1781 as a member

---

98   Andrew Sherburne, *The Memoirs of Andrew Sherburne.* (Connecticut: Linnet Books, 1993), 66-82. First published in 1824.
99   James M. Volo, *Blue Water Patriots: The American Revolution Afloat.* (New York : Rowman & Littlefield, 2006), Franklin bounties on 47, 249 Howe's prisoners exchanges.

of her prize crew.[100] This was common, as thirty-nine percent of all rebel prizes were recaptured by the Royal Navy.[101] Six months later Sherburne landed in Mill Prison, where he spent nearly a year before being exchanged in a cartel of 400 other prisoners. The teenager would soon be captured for the third time while serving aboard the privateer *Scorpion* in 1782, which was promptly taken by the Royal Navy. This time, Sherburne would be confined aboard the notorious *Jersey* in New York harbor, serving nearly a year of captivity until sprung in March, 1783 by the war's end. On this occasion, the young man was lucky to leave with his life, as he was emaciated by sickness and hobbled by frostbite. Still, thousands of others were much less fortunate, as a sentence aboard a British prison ship was a near-death sentence.[102] Conditions aboard the *Whitby* were so heinous that the prisoners set her afire in 1777.[103] While disease was a big killer, so was starvation. Sherburne noted that his provisions;

> "... consisted of worm eaten ship bread and salt beef. It was supposed that this bread and beef had been condemned in the British navy. The bread had been so eaten by weevils, one might easily crush it in the hand and blow it away."[104]

100   Andrew Sherburne, *The Memoirs of Andrew Sherburne*. (Connecticut: Linnet Books, 1993), 35 details number of boys aboard the privateer Greyhound, 26-31 covers Charleston capture, 46-47 capture aboard prize.

101   James M. Volo, *Blue Water Patriots: The American Revolution Afloat*. (New York : Rowman & Littlefield, 2006), 48.

102   Andrew Sherburne, *The Memoirs of Andrew Sherburne*. (Connecticut: Linnet Books, 1993), 66-81 Mill Prison, 85-86 *Scorpion* and confinement aboard *Jersey*. First published in 1824.

103   Robert H. Patton, *Patriot Pirates*. (New York: Random House, 2008), 99.

104   Andrew Sherburne, *The Memoirs of Andrew Sherburne*. (Connecticut: Linnet Books, 1993), 85. First published in 1824.

Such provisioning aboard the *Jersey* and other prison ships is disquieting, but was not something directly inflicted by the British as a matter of policy. Instead, it is a classic example of greed, for many individuals responsible for procuring food supplies either pocketed the money directly or sold much of the supply to someone else. General Howe had made Joshua Loring his commissary of prisoners, in an effort to reward the husband of his mistress.[105] Loring later admitted to starving to death 300 men by shorting their rations. Loring's provost martial, William Cunningham, was haunted by his complicity until his death, confessing;

> "I shudder at the murders I have been accessory to, both with and without orders from the government, especially while in New York, during which time there were more than 2,000 prisoners starved in the different churches, by stopping their rations, which I sold." [106]

While the Americans certainly paid a high price for their independence, the British suffered their own misfortunes, not the least of which was the loss of a sizeable chunk of her Empire. Wishing to avoid a protracted, costly war in America and the further expansion of the war to include France and Spain, this is not at all what Britain got, as events spiraled such as to even make an enemy of their longest-standing ally, Holland. Lack of a central plan for handling the American rebellion, coupled with a high rate of turn-over among British leaders in that theater only exasperated the problem and did much to see

---

105   Benson Bobrick, *Angel in the Whirlwind: The Triumph of the American Revolution.* (New York: Penguin, 1998), 308.
106   James M. Volo, *Blue Water Patriots: The American Revolution Afloat.* (New York : Rowman & Littlefield, 2006), 249-250, quote on 250.

independence won.[107] Throughout the war, the Royal Navy was seriously under-manned, which hampered both morale and operational ability.[108] The American rebellion played a large part in British naval woes, for in conjunction with losing a prominent supplier of naval stores and manufactured ships, some 13,000 Americans had previously filled the ranks of the Royal Navy.[109] This number is arguably higher, since many of the 42,000 British sailors who deserted during the eight year conflict did so in America. Along with ever-present desertion rates, disease claimed the lives of 18,000 British sailors.[110] The loss of such manpower from the Royal Navy would become the catalyst for Britain's continued impressment of American sailors from merchantmen stopped at sea. Even with war ended, American shipping was not safe, as both British trade policy and contempt for the former rebels allowed for the continued seizure of large numbers of American vessels and cargo. Indeed, as the last ship in the Continental Navy, *Alliance*, was sold-off in 1785, the new nation's banner was nearly an invitation to piracy.[111]

Had France harbored the same doubt and unease toward American independence as had Spain, the French monarchy would have greatly benefited. The war with Britain which spawned from the American rebellion bankrupted France

---

107   John A. Tilley, *The British Navy and the American Revolution.* (University of South Carolina Press, 1987), 280.

108   David Syrett, *The Royal Navy in European Waters during the American Revolutionary War.* (University of South Carolina Press: 1998), 31, 66-67.

109   Robert H. Patton, *Patriot Pirates.* (New York: Random House, 2008), 141.

110   James M. Volo, *Blue Water Patriots: The American Revolution Afloat.* (New York : Rowman & Littlefield, 2006), 64.

111   William M. Fowler, Jr., *Jack Tars and Commodores: The American Navy, 1783-1815,* (New York: Houghton Mifflin, 1984), 8. *Alliance* was sold for $26,000.

and did much to help usher in the French Revolution, which not only plunged the entire French Empire into bloody chaos and war, but also allowed for the emergence of Napoleon. The famed Emperor's later invasion into Spain would cause yet another empire to crumble into revolution. The majority of these subsequent rebellions would have much in common with the American version, especially in the categories of fast American vessels and outright piracy committed on the high seas.

**Napoleon on his imperial throne by
Jean Auguste Dominique**

Tory Picaroons

While the worst atrocities of the American Revolution were generally suffered by North America's native tribes, the strife and friction which ran between Patriots and those they labeled Tories -- whether or not they actually had Loyalist leanings -- did not lag far behind and was certainly more widespread. As historian Mark E. Lender notes, "Most striking about the soldiers' reactions to the Loyalists ... was the virulence of the hatred, a hatred far greater than any anti-British senti-ments."[112] As a result, it is not surprising that the Continental Congress urged each state to enact laws which allowed for the confiscation of loyalist property, most of which also met-ed-out a variety of punishments in conjunction. As historian Benson Bobrick notes, "There was often more than a touch of mercenary greed or "sordid interest" in such reprisals..."[113] Civil wars and revolutions often legitimized theft and piracy, along with allowing for the settling of old grudges. In many ways, this was a key feature of the American Revolution.

Land claims were a common dispute at the time and were generally the result of different dukes and Royal Governors who sold or granted the same land in an area of disputed boundaries. While many states would have border disputes and corresponding skirmishes, the most prominent example of such disputed land can be found with Vermont. The area was mostly settled by New Hampshire frontiersmen who

---

112   Mark E. Lender, "The Mind of the Rank and File: Patriotism and Motivation in the Continental Line," from William C. Wright, ed, *New Jersey in the American Revolution*, vol.3, 1976. Excerpted from *Major Problems in American Military History*. (New York: Houghton Mifflin, 1999), 80-81.

113   Benson Bobrick, *Angel in the Whirlwind: The Triumph of the American Revolution*. (New York: Penguin, 1998), 322-223, quote on 323, in which Bobrick quotes Alexander Hamilton.

bought portions of claims granted by their Royal Governor, Benning Wentworth, who brazenly christened the grant closest to New York after himself, Bennington. However, New York had always claimed the land as its own -- since it actually was -- which quickly led to disputes and the eventual burning-out of settlers. Ethan Allen's Green Mountain Boys were formed as a sort of minuteman militia, but not for protection against the British. Instead, they were to harass anyone --especially "Yorker" surveyors or sheriffs -- who hassled them over their lands. Disputed land is the reason why Allen and the Green Mountain Boys took Fort Ticonderoga, for use as a potential bargaining chip to ensure clear title to their Vermont lands. The Massachusetts Committee of Safety attached Benedict Arnold to the undertaking only at the last minute; mostly to give the action a shred of legitimacy and also claim the fort's captured powder and artillery for the revolution and not the aspirations of Ethan Allen.[114] Always looking for leverage, Allen tried for some years to work a deal with British Canada for Vermont autonomy, which proved to be too much to pull off. However, in 1796 his brother Ira was captured by the Royal Navy while transporting gunpowder, muskets and artillery to the upstart state after purchasing the goods in France. Even five years after achieving statehood, Ira Allen dreamt of an independent Vermont re-christened *United Columbia*.[115]

Delaware would achieve statehood in 1776 after years of battling the claims of William Penn, which had attached the "three lower counties on the Delaware" to Pennsylvania.[116] In southern Sussex County, many farmers suffered the same

114   Pauline Maier, *American Scripture*. (New York: Knopf, 1997), 9.
115   Charles T. Morrissey, *Vermont: A History*. (New York: W.W. Norton, 1984), 86-99. Ethan Allen and his brothers had formed the Onion River Land Company in 1773, representing some 60,000 disputed acres.
116   Carol E. Hoffecker, *Delaware: A Bicentennial History*. (New York: W.W. Norton, 1977), 140.

problem Vermont was experiencing with disputed land grants, mostly on parcels granted by Lord Baltimore. Among other reasons, this resulted in a large Loyalist population on the Delmarva Peninsula, many of which were devout Tories or out-right criminals who swarmed the many inlets, creeks and rivers along the Chesapeake shore and raided towns practically at will. At the state's northern end, the situation was little better, as dislocated Loyalists from Philadelphia and New Jersey banded together in roving gangs and took to the Delaware River in "refugee galleys" -- whaleboats and barges which darted out from places such as Reedy and Pea Patch Islands to attack rebel shipping. Thomas Truxtun, the future U.S. Navy Commodore who would wreak havoc among the French during the Quasi-War, spent the revolution alternating between smuggling and serving aboard privateers. Sailing from Philadelphia, Truxtun engaged Tory picaroons off Reedy Island at least twice; once in a ten-gun merchantman in 1779 and again in the twenty-gun *St. James* in 1781 as he sailed with Thomas Barclay aboard as a passenger, the American envoy to France. Shortly after clearing Delaware Bay, Truxtun was then forced to beat-off a New York Loyalist privateer of some twenty-four guns. In September of the following year, Truxtun suffered a loss as part-owner of the privateer schooner *Harlequin*, which was captured on the Delaware by "refugee galleys." The mouth of the Delaware would prove treacherous throughout the war.[117] Even the coast of the new state witnessed sporadic raiding from similar pirates, such as in August, 1781 when John Dickinson's home was plundered by sixteen water-mobile Tories.[118] Dickinson had drafted the

117   Eugene S. Ferguson, *Truxton of the Constellation: The Life of Commodore Thomas Truxton, U.S. Navy, 1755-1822.* (Baltimore: Johns Hopkins University Press, 2000), 33 details 1779 fight, 42-45 covers 1781 action, *Harlequin* on 48. Originally published 1956.
118   Carol E. Hoffecker, *Delaware: A Bicentennial History.* (New York:

Continental Congress' July, 1775 "Olive Branch Petition" to King George III and was the sole delegate not to sign the Declaration of Independence.[119] While Dickinson was no Loyalist, the irony is inescapable. As the war progressed, the picaroons on both Chesapeake and Delaware Bays would wage war mostly for themselves, targeting rebels and Loyalists alike.

**Flight of Lord Dunmore —
Library of Congress**

The actions of Lord Dunmore, the last Royal Governor of Virginia, proved to be of key importance to piracy on the Chesapeake. Indeed, many historians credit Dunmore with doing more than anyone else to cement the Southern and Northern colonies together in rebellion. In October, 1775, Dunmore began to openly speak of freeing all rebel slaves who wished to bear arms for the crown, and on November 7, offered an official decree making it so. Not only did Dunmore manage to turn many potential Loyalists to the rebel camp,

W.W. Norton, 1977), 167.
119   Pauline Maier, *American Scripture*. (New York: Knopf, 1997), 24, 150.

but also did much to stiffen the rebellion of the Southern colonies. One Pennsylvanian declared, "Hell itself could not have invented anything more black than this design of emancipating our slaves." Even George Washington shared such outrage.[120] The effect of Dunmore's policy -- which became British policy -- was to add a special twist to the age-old piratical practice of raiding plantations.

On Chesapeake Bay piracy, Donald Shomette notes, "There would be no sanctuary for either patriot or Tory anywhere along the thousands of miles of shoreline, or on the waters of the Bay itself."[121]

Shommete further elaborates,

> "It was a conflict whose principle weapons were the barge, whale boat, row galley, and schooner. There was no strategy, and tactics consisted of little more than brutal, lightning raids launched from remote islands, no-holds-barred skirmishes, and the wanton plunder of innocent civilians."[122]

When Lord Dunmore fled to the safety of his ships and then sailed up the Chesapeake, he loosely commissioned several Loyalists to scour the countryside and appropriate food for his troops. One such man was Joseph Wheland, Jr., who would become the scourge of the Bay. The main attraction to such a position was that a man could plunder for himself while he plundered for the King. Somerset County, Maryland was overrun with Tory raiders, who quickly fanned out across the Bay in the summer of 1776. Many personal scores were

120   Robert Harvey, *A Few Bloody Noses: The Realities and Mythologies of the American Revolution.* (New York: Overlook Press, 2001), 183-185, quote on 183.
121   Donald G. Shomette, *Pirates on the Chesapeake.* (Centreville, MD: Tidewater, 1985), 255.
122   Ibid, 256.

settled in the process. When plantations were raided, the majority of the slaves encountered -- who normally would have been prized captures worth good money -- were instead set free, with a large number of them joining the picaroons. Certainly, the lure of vengeance over other masters must have been a strong attraction, along with feelings of loyalty toward those who had freed them. In turn, black picaroons would terrify the peninsula and Bay with the slaveholder's worst fear -- armed slaves in rebellion.

Joseph Wheland, Jr. would experience a very short few months in his new profession before being captured aboard his sloop by militia Major Daniel Fallin and thirty patriots in late July, 1776 off of Hooper's Strait. Wheland would spend five years in jail and earn his freedom with a 10,000 pound bond -- posted by others -- and a pledge of fidelity. However, after moving his family up the Wicomico River in 1781, he would resume his former career with a vengeance.

After Wheland's capture, the situation on the Chesapeake calmed down to sporadic raids, visits from New York Loyalist privateers and small-scale piracies. To some degree, the miniscule Maryland and Virginia state navies played a part in deterring picaroon activity until 1779. However, most of the fleet was sold at auction in early 1780, as the vessels had become rather worn-out -- excepting for the schooners *Dolphin* and *Plater*, who would be involved in future operations.[123]

The appearance of a Royal Navy Squadron under Sir George Collier in the spring of 1779 provided much of the reason for the resurgence of raiding. Lord Dunmore had departed the region in early 1776, negating the need for local supplies. However, Collier's ships would provide the same market. As a result, Stephen Mister from Smith Island took up where his former accomplice Wheland had left off and

123   Ibid, 256-258 Wheland, 264 Maryland and Virginia state navies.

led a wave of picaroon activity across the Bay. *Dolphin* and *Plater* were ordered to root him out of Tangier Sound on April 4, 1779. Neither the schooners nor a detachment of the Dorchester County militia found any picaroons, however, due to the myriad of waterways, creeks, rivers and islands that comprise the region. In many respects, the Eastern Shore and areas bordering the Bay are a pirate's dream because of the terrain, which not only offers abundant escape routes and hiding places, but also numerous spots to ambush prey. Mister would roam free for another year until being captured by Virginia patriots in August, 1780. Regardless, until the war's end in 1783, a variety of local agencies "applied for measures to stop the pirates" to the Maryland government.[124]

The Eastern Shore would fall into sharper focus the following year, as the summer of 1780 witnessed a rash of picaroon and privateer activity which hit Somerset and Worchester counties particularly hard. Once again, the appearance of yet another Royal Navy Squadron kicked events into high-gear that summer, especially as the ships brought 2,000 soldiers under General Alexander Leslie to destroy rebel munitions stored at Richmond and Petersburg, Virginia. Within days of the fleet's arrival, the lower Bay and Eastern Shore "literally swarmed with the predatory barges, galleys, and privateers of the enemy."[125]

The Chesapeake mainland would not be overlooked, however, especially the Patuxent River, one of Maryland's most important commercial waterways. The plantations running along this river were not only some of the richest in Maryland, but were practically undefended. Making off with two vessels loaded with tobacco, the raiders sought provisions from patriot Colonel William Fitzhugh's estate. When the

---

124   Ibid, 259-261, quote on 260.
125   Ibid, 264, author quoted.

request was refused, the picaroons shot his house to rubble with cannon fire and burned what remained. For the last two months of the year and into 1781, the Patuxent would fall victim to what amounted to a picaroon blockade, as the raiders made off with a number of vessels loaded with goods for market.

In January, 1781 the Maryland Council learned that Benedict Arnold had arrived in Virginia with a force of 3,000. At roughly the same time, Joseph Wheland, Jr. had been released from captivity and wasted no time in getting back to work. Along with the Timmons brothers, Wheland led a flotilla of four barges which roamed the shoreline, capturing and occasionally burning vessels while dashing inland to plunder small towns and plantations. It seemed the blow could fall anywhere, at anytime -- the Patuxent, the Potomac, St. Mary's County, Point Lookout, the entire Eastern Shore and even into Delaware.

One of the more notable instances at that time concerned a joint privateer-picaroon plan to sack Vienna on March 10, 1781. Sailing up the Nanticoke with a brig and two sloops -- one armed with fourteen 18-pounders -- the raiders bombarded the town and then began to row ashore. However, they reaped lead instead of plunder, as local militia hotly contested the landing. Due to the shipboard artillery, a landing was finally forced, with the raiders suffering three or four men killed and the patriots losing one man while both sides counted several men wounded. After landing, the attackers ran up a flag of truce and brokered a deal for the town's grain supply, with payment at market price. If the terms were found unacceptable, then Vienna would be put to the torch. As the militia was outnumbered and out-gunned, the terms were agreed to. The raiders were good to their word, however, and left after loading up the grain.[126]

While such deals with the enemy for food might seem strange, especially as many port towns stopped such sales to British forces either voluntary or through patriot coercion, such practices were not an uncommon feature of the American Revolution.[127] As the war dragged on, many farmers -- even conflicted patriots -- would be forced to sell provisions to British forces for the simple fact that they paid for supplies in gold and silver, while the farmer who sold to the Continentals either went unpaid or was given over-inflated and worthless currency. The events at Machias, Maine (part of Massachusetts at the time), in June, 1775 began as a patriot lumber for British food deal which utterly collapsed when the local Tory who brokered the transaction, Ichabod Jones, announced his desire to exclude townsmen who had voted against the deal. The people of Machias -- a small lumber town which had always been dependent on imported food goods, a situation made worse by a drought in 1774 -- had written the Massachusetts Provincial Congress in May, in order to broker a lumber-for-food deal with the patriots. Having yet to be answered, and with Jones arriving in June with provisions for a similar deal in order to procure wood for the British in Boston, a vote was taken and bargain struck. However, the smugness of Jones was too much to swallow. Jones and Midshipman Moore fled from church when they spotted an armed mob coming for them. Jones' *Polly* was stripped of her sails and later confiscated, while *Unity* was taken by locals and used with *Falmouth Packet* to chase down the tiny Royal Navy sloop *Margaretta* and take her with a swift boarding

---

126   Ibid, 265-268.

127   James L. Nelson, *George Washington's Secret Navy*. (New York: McGraw-Hill, 2008), 8 illustrates the steps taken to prohibit provision sales to any "ministerial forces."

action. Midshipman Moore was shot twice during the action and died the next morning. *Margaretta* would be stripped of her pivot guns and stored 3-pounders, which were used to arm the captured *Polly*, renamed *Machias Liberty* after she was taken into service by the Massachusetts Provincial Congress for the protection of Machias a few weeks later.[128]

Most of the provisioning in the Chesapeake area would be done with either threats or outright violence, as plantations, farms and towns were plundered and put to the torch. By March of 1781, the citizens of Somerset County petitioned the state to build a barge large enough to carry sixty men and a 24-pound gun, at a cost of 150 pounds. When the cash-strapped government failed to act, locals built it themselves at Snow Hill, christening the craft *Protector*. The barge did well and captured a few prizes while driving off several picaroons, undoubtedly aided by the zeal of her crew. Such action sparked other communities to follow suit, with Queen Anne and Talbot counties paying for *Experiment* while Dorchester County built the barge *Defence*. Other vessels would appear in a similar fashion, like *Intrepid*, *Terrible* and *Fearnaught*, some of which were captured pirate craft.[129]

In late April, two patriot privateer schooners cruised the Bay and captured the New York Loyalist privateer *Jack-A-Lanthorn*(6) and her prize, after having already taken the *Resolution*. However, such captures provided little respite from the near-daily piracies and plunder which overran the peninsula that summer. Even Lord Cornwallis was shocked by the activity and ruthlessness of the picaroons. Salisbury was nearly blockaded by a force of such pirates, with Joseph

128   Ibid, 23-35.
129   Donald G. Shomette, *Pirates on the Chesapeake*. (Centreville, MD: Tidewater, 1985), 270-271. A merchant-backed "Board of Patuxent Associators" attempted to fit-out a vessel, but the plan sunk when the schooner *Nautilus* proved to be unserviceable.

Wheland, Jr. right in the thick of it all.[130]

By late July, the Maryland government was able to patch together a small naval force, having been seriously handicapped throughout the war by a lack of funding. A paucity of sailors proved problematic as well, for many seamen had either signed-on with privateers, Continental ships, or had joined the ranks of the picaroons. However, under the activity of Commodore George Grason of the Maryland State Navy, a three-barge flotilla encountered a similar-sized picaroon force, commanded by Wheland himself. While Wheland escaped in a whaleboat, two other boats and the pirate barge *Restoration* were captured, along with a pirate leader named McMullen. Such action did not dissuade the bandits, however, who continued to raid the local rivers, seizing a number of tobacco-laden vessels and launching an abortive attack of Vienna. That attack failed, costing the pirates one barge and three captured picaroons.[131]

The tale of John Greenwood says much about conditions on the Bay. At fifteen, Greenwood served as a fifer for a Massachusetts regiment which saw action at Bunker Hill and Trenton. When his term of enlistment expired, he joined the crew of a privateer, which was eventually captured by the British in the Caribbean. After spending five months in a Barbados jail, Greenwood came to the Chesapeake and bought a small schooner with a partner, hoping to engage the local coasting trade. A victim of poor timing, Greenwood's schooner fell victim in August, 1781 to two row galleys holding ninety men, commanded by Joseph Wheland, Jr. Not long after a pirate prize crew was put aboard his schooner, the picaroons spied a tobacco trader heading down the Bay and took off after her. During the chase, Greenwood and his partner were

---

130   Ibid, 272-273.
131   Ibid, 274-275.

able to overpower the prize crew and sail to Baltimore, where he sold his share of the vessel as soon as he could. He gave a brief description of the men who captured him:

> "…a set of gallows-marked rascals, fit for nothing but thieves; hellhounds and plunderers from inoffensive, unarmed people, they seemed to be without any kind of principle… Their whole object was plunder and they paid no manner or regard to the vessel they despoiled, be it loyal or otherwise; gain was all they sought, and to acquire from others what they were through mere laziness unable to obtain for themselves…"[132]

Greenwood certainly gave an apt description, for by late summer, 1781 the picaroons were targeting former Tory Loyalist allies, launching raids from Gwynn's Island at the mouth of the Piankatank. However, there was a brief lull in piracy when Lord Cornwallis surrendered his forces at Yorktown in mid-October, although the presence of the French fleet in the Chesapeake likely had more to do with the down-turn in activity. Coincidently, Joseph Wheland, Jr. and his "lieutenant" Timmons were captured in North Carolina at this time. Ever slippery, both men would escape in relative short-order. In November, the Maryland privateer *Porpoise* captured a pirate schooner, although much of the Maryland state navy was again lashed to the docks due to financial problems after the surrender of Cornwallis. The French did make at least two captures, one of them being the *Tarleton*, which was taken into French service. While promising four corvettes, France did not deliver them and placed the responsibility of clearing the Chesapeake squarely on the Maryland government.[133]

---

132   Ibid, 277-281, quote on 281.
133   Ibid, 275, 283-284.

With Tangier Island again becoming a notorious pirate base, as a rash of piracy swept across the Bay during the winter, Commodore Grason was ordered to depopulate the island, but the plan fell apart due to insufficient manpower. However, Maryland ordered their small flotilla into action in May, 1782, but still found themselves severely short of hands. Frustrated, Grason gathered what men he could and loaded them into his "flagship," the barge *Revenge*, and made for the Potomac. Grason found three picaroon barges and was killed engaging them, along with several of his men, as the *Revenge* was taken as a prize.

Outraged, Maryland passed a new Act for the Protection of the Bay Trade, which not only providing funding for four barges, a galley and their respective crews, but for the first time allowed captured British property to be paid-out in prize money.[134] This provision alone might have been the act's best feature, as the Continental Navy -- which paid only up to half of the prize value to the crew for most of the war -- had long suffered crew shortages due to the sailors' relative flocking to man privateers, who were eligible for all of a prize's worth.

However, the Maryland state navy was still slow in preparing, although their plan of action was in line with George Washington's advice on the matter, which called for barges and galleys as the picaroons themselves used.[135] In the matter of hunting pirates, the "fight fire with fire" method of operating had historically produced the best results.[136] In the meantime, the pirates continued their depredations, growing so bold as to attack a Massachusetts privateer at night while lying at anchor off St. George's Island on July 2. The *Ranger* had seven guns

134   Ibid, 286, both Grason's fight and Protection Act.
135   Ibid, 287-288.
136   Peter Earle, *The Pirate Wars*. (New York: St. Martin's, 2003), 187. Oared vessels were especially useful both to pirates and smugglers along with those hunting them.

with a crew of only twenty and yet managed not only to repel two picaroon barges which attempted to board, but killed or wounded nearly half of the sixty attackers. *Ranger* lost one man, but had several others badly wounded. By late summer, 1782 the Maryland navy sailed, under Commodore Zedikiah Walley, and almost immediately recaptured four vessels taken as picaroon prizes in September. For a short while, it seemed that the pirates were on the run, as the Maryland state flotilla was augmented by a variety of the locally-built Eastern Shore barges. Together, this flotilla would take the barge *Jolly Tar* with eighteen picaroons in mid-November, while giving chase to three others. When word arrived that the picaroons were spotted off Tangier Island, Walley gave immediate chase.[137]

On the morning of November 30, six picaroon sails were sighted. As the Maryland flotilla approached, the pirates formed their five barges into a line of battle, which was exactly what Walley had hoped for. Battle was quickly joined off Cager's Strait and for the first few moments, as Walley's *Protector* pounded away with her eighteen-pounder and *Defence* poured in her twelve-pound shot, it appeared that the pirates were on the verge of breaking. The tide turned when loose powder from a broken paper charge caught fire aboard *Protector*, igniting the powder supply. A second explosion occurred moments later, which nearly evaporated three men. *Protector* was then engulfed by picaroon barges, who boarded in an angry surge. Vicious hand-to-hand combat broke out, which claimed the life of Commodore Walley, his lieutenant, a militia captain and twenty-five crewmen. Colonel Cropper of the state militia was wounded, as were twenty-nine others, four of which later died from their wounds. Seeing their flagship fall prize to the picaroons, the majority of the Maryland

---

137   Donald G. Shomette, *Pirates on the Chesapeake.* (Centreville, MD: Tidewater, 1985), 287-291.

flotilla fled, causing *Defence* to break off the engagement or become a prize herself. The pirates chased after the state ships for the rest of the day. The battle would stand as the bloodiest day of the American Revolution for the Maryland State Navy. The pirates suffered as well, however, with a "Captain Kidd" -- long a piratical pseudonym -- of the barge *Kidnapper* tallying twenty-two killed and wounded on his vessel alone. While "Kidd" was kind enough to parole the wounded Colonel Cropper and other prisoners, many of the patriot wounded had been given no quarter and were slaughtered on deck of the *Protector*. It was latter learned that Wheland himself had commanded the pirates.[138]

With the defeat of law and order, piracy on the Bay and the pillage of the surrounding countryside continued nearly unchecked for the next few months. It was common knowledge that an official peace was forthcoming, which made the picaroons eager to plunder and steal from anyone, while the getting was good.

It would not be until March 22, 1783 that Maryland could launch another expedition against the picaroons. Certainly, the utter defeat suffered during the last engagement was not much of an inducement in recruiting for another. Fittingly enough, the picaroons were now reputed to have infested Devil's Island (today's Deal Island), and Captain Solomon Frazier -- who had commanded *Defence* in the previous action -- led a small flotilla which was determined to crush the picaroons once and for all.

What truly occurred is less than clear. Word of the official end of the American Revolution reached Annapolis on March 23, but on March 31, Captain Bryan and the officers of *Defense* were charged with misconduct for boarding and plundering a vessel. Additionally, they were charged with "Plundering the

138   Ibid, 294-299.

Citizens of this State on some one of the Islands on the Bay of Chesapeak."[139] The lack of records -- other than the charges levied against the men of the *Defense* -- make it seem likely that picaroons were not only found on Devil's Island, but were attacked and plundered, probably after news of the treaty had arrived. As records would only incriminate those involved, they probably weren't kept. Perhaps only the *Defense* was involved, but this seems unlikely. What seems more reasonable is that -- after suffering years of piracy, pillaging, death and burning -- when the patriot forces finally got the drop on the picaroons, the official date of incident was of little concern to them. Either way, the "official" end to the war is harder to pin down than the January 20, 1783 Treaty of Paris date. Certainly, enemy prizes captured past that date should lawfully have been deemed unfit captures by prize courts. However, due to the time lag surrounding information coming from Europe, neither the Continental Congress nor Sir Guy Carleton's British troops declared a cessation of hostilities until roughly April. News of the peace was not presented to the Continental troops until April 19, eight years to the day from the opening volleys fired at Lexington and Concord.[140]

One of the better examples depicting the level of strife between patriots and Tories in the Chesapeake region can be seen with the punishment handed down for the eight ringleaders of the "Black Camp Rebellion" of 1780 in lower Sussex County, Delaware, although no rebellion actually occurred. These eight Tories were sentenced to be hanged as follows:

> "By the neck but not until dead, for then your
> bowels must be taken out and burnt before

---

139   Ibid, 302-304, quote on 304.
140   Benson Bobrick, *Angel in the Whirlwind: The Triumph of the American Revolution.* (New York: Penguin, 1998), 476.

your face, then your head must be severed from your body, and your body divided into four quarters, these must be at the disposal of the supreme Authority in the State."

To their great fortune, these men would be pardoned by the Delaware General Assembly on November 4, 1780. After all, cruel and unusual punishment was a point of contention held against the British.[141] However, Delaware would hand out harsh discipline for quite some time. Flogging with a cat-o'-nine tails was routinely dealt out as punishment until 1952, although the law remained on the books until 1972.[142]

**Rhode Island, 1780 Rochambeau —
Library of Congress**

141   Michael Morgan, *Pirates and Patriots: Tales of the Delaware Coast.* (New York: Algora: 2005), 43-44. Quote on 43.
142   Carol E. Hoffecker, *Delaware: A Bicentennial History.* (New York: W.W. Norton, 1977), 129. From 1900-1942, 1,604 prisoners were flogged,

It should be noted that while there was abundant whale-boat activity surrounding Boston early in the war and across Long Island and the Sound throughout the war, these actions were not piratical as much as they were tactical. The same can be said of the whaleboat fleet which "blockaded" Savannah in the summer of 1775, although these men were prone to plundering captured vessels.[143] While some out-right theft undoubtedly occurred -- as it seemed to happen nearly every-where during the war -- these whaleboat actions were more in line with activities concerning a waterborne militia looking to harass the enemy. Similar endeavors would be found in Connecticut and Rhode Island waters as well. Many soldiers had been former sailors, particularly in this instance, and so the whaleboat was a natural means of transportation for them. Early in the war, George Washington utilized the flotilla of whaleboats surrounding Boston as a reconnaissance force.[144]

One final escapade is worth noting. While the war ended for America on January 20, the final treaty between Britain, France and Spain wouldn't become official until its signing on September 3, 1783. The preliminary treaty of January 20 made it clear that a number of captured British island colonies -- such as the Bahamas -- would be returned, while Spain would be given Florida. The Bahamas had been sacked twice by the Americans, and on May 7, 1782 fell to a force of American vessels and Spanish troops, with a shot never being fired during any of the "attacks." Spain chose to occupy

22% of the total prison population, page 128.

143   Robert H. Patton, *Patriot Pirates*. (New York: Random House, 2008), 24. These men were so bold as to capture a letter from Georgia's Royal Governor, which requested aid from the Royal Navy to clear the harbor of patriot whaleboats. The patriots re-wrote the letter to declare that everything was fine and no ships were needed.

144   James L. Nelson, *George Washington's Secret Navy*. (New York: McGraw-Hill, 2008), 53-54.

the Bahamas and garrisoned over 700 men on the island of New Providence, on which was located the capital, Nassau. Meanwhile, a number of Loyalists had fled to Florida, and with the unsettling news of the coming treaty which would return Florida to Spain, many dislocated Tories simply didn't know where to turn.

Andrew Deveaux was such a displaced loyalist, the Lt.-Colonel of a South Carolina Loyalist militia unit. In April, 1783, Deveaux and "a handful of ragged militia" sailed to New Providence in two armed brigantines and launched an attack on Nassau. Fort Montagu was taken during the night without a shot fired, as were the heights surrounding the city. Due to impending peace, the Spanish were not expecting attack. By sheer bluff and maneuver, Deveaux tricked the Spanish governor into surrendering by building scarecrows on the heights and ferrying troops from the brigs in an unending cycle by having them lie down in the boats for the return trip -- out of sight -- climbing aboard the brig from the far-side and then boarding another boat back to shore on the other. After the surrender, when the ruse became apparent, the Spanish were shocked. Historian Michael Craton sums up the result:

> "Naturally enough, no-one gained more from this brilliant exploit than Andrew Deveaux himself. Carving out an estate of 250 acres in eastern New Providence and another 1,000 acres in Cat Island, he became a prominent Member of the reconstituted House of Assembly."[145]

Following the war, a large number of Loyalists would flock to Canada, with a great many Southern Loyalists bringing their slaves with them to the Bahamas, more than tripling

---

145   Michael Craton, *A History of the Bahamas*. (San Salvador Press, 1999, first printed 1962),143-147, quote on 147.

the population by 1788. This resulted in one of the sweetest ironies of the American Revolution. In October, 1787, Lord Dunmore -- the very same man who as Virginia's last Royal Governor had done so much to inflame Southerners in 1775 -- arrived in Nassau as the new Royal Governor. His leadership would be nearly as inept in the Bahamas as it had been in Virginia, although this time he freed no slaves.[146] Those slaves who had heard Dunmore's call and flocked to his banner during the revolution suffered perhaps the worst irony of the war, as Dunmore sold roughly a thousand of them back into slavery after fleeing Virginia for the West Indies.[147] Regardless, one can only imagine the thoughts and emotions of the former Americans.

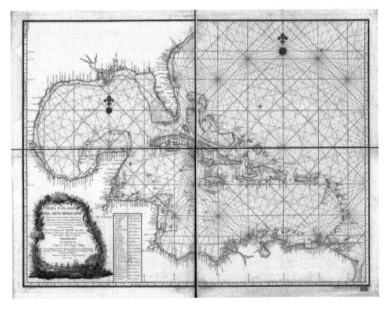

Caribbean, 1787

146   Ibid, 148, 159.
147   Benson Bobrick, *Angel in the Whirlwind.* (New York: Penguin, 1998), 163.

King George III
U.S. National Archives

British Isles, 1783
U.S. National Archives

Top: Lyon vs. Griswold — Library of Congress
Bottom: British Portrayal of XYZ Affair — Library of Congress
Background: Bill which established the U.S. Navy, 1798 —
U.S. National Archives

Chapter Two

Quasi-War Piracy

From 1797-1801, France and the United States waged an undeclared war on the high seas, the vast majority of which was fought in the Caribbean. The Jay Treaty, ratified by the Senate in 1795 as an effort to end British seizures of U.S. merchant shipping and tie up a variety of loose ends leftover from the American Revolution, was the primary cause for this naval friction. The Revolutionary French government took offense at what they perceived as a pact between the U.S. and Britain, their enemy since February, 1793. As a result, both France and her Caribbean colonies issued an immense number of privateer commissions and began seizing large numbers of American merchant vessels in 1796. In order to combat these piratical seizures, as the last Continental warship had been sold-off in 1785, Congress passed legislation in 1798 which not only created the United States Navy and Marine Corps, but authorized funds for both the construction of warships as well as the conversion of purchased merchantmen.

With the exception of Commodore Thomas Truxtun's battles with two French frigates, much of the hard-fought naval actions which occurred during this period have been little discussed. Instead, the Quasi-War is renowned for the partisan politics of the Federalists and Republicans -- easily illustrated by the Lyon-Griswold fight on the floor of Congress, which utilized fire-tongs and a hickory walking stick -- as well as the infamous XYZ Affair and the notorious Alien and Sedition Acts. Also largely overshadowed by the period's political intrigues has been the covert support given to the revolution in Saint Domingue -- modern day Haiti -- specifically the aid given to the black revolutionary Toussaint Louverture by the administration of President John Adams.

Revolution

On February 1, 1793, Revolutionary France declared war on Britain, Spain and Holland. President Washington, not wishing for the young nation to become entangled in European wars, would issue a proclamation of neutrality. Along with declarations of war, France also opened trade with previously closed West Indies colonies to merchants of any nation. American shipping -- already restricted from the British West Indies -- flocked to these French islands. As a result, American merchant vessels would fall victim to seizure by the Royal Navy in large numbers, as Britain invoked the Rule of 1756, which stated that items previously banned from trade during peace could not be traded in war.[148] These captures would cause Washington to send Chief Justice John Jay to London, which would result in the Jay Treaty, ratified in 1795 only after an appeal to the Senate from Washington himself. While the treaty cleared up some border disputes and would lead to the British evacuation of most of their forts in the Northwest Territory, it also bound the U.S. to a lop-sided trade agreement with Britain.

France considered the Jay Treaty to be a slap in their revolutionary faces, for the Franco-American Alliance of 1778 was not only still valid, but even allowed French privateers to be fitted out in American ports, along with the institution

---

148   Alexander DeConde, *The Quasi-War: The Politics and Diplomacy of the Undeclared War with France, 1797-1801.* (New York: Scribners, 1966), 199.

of prize courts to condemn captured goods and vessels. The French consul to the U.S., "Citizen" Edmond Genet, not only passed along French letters of marque, but also lent a hand in directly fitting out privateers in Charleston and Philadelphia. By August 1793, Genet would be recalled to France due to President Washington's outraged insistence,[149] and in late June, the Treasury Department ordered customs houses and revenue agents to deny entry to privateers from all nations. Once again, the Jay Treaty could be blamed, as Article 24 prevented the U.S. from providing privateers for any nation at war with Britain.[150] While the Jay Treaty was derisive to many Americans, to Revolutionary France it was an outrage.

In a rapidly-deteriorating political situation, the French Directory declared in July, 1796 that neutral vessels should be treated by France as they were treated by Britain. The following month, colonial French privateers would begin seizing American merchants hauling British goods in the Caribbean. On March 2, 1797, the French decreed that U.S. merchant ships must carry a *role d'equipage* -- a list of all crewmen and their nationalities -- along with tightening up on what cargo was considered contraband. The *role d'equipage* rule had been a part of the 1778 Treaty of Amity and Commerce, but had never been enforced. As a result, scores of American ships were seized by the French -- particularly by their privateers, already active against Britain.[151] Certainly, many of these merchants were indeed "smuggling" and liable to seizure -- as

---

149   Joseph J. Ellis, *American Creation: Triumphs and Tragedies at the Founding of the Republic.* (New York: Knopf, 2007), 190.
150   Irving H. King, *The Coast Guard Under Sail: The U.S. Revenue Cutter Service 1789-1865.* (Annapolis, MD: Naval Institute Press, 1989), 20-21.
151   Michael A. Palmer, *Stoddert's War: Naval Operations during the Quasi-War with France, 1798-1801.* (Annapolis, MD: Naval Institute Press, 2000), 4-5. Originally published by South Carolina Press, 1987.

was still the case with many on-going British seizures -- but most merchants were being seized and condemned for no reason at all. The situation would only worsen the following year, when a French decree on January 18, 1798 authorized the seizure of any vessel carrying British goods. Often, this resulted in vessels being seized if *any* British item was found aboard, even things like sextons or navigational equipment.[152]

Victor Hughes, *commissair civil* of French Guadeloupe, was firm in his revolutionary beliefs and turned the colony into a microcosm of Paris as he mirrored the violence and butchery done to Royalists. Not surprisingly, Hughes was quite emotional about American shipping and the Jay Treaty, taking it upon himself to cover the Caribbean with blank privateer commissions starting in August, 1796. That the situation "degenerated rapidly into piracy" was even recognized by the French Directors by July, 1798, who admitted that many French privateers "have infringed the laws of the republic relative to cruising and prizes ... that foreigners and pirates have abused the latitude allowed at Cayenne."[153] Cayenne, oddly enough, is where Victor Hughes would be sent by the French government in December, 1799. The following year, American losses would triple in the surrounding area.[154] Having been replaced at Guadeloupe by General Desfourneaux in 1798, as France attempted to tighten up control, Hughes would be arrested, sent back to France for trial, cleared and eventually sent to Cayenne. Upon his arrival at Guadeloupe, Desfourneaux noted, "a system of piracy almost general, sustained by a commercial tribunal which condemns without reserve and without exception..."[155]

---

152   Ibid, 6.
153   Ibid, 75, quotes on 76.
154   Ibid, 148-49.
155   Ibid, 76.

Under such conditions, from October, 1796 to June, 1797 the U.S. lost 316 merchant vessels due to French privateer/pirate seizures, the majority captured in the Caribbean -- out of an American merchant fleet roughly 5,000 strong.[156] By September, 1800, the French would tally 2,309 American vessels. The U.S. government would eventually deal with 6,479 total claims concerning goods and vessels.[157]

A Call To Arms

John Adams —
White House

John Adams had advocated American naval strength since the early days of the revolution. When he became the nation's second president in March, 1797 the U.S. had no navy, nor were American merchants allowed to arm their vessels in defense. President Washington had forbade the arming of merchant vessels because he realized it would only invite Britain -- or potentially any other nation -- to seize U.S. merchants under a claim of "piracy." In July, 1797 Congress provided for the completion of three of the six frigates begun in 1794 and gave approval for the Treasury's Revenue Cutters to be used as a naval force. However, President Adams had nothing else to work with in the meantime,

---

156   William M. Fowler, Jr., *Jack Tars and Commodores: The American Navy, 1783-1815*, (New York: Houghton Mifflin, 1984), 31.
157   Michael A. Palmer, *Stoddert's War: Naval Operations during the Quasi-War with France, 1798-1801*. (Annapolis, MD: Naval Institute Press, 2000), 6. Merchant fleet estimate on 5.

and as the number of French captures rose, he petitioned Congress on March 19, 1798 to allow American merchant vessels to arm themselves.[158]

The fight over arming merchants would betray the heart of the Republican-Federalist fight, which boiled down to whether or not you "backed" France or England. The issue was cleared when Adams released the "XYZ papers," which told the tale of France demanding bribe money -- $250,000 worth -- in order to treat with U.S. diplomats, along with a corresponding loan to France worth some $6 to $13 million. News of the "XYZ Affair" was released under Republican pressure and immediately back-fired against them, unleashing a wave of anti-French feeling across the nation.[159]

Adams would use the political momentum to great advantage, signing a series of bills in the next few months which would create the Department of the Navy (April 30), a permanent Marine Corps (July 11), allow for arming merchantmen (June 25), revoke all previous French treaties (July 9), provide $950,000 to buy, build or lease twelve 22-gun ships, as well as funding to finish the last of the six frigates begun in 1794. Finally, on July 9, 1798, President Adams signed the act which permitted the Navy to take armed French ships anywhere on the high seas. Originally, Congress had only allowed for the seizure of armed French ships off the U.S. coast on May, 28. This is indicative of the degree of strife and partisanship which raged in Congress, even after the release of the XYZ papers.[160]

---

158   Alexander DeConde, *The Quasi-War: The Politics and Diplomacy of the Undeclared War with France, 1797-1801*. (New York: Scribners, 1966), 15, XYZ Affair and merchant arming, 70. The "loan" was an odd money-exchange scheme involving Dutch currency at a discounted rate.

159   Ibid, 71-73.

160   William M. Fowler, Jr., *Jack Tars and Commodores: The American*

There were other strange stipulations in many Congressional acts, such as only *armed* French vessels could be targeted by U.S. forces on the *high seas*. As a result, few actual American privateers would be commissioned, since no unarmed merchant vessels were allowed to be captured. Armed American merchants were only allowed to defend themselves against French vessels -- which explains why the majority of commissions were obtained by merchantmen, as "insurance" against claims of piracy.[161] Such merchants would prove to be wise, for even while there would be a degree of U.S.-British cooperation throughout the Quasi-War, this can be attributed to sharing a common enemy, not common trade beliefs. The British would continue to seize American vessels and cargos throughout the two and a-half active years of the Quasi-War. The Royal Navy continued to press American sailors into service from merchantmen intercepted at sea and even attempted to force them from the decks of the fledgling U.S. Navy -- which only worked the first time.

By late spring, 1798, the U.S. Navy was still in the making, as merchantmen were being converted and frigates finished construction. The Revenue Cutter Service would not only receive a larger breed of freshly-built

Frigate *Essex*, 1799

Navy, 1783-1815, (New York: Houghton Mifflin, 1984), 32-36.

161 Alexander DeConde, *The Quasi-War: The Politics and Diplomacy of the Undeclared War with France, 1797-1801.* (New York: Scribners, 1966),127. Over 1,000 merchant vessels would be commissioned.

cutters that year, but also an expanded service role. Congress also authorized the president to receive up to twelve ships as "gifts." These "subscription ships" were built from local or regional donations and would include the frigate *Essex*, christened for Essex County, Massachusetts. Fort Pinckney would be built in Charleston by similar funding.[162] Not until late spring, 1798, did any U.S. warships began cruising. Just a short while later -- July 7 -- Stephen Decatur, Sr. captured the French privateer *la Croyable* (12) off the Delaware coast with the converted merchantman *Delaware*(20). *la Croyable* would be condemned in Philadelphia and taken into the U.S. Navy as *Retaliation*.[163] The French captain, taken after failing to fire a shot, declared, "I wish I had been sunk."[164]

Three Forms Of Piracy

Jolly Roger

The brutalities committed by French "privateers" against American merchants trading in the Caribbean during the mid-to-late 1790's -- along with some Spanish vessels operating under loose letters of marque -- is little different than accounts from the Golden Age. Some of these "privateers" would even fly the Jolly Roger, such as those spotted off Curacao in autumn, 1799 who flew "a dark (flag) with a skull and cross bones painted on it."[165] On Christmas

---

162   Ibid, 85.

163   William M. Fowler, Jr., *Jack Tars and Commodores: The American Navy, 1783-1815*, (New York: Houghton Mifflin, 1984), 36.

164   Michael Morgan, *Pirates and Patriots: Tales of the Delaware Coast.* (New York: Algora: 2005), 56.

165   Michael A. Palmer, *Stoddert's War: Naval Operations during the Quasi-War with France, 1798-1801.* (Annapolis, MD: Naval Institute Press, 2000), 147.

Day, 1796 the ship *Commerce* heaved-to at the command of a French privateer and received a full broadside shot into her for complying, wounding four men. Headed back to New Hampshire from Tobago, the schooner *Zilpha* was captured by the privateer *Hirondale*, which pillaged the schooner and forced the crew to abandon her. In March, 1797 the ship *Cincinnatus* was boarded by the crew of a French brig, who tortured the American captain with thumbscrews in an effort to make him declare his cargo to be English. The captain held firm and was robbed of his personal effects and ship's provisions instead.[166] As can be seen with *la Croyable*'s capture, the French were not afraid to operate in American waters. Of course, as there was no navy opposing them prior to late May, 1798, why should they have been frightened? Delaware Bay and Long Island Sound were hot-spots for French privateers throughout 1797.[167] The Delaware coast would also be targeted by German U-boats during WWII and would be fortified by a series of watchtowers and shore batteries, particularly at Cape Henlopen..[168]

Submarine Watchtower, Ft. Miles, Cape Henlopen, Delaware

Overall, there were three sorts of pirates faced by American merchants plying their wares in the Caribbean. The most common variety were French privateers loosely commissioned from the colonial islands of Guadeloupe and Cayenne, as well as those commissioned in France. Early on, in 1796-

---

166   Alexander DeConde, *The Quasi-War: The Politics and Diplomacy of the Undeclared War with France, 1797-1801*. (New York: Scribners, 1966), 9.

167   Ibid, 125.

168   Michael Morgan, *Pirates and Patriots: Tales of the Delaware Coast*. (New York: Algora: 2005), 182-3.

1797, the port of Cap Francais (also called Le Cap) in Saint Domingue (modern Haiti) would also be active in French privateering. Of the 280 merchants captured in the Caribbean in 1797, 200 would fall victim in or around the Windward Passage, the highly-trafficked channel separating Cuba from Saint Domigue, which comprised the western portion of the island of Hispaniola.[169] It is not by accident that Guantanamo Bay would later be chosen as a U.S. naval base after the Spanish-American War of 1898, in order to protect this busy passage. However, a massive slave revolt, combined with the French revolution and subsequent military campaigns involving British and Spanish forces on Hispaniola, put an end to Cap Francais privateering and replaced it with out-right piracy. The Saint Domingue slave insurrection would account for the second strain of pirates plaguing American shipping -- bloodthirsty picaroons who haunted becalmed vessels in the Windward Passage and along the shores of Hispaniola.

While a much smaller example of piracy at the time, it

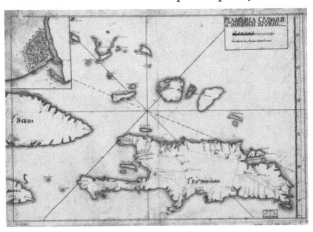

Hispaniola, late 1700s — U.S. National Archives

---

169   Michael A. Palmer, *Stoddert's War: Naval Operations during the Quasi-War with France, 1798-1801.* (Annapolis, MD: Naval Institute Press, 2000), 74-5.

is important to note how Spanish pirates -- whether or not they bore French commissions -- fit into a different category during the Quasi-War. Nearly all of the French sailors found aboard captured vessels were more or less treated as prisoners of war, with many being exchanged for captured Americans. Only one thousand or so French prisoners were shipped to the U.S., as room for holding them in the Caribbean was rather limited. However, the Adams administration issued clear instructions that any captured Spanish pirates were to be shipped to the U.S. for trial. When reports in early 1799 told of a pirate lair fortified with two-dozen cannon on a small key east of Matanzas, Cuba, Navy Secretary Stoddert wished to land forces and crush it. Several American vessels had been taken by the Matanzas pirates, including a New York ship which was forced to surrender after a spirited fight. As the Americans had killed a reported ten pirates during their defense, they in turn were slaughtered by their captors. However, high politics and war powers limited only to armed French vessels would constrain President Adams from authorizing a landing against the Matanzas pirates.[170] Fortunately, a small squadron under William Bainbridge would arrive in December, 1799, and with constant cruising manage to drive off the Matanzas pirates by the following spring. As added incentive, Bainbridge ran-down a privateer flying French colors near Havana and squeezed the vessel between the shore and his brig *Norfolk*(18), blasting the pirate to pieces.[171]

---

170   Ibid117-118.
171   Ibid, 228.

American Naval Operations

Navy Secretary Benjamin Stoddert by E.F.Andrews — Naval History and Heritage Command

Benjamin Stoddert, sworn into office as the nation's first Secretary of the Navy in May, 1798, was the second choice for the position and in many ways an unlikely one. During the Revolution he had served with the Continental Army and was seriously wounded at the Battle of Brandywine. Later, he would spend much time fighting Indians along the Susquehanna with Pennsylvania troops, before serving the Continental Congress as the Board of War's secretary. Undoubtedly, this was where the ties formed which twenty years later secured his selection as Navy Secretary. Stoddert's merchant ventures -- though bankrupting him -- seemed to teach him all he would need to know about naval logistics, for he never captained a ship in his life. Much of America's success during the Quasi-War can be attributed to the efforts of Benjamin Stoddert.[172]

By the summer of 1798, as freshly-built vessels came off the ways and hastily-converted merchantmen were at last armed and manned, Stoddert finally had some weapons to work with. The Navy would have fourteen vessels operating by the end of the year[173]-- twenty when including the attached

172   Ibid, 10-14.
173   William M. Fowler, Jr., *Jack Tars and Commodores: The American*

revenue cutters.[174] The new generation of revenue cutters -- capable of holding seventy men and 10-16 guns -- were also becoming available for use with the Navy. This should not be overlooked, as these smaller brigs and schooners would prove integral to suppressing Caribbean piracy and eventually score twenty-six captures.[175] If one "weak point" of Stoddert's naval planning can be found, it is here, as he pressed for frigates and 74-gun "liners" while preparing for a possibly larger naval conflict. Accordingly, fewer smaller vessels were built for the Navy, which would result in the transfer of many revenue cutters to the Navy Department; three of which -- *Eagle*, *Pickering* and *Scammel* -- served for the duration of the Quasi-War.

Stoddert split the eastern seaboard into three zones and assigned ships to cruise on station while putting a large emphasis on convoying merchants. It would become apparent, especially as the tough winter months set in, that the American coasts had been abandoned by French

Pickering, 1798

corsairs in favor of the warmer Caribbean climate. In order to catch the privateers themselves, four cruising squadrons would eventually become operational.[176] Two squadrons would be sent to patrol both ends of Cuba -- one of which would even-

Navy, 1783-1815, (New York: Houghton Mifflin, 1984), 38.

174   Michael A. Palmer, *Stoddert's War: Naval Operations during the Quasi-War with France, 1798-1801.* (Annapolis, MD: Naval Institute Press, 2000), 73. Twenty vessels all-told.

175   Ibid, 55. Revenue cutters were also credited with recapturing at least ten merchant vessels.

176   Ibid, 56-57.

tually be stationed at Cap Francais -- while another two would lay off Guadeloupe. One of those squadrons would later be sent to patrol the Caribbean along the northern portion of South America, particularly around Dutch and Spanish colonies who traded with American merchants. Overall, it was a sound plan that would soon reap rewards, but there would also be a bit of a learning curve for the nascent U.S. Navy.

**USS Constitution —
U.S. National Archives**

British Involvement

Mistakes in identifying the proper nationality of a ship met at sea were common during the age of sail, especially as state ships, privateers and pirates alike would all fly false flags in order to deceive potential enemies. This was all perfectly "legal," providing that your proper national banner was raised -- and the false one lowered -- prior to engaging an enemy. Such troubles with identification would lead to a short night engagement in which the schooner *Experiment* practically pulverized a British privateer.[177] The revenue cutter *Unanimity* would swap cannonballs with a British sloop-of-war, although this encounter was largely the fault of the revenue cutter's commander, for instead of communicating, he ran from the British and was mistaken for a French privateer. While the *Experiment* incident is understandable, the *Unanimity* episode serves to illustrate how "green" much of the U.S. naval forces

---

177   Claude G. Berube and John A. Rodgaard, *A Call to the Sea: Captain Charles Stewart of the USS Constitution.* (Washington: Potomac Books, 2005), 19. Vessel was 8-gun *Louisa Bridges* out of Bermuda.

were, which in a round-about way is also understandable. Then there's the case of Captain Nicholson.

Samuel Nicholson had a large family and was badly in debt. He had served in the Continental Navy as a captain and took scores of prizes with the *Dolphin*(10) and frigate *Deane*(32). However, late in the war a court of inquiry would find him guilty of many charges, including waste of public property, dishonorable and ungentlemanly conduct along with neglect of duty.[178] Regardless, in 1798 he would be given command of the new *Constitution*(44) and almost immediately capture the British ship *Niger* of 24-guns, commanded by a French Royalist who had been in British service for five years. Nicholson took the ship as a prize anyway, locked the crew in chains and sailed for Norfolk. While realizing that condemnation took time, Nicholson kept *Constitution* in port for a month and didn't set sail until October. Not only would his "prize" later go free, but the U.S. government would pay the $11,000 indemnity charged for the reckless capture of the *Niger*.[179]

So badly were captains needed that Nicholson wasn't fired. As a result, he took it upon himself to organize a merchant convoy to Havana, although it is likely he was bribed by merchants. As an added bonus, there was a shipment of specie lying at Havana waiting for transport to America in a warship. At the time, captains of warships (generally frigates or larger) received a lucrative commission for hauling such gold and silver. Ready to sail, Nicholson then further expanded his authority and "attached" the *Baltimore*(20) to his convoy, under the command of Isaac Phillips. The *Baltimore*

---

178   Michael A. Palmer, *Stoddert's War: Naval Operations during the Quasi-War with France, 1798-1801.* (Annapolis, MD: Naval Institute Press, 2000), 45.

179   Ibid, 47-49.

had just arrived in Norfolk, having been part of a convoy under Thomas Truxtun. The British privateer *Nancy* managed to infiltrate the convoy and was boarded by Phillips, during which time some U.S. citizens serving aboard the privateer volunteered to join the U.S. Navy.[180] After getting under way with Nicholson's convoy to Havana, the *Constitution* snapped her bowsprit and turned back, leaving Phillips in charge.

On November 16, 1798 as the convoy approached Havana, the British Jamaica Squadron under command of expatriated Tory John Loring -- whose sister-in-law was General Howe's mistress throughout the American Revolution -- stopped the *Baltimore* and ordered Phillips to hand over fifty-five men from the warship. Phillips complied, none-too-happily, as he complained about having insufficient men to crew his vessel. Generously, Loring returned fifty men and only kept five. When word reached the U.S. about subjects being impressed from American warships, the Adams administration turned livid and issued instructions to all commanders that such further attempts were not to be complied with, even if it meant

Impressment
Library of Congress

---

180   Ibid, 59.

engaging the Royal Navy. Phillips would soon be dismissed by Adams' executive order. As for the British, they would attempt to impress sailors from the decks of U.S. warships at least twice more during the Quasi-War, both times without success. Replying to the British demand, Captain Tingey of the *Ganges* retorted, "I shall die at my quarters before a man shall be taken from the ship."[181] While Adams issued firm instructions denying British impressments from American warships, he did not follow the same course when such attempts targeted merchant vessels and had previously ordered commanders not to interfere with British seizures of U.S. shipping.[182] While such British actions would provide much of the reason for the future War of 1812, Adams realized that it would be impossible to engage both British and French forces with the nascent Navy, in effect deciding on one war at a time. As for Nicholson, he would not be dismissed. To get him out of the way, Stoddert appointed him superintendent to one of the 74-gun "liners" when construction finally began.[183]

U.S.-British cooperation would prove to be a convenience as well as a strain during this period. Signal books would be given to the Americans in order to easily identify Royal Navy vessels, and more importantly, U.S. naval forces were allowed to use the island of St. Kitts -- not far from French Guadeloupe -- as a major base for provisions, repairs and a place to hold prisoners.[184] When a British mutineer was found aboard *Constellation*, he was handed over to the British, as

---

181   Alexander DeConde, *The Quasi-War: The Politics and Diplomacy of the Undeclared War with France, 1797-1801.* (New York: Scribners, 1966), 202-203. Quote on 203.
182   Ibid, 200.
183   Michael A. Palmer, *Stoddert's War: Naval Operations during the Quasi-War with France, 1798-1801.* (Annapolis, MD: Naval Institute Press, 2000), 111.
184   Ibid, 38, 95.

was another found in Charleston, although an American who had served aboard the frigate *Hermione* with them was not.[185] However, no military intelligence was shared. Both nations did allow each other's vessels to join merchant convoys, which was certainly helpful to U.S. merchants early in the war, providing that their seamen weren't impressed or their cargos confiscated.[186]

The Jamaica Station, under command of Admiral Sir Hyde Parker, would also prove to be a blessing and a curse. Parker had been knighted for fighting against "rebels" during the American Revolution and if anything, did much in permitting -- if not encouraging -- British seizures of American shipping. This suited him because he received a percentage of all prizes taken by the Jamaica Squadron, which accounted for one-third of all British captures, while the squadron totaled a mere five percent of Royal Navy strength. After *Constellation* engaged *la Vengeance*, Parker refused to give Truxtun

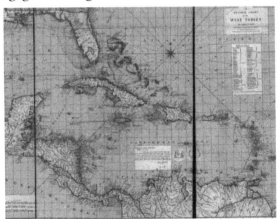

West Indies 1796
Library of Congress

185   Alexander DeConde, *The Quasi-War: The Politics and Diplomacy of the Undeclared War with France, 1797-1801.* (New York: Scribners, 1966), 205.
186   Ibid, 200.

a mainmast, stating none were available. When a trade deal was struck in 1799 between Britain, the U.S. and Toussaint Louverture, leader of revolutionary Saint Domingue, Parker allowed some of Toussaint's transports -- full of valuable war materials and provisions -- to be seized and condemned at Jamaica, which brewed fears that such action would increase Saint Domingue piracies. At the same time, however, the Royal Navy captured 78 French privateers in the Caribbean during 1798. While this number dropped to a mere nine in 1799, the previous year's catch was undoubtedly helpful to American merchants.[187]

Dutch Caribbean colonies, while allied with France, were never embargoed by the U.S., as they desperately needed trade for food stuffs and certain raw materials. When Britain captured Surinam and Curacao, this trade was practically ended. This is notable because Curacao was captured largely due to American assistance, since the French wished to fortify the island, but the operation was postponed when USS *Merrimack* and *Patapsco* arrived before the French could land. *Patapsco* stood in the harbor channel and shelled the French-occupied fort, who withdrew after losing 150 men, while *Patapsco* lost only two. This cleared the way for a British invasion -- after Captain Watkins of the Royal Navy fed the U.S. warships false information about French privateers in the area. When *Merrimack* and *Patapsco* sailed for the imaginary privateers, the British occupied the island and seized several American merchant vessels anchored in the harbor.[188]

Friction between the U.S. and Britain, never truly cleared-up by the Jay Treaty, would provide much ammunition for

187   Michael A. Palmer, *Stoddert's War: Naval Operations during the Quasi-War with France, 1798-1801.* (Annapolis, MD: Naval Institute Press, 2000), Parker note on 172-3, RN strength on 62, Truxtun mainmast 190, Toussaint's transports on 161, RN captures on 74-5, 131.
188   Ibid, 200-201.

Republican arguments concerning operations against French warships. During the spring of 1798, as tempers flared over the possibility of war with France, the Republicans pointed out that the British "despoiled" nearly as much shipping as the French did.[189] While this was accurate, it is also important to note that the Royal Navy was by far the strongest navy in the world, while France was not, especially while at war with Britain. It would prove much easier to construct a navy to fight French piracy than it would be to engage British ships-of-the-line. However, Federalists neither liked nor ignored British seizures. A report from Alexander Hamilton in 1800 stated, "…the British capture all American vessels that afford the slightest pretext for condemnation and impress (our) seamen without discrimination."[190] Not surprisingly, the information had been provided by an American merchant captain from Jamaica.

Engagements

Certainly, the most celebrated victories during the Quasi-War belonged to Thomas Truxtun and the frigate *Constellation*, which captured the slightly smaller frigate *l'Insurgente* in February, 1799 and fought the larger frigate *la Vengeance* the following February to a near-mutually destructive standstill. The second battle occurred at night, which obscured the fact that the French had twice struck their colors, which concluded in one of the most ironic endings in naval history. As *Constellation* moved in to claim her prize, her battered mainmast snapped and toppled to sea a mere

---

189   Alexander DeConde, *The Quasi-War: The Politics and Diplomacy of the Undeclared War with France, 1797-1801.* (New York: Scribners, 1966), 92.
190   Ibid, 276.

twenty-five yards away from *la Vengeance*, which was able to limp away.[191] *l'Insurgente* would be the only French warship to capture a U.S. Navy ship, *Retaliation*, which had been the first U.S. prize of the war, *la Croyable*. She would later be captured again by the Americans, with her new moniker, *la Magiciennne*(12), providing no special tricks.[192] Each time the French were engaged, their commanders would not only be shocked by the presence of American warships, but absolutely stunned by American gunners, whose accuracy and high rate of fire rivaled even the British. Such efforts are a credit to U.S. captains, who were responsible for the training of American sailors. While the official end of the Quasi-War would arrive in 1801, after the Treaty of Mortefontaine was officially ratified, for all intents and purposes the war was over by September, 1800.[193] In roughly thirty months, the U.S. Navy and Revenue Cutter Service would take nearly 100 French prizes and recapture scores of merchant vessels.[194]

The schooner *Experiment* would see much action and take part in one of the most dramatic engagements against pirates. *Experiment* would be attached to the Cap Francais station after an unofficial trade agreement had been brokered between Saint Domingue, Britain and the U.S. Since the

---

191   Eugene S. Ferguson, *Truxton of the Constellation: The Life of Commodore Thomas Truxton, U.S. Navy, 1755-1822.* (Baltimore: Johns Hopkins University Press, 2000), 167, 189-193. Originally published 1956.

192   Michael A. Palmer, *Stoddert's War: Naval Operations during the Quasi-War with France, 1798-1801.* (Annapolis, MD: Naval Institute Press, 2000), 116.

193   Alexander DeConde, *The Quasi-War: The Politics and Diplomacy of the Undeclared War with France, 1797-1801.* (New York: Scribners, 1966), 256.

194   Michael A. Palmer, *Stoddert's War: Naval Operations during the Quasi-War with France, 1798-1801.* (Annapolis, MD: Naval Institute Press, 2000), 235. Other historians record captures from low 90's to 99.

**Constellation vs L'Insurgent —
Naval History and Heritage Command**

slave insurgency on the island was the slave-holding South's worst nightmare, the U.S. would not sign official agreements and in order to assuage many Republicans, prevented Toussaint from sending ships to American ports, lest black sailors infest the South with revolutionaries.[195] While not surprising, as this agreement also forbade Toussaint from issuing privateer commissions in order to combat piracies, it is notable because many of the Saint Domingue revolutionary leaders had fought with the French during the Savannah campaign of the American Revolution.[196] While President Adams would embargo trade to all French colonies in 1798, specifically to limit piracies in the Saint Domingue area, he reopened this trade the following year in a dual effort to weaken France -- as the revolutionary colony had been France's most valuable possession -- as well as the chance to reap a sort of "indemnity" from France. A similar attempt would be made during the Mexican War, when part of the war's cost was to be financed from customs duties collected off Mexican ports.[197] In both

195   Ibid, 155.
196   Madison Smartt Bell, *Toussaint Louverture: A Biography*. (New York: Random House, 2007), 31.
197   Daniel Walker Howe, *What Hath God Wrought: The Transformation of America, 1815-1848*. (New York: Oxford, 2007), 781.

cases, the money would not add up to very much, especially when the cost of the arms given to Toussaint was factored in.

The reopening of Saint Domingue trade and subsequent support to Toussaint (mostly "covert") would lead to the shelling of Rigaud's forces at Jacmel by the frigate USS *General Greene*, which mostly ended Saint Domingue's civil war.[198] Rigaud's supply ships would prove to be the only unarmed merchant vessels captured by U.S. forces. However, due to the local warlords on the island, piracy would not only be difficult for Toussaint to control, but would also provide the most bloodthirsty pirates of the period.

Experiment, convoying four merchant vessels through the Windward Passage on New Year's Day, 1800 would find herself involved in an all-day engagement. Becalmed close to shore by a lack of wind, at six in the morning eleven large barges -- much like large longboats -- holding roughly forty pirates each, armed with small swivel guns and muskets, appeared from shore and swiftly rowed toward the stranded vessels. The shores of Saint Domingue were famous for such picaroons, whose penchant for violence was unmatched. The picaroons spread out and headed for each vessel, not realizing *Experiment* was a warship, as her gun ports stayed closed. When the pirates reached musket range, *Experiment* ran out her six-pound carronades and pounded the oncoming barges with a hail of grapeshot and musketry, sinking at least two. The merchants joined the fight as well, using what few muskets they possessed. As the *Experiment* was equipped with oars, this allowed her to turn about and fire her starboard battery while the port-side reloaded, allowing full use of her twelve guns. The picaroons broke off and rowed to the island

---

198   Michael A. Palmer, *Stoddert's War: Naval Operations during the Quasi-War with France, 1798-1801.* (Annapolis, MD: Naval Institute Press, 2000), 162.

of Gonave to re-group.

Within ninety minutes the attack resumed, with three additional barges joining the fray. This time, the picaroons split into groups and made directly for *Experiment*, hoping to knock her out of commission. This would not be the case, however, as during the next three hours two more barges would be sunk and then a third that was making for the merchant *Mary*. The *Mary's* captain would fight the pirates by himself and be butchered for his effort, although the forty picaroons who swarmed the deck would be beaten off by a shower of grapeshot from *Experiment*. By four that afternoon, two of the merchant vessels which had drifted close to shore were taken when the pirates launched another attack, after their crews abandoned ship and rowed longboats to *Experiment*. Early that evening a breeze finally arrived and carried *Experiment* and her two wards out of harm's way, after a ten-hour fight which nearly drained the schooner's ammunition supply. Accounts put U.S. Navy casualties between one and three men, none seriously injured, with Lt. David Porter being among the wounded.

There would be some debate over this attack in future years, mostly as a result of Porter's son, Admiral David Dixon Porter, who put together his father's autobiography long after his death. In this account, David Porter is credited for relieving Lt. Maley of command, who supposedly wished to surrender. While Maley would later be relieved of command -- he wasn't much good, and only four of the fourteen prizes he took were judged to be "good prizes" -- any account of his desire to surrender is incorrect. Dr. Edward Stevens, U.S. consul to Cap Francais, was aboard *Experiment* at the time and never made mention of it, nor did anyone else. Porter did report Maley for negligence after a later encounter and this is probably where the confusion derives from. Oddly enough, Josiah Blakely -- Stevens' counterpart in Santiago, Cuba -- had abandoned ship not far from this location a year prior when the merchantman he was traveling on was taken by a French privateer, which boarded his vessel just as Blakely's longboat made the Cuban coast.[199]

Destiny would seem to tie *Experiment* to Saint Domingue. Under command of Lt. Stewart, *Experiment* captured *les Deux Amis*(8) in August, 1800 and was later chased by two French privateers in September. After outrunning them, *Experiment* turned about and gave chase, capturing the 14-gun privateer *la Diana* off of St. Bartholomew's, an island with a long history of fencing pirated wares and vessels. Aboard *la Diana* were several French soldiers and the Haitian General Andre Riguad. Riguad had been linked to picaroons for some years, along with being notorious for butchery and torture during his time on Saint Domingue. Stewart pointed him out, declaring, "That is the man, sir, that has wrested millions from my countrymen. The depredations, the piracies, plunder and murders he has committed are too well known."[200]

The fast schooners and brigs of the U.S. Navy, such as the oared *Experiment* and *Enterprise*, proved to be excellent at the task of running down and capturing French privateers and the related pirate vessels of the period. In all, such Navy vessels accounted for twenty-five captures during the war. When added to the victories of the similarly-sized Revenue Cutters, this number would account for more than half of all captures made during the Quasi-War. This should not be surprising, however, for smaller, low-draft sloops and schooners equipped

---

199   Ibid, 165-168 details *Experiment* vs. picaroons, Blakely note 120.
200   Claude G. Berube and John A. Rodgaard, *A Call to the Sea: Captain Charles Stewart of the USS Constitution.* (Washington: Potomac Books, 2005), 17-18.

with sweeps had proven their worth in pirate hunting since the early eighteenth century. Commodore Thomas Truxtun had urged Benjamin Stoddert to construct more of these vessels, but the advice fell on deaf ears, as the Navy Secretary was preoccupied with producing larger warships. The new American frigates would catch and sink their share of pirates as well, with even the "heavy" 44-gun frigates *United States* and *Constitution* proving their flexibility by running down enemy schooners and brigs. Also, the U.S. Navy would find excellent leadership under Silas Talbot and Thomas Truxtun. The Quasi-War was an unqualified success for the Americans, as the presence of the nascent Navy cut merchant losses to French vessels by two-thirds in 1799 and took 58 vessels in 1800. Each U.S. warship averaged better than five captures apiece.[201]

USS United States, **1797-1861**
Naval History and Heritage Command

On March 23, 1801, all U.S. warships would be recalled and on July 31, the final ratified version of the Treaty of Mortefontaine would be exchanged between the U.S. and France, bringing an official end to the Quasi-War. The Senate would ratify this version on December 19, but it would not include an indemnity payment from France for captured American cargos or vessels and also required the U.S. to return all captured French national warships. Neither of these stipulations were

201   Michael A. Palmer, *Stoddert's War: Naval Operations during the Quasi-War with France, 1798-1801.* (Annapolis, MD: Naval Institute Press, 2000), 238 small-vessel captures, Truxtun's advice 79, reduction on losses 128, take in 1800 and average ship captures, 235.

popular.[202] USS *Insurgent* would not be given back, however, as she sank in a gale along with the store ship *Florida* and cutter *Pickering* in September, 1800.[203]

While more than proving their worth on the water, the Navy would suffer severe budget cuts under the forthcoming administration of Thomas Jefferson. All of the 74-gun battle-ships would lose their funding and be left to rot on the stocks. This is certainly the saddest legacy of the Quasi-War, for had those American ships-of-the-line been available for the War of 1812, their impact may have been quite dramatic.

202   Alexander DeConde, *The Quasi-War: The Politics and Diplomacy of the Undeclared War with France, 1797-1801.* (New York: Scribners, 1966), 320-325.

203   Michael A. Palmer, *Stoddert's War: Naval Operations during the Quasi-War with France, 1798-1801.* (Annapolis, MD: Naval Institute Press, 2000), 218.

The Revenue Cutter Service: Predecessor of the U.S. Coast Guard

On August 4, 1790, Congress enacted a bill presented by Treasury Secretary Alexander Hamilton which authorized funding for the construction of ten small vessels. These "cutters" would be used to enforce the payment of custom duties and prevent smugglers from dodging tariff laws, beginning in 1791. Or, as Hamilton himself stated, "A few armed vessels, judiciously stationed at the entrances to our

Alexander Hamilton, First U.S. Treasury Secretary

ports, might at a small expense be made useful sentinels of the laws." Americans had a long history of smuggling, particularly during the colonial period, when it was considered to be nearly patriotic -- or at least good business -- to evade the various taxes and custom duties enacted by Britain. As the newly created Federal Government received the vast majority of its funding from such trade taxation, these laws had to be enforced. Often referred to as the Treasury Navy or the Revenue Marine, the Revenue Cutter Service employed these ten small schooners -- manned with two masters and only six hands -- in various ports along the coast. Relatively fast and nimble, these small craft performed a remarkable service in deterring smugglers, which enabled the bankrupt nation to pay off its debts in a few short years.[204] You could run from

---

204   www.uscg.mil/history/first10cutters/ Unknown Author

the tax man, but you would be chased.

Hamilton largely based these cutters along the British model, which is where the term "cutter" comes from. In 1674, King Charles II began using custom house agents aboard small vessels in order to collect duties as well as enforce their payment.[205] The first ten U.S. revenue cutters were very lightly armed with only three small swivel guns each. A good portion of the original masters had served in the Continental Navy and were commissioned by George Washington. Due to the state of American industry at the time, the cutters did not have copper sheathing over their hulls. As a result, by the time of the Quasi-War, many of their hulls were badly deteriorated by sea worms, *Teredo navalis*, which left only two cutters seaworthy by 1797. Paul Revere would eventually provide copper bottoms for many ships of the U.S. Navy built at this time, beginning in 1799.[206] As the last Continental Navy ship had been sold in 1785, these two small cutters were the only "warships" available at the onset of the Quasi-War, constituting America's "first line of defense" while the future ships of the U.S. Navy were being built or converted from merchantmen.[207]

Due to the deterioration of the original revenue cutters, most of them were sold-off in 1798 and replaced with ten new cutters, constructed between 1797-1798. This new generation of cutters was built with a dual role in mind. These vessels were considerably larger and better armed than their predecessors, capable of carrying seventy men and ten to sixteen cannons, generally a mixture of four and six-pounders.

205   E. Keble Chatterton, *King's Cutters and Smugglers*. (London: BiblioBazaar, 2007), 23. Originally published in 1912.
206   Michael A. Palmer, *Stoddert's War: Naval Operations during the Quasi-War with France, 1798-1801.* (Annapolis, MD: Naval Institute Press, 2000), 121. Originally published by South Carolina Press, 1987.
207   Ibid,53. Worm note on 121.

Able to cruise in shallows, they were rigged as double-topsail schooners -- commonly called "Jackass Brigs"-- which made them quick handling and fast on the water. In reference to their abilities, historian Michael A. Palmer states, "The fine sailing qualities of the cutters, designed to catch smugglers, made them equally suited for work against privateers."[208]

Revenue Cutter *Eagle* Captures *Bon Pere*, April 1799 by Wende

On July 1, 1797, Congress authorized President Adams to employ the revenue cutters as a naval force.[209] Once enough merchantmen had been converted for use by the newly-created U.S. Navy, the freshly-built cutters would begin to patrol with them in the summer of 1798.[210] On October 10, 1798, Benjamin Stoddert, Secretary of the Navy, notified the various collectors of customs that the following seven revenue cutters would sail under his command, *Eagle, Scammel, Diligence, Pickering, Virginia, Governor Jay* and *General Greene* (not to be confused with the frigate). By late 1798, nine of Stoddert's twenty-one operational vessels would be revenue cutters, although by mid-1799 many would be transferred back to the Treasury Department. Further authorization would come in February, 1799 to officially transfer both cutters and crew to the navy, which would also provide equal pay and compensation for the two services. Due to subsequent transfers, only *Eagle, Pickering* and *Scammel* would be retained by the navy

---

208   Ibid, 53. Also, www.uscg.mil/history/ Unknown Author

209   Alexander DeConde, *The Quasi-War: The Politics and Diplomacy of the Undeclared War with France, 1797-1801.* (New York: Scribners, 1966), 15.

210   Ibid, 126.

for the duration of the Quasi-War.[211]

Robert Cochran was master of the revenue cutter *South Carolina*, operating from Charleston. As the vessel was practically worn-out, his command was switched to the new cutter *Unanimity* when the cutter was completed in May, 1798. On July 29, just up the coast from Charleston, Cochran ran across the 16-gun Royal Navy schooner *Mosquito*, commanded by Lt. White. After each vessel raised their national banner, Cochran made no attempt to communicate with *Mosquito*, but ran away from her instead. Thinking the cutter to be a French privateer, Lt. White gave chase and fired a shot across *Unanimity's* bow, but Cochran continued to run. Closing, as the cutter was now trapped between the shore and *Mosquito*, Lt. White fired a broadside, which did little damage. Cochran returned fire to no effect and then grounded the cutter on a sandbar a short while later as he continued to flee. Not wishing to ground the *Mosquito*, Lt. White stood off to sea, where he met an American pilot boat which informed him of the cutter's identity -- much to White's surprise. As no real damage was done, the incident was quickly smoothed-over, with the exception of Cochran, who was soon discharged from service.[212] In the following year, 1799, the Revenue Service would adopt its own ensign, which would not only

Original Ensign of 1799

help to clear up the future identification of revenue cutters, but is still flown by the Coast Guard to this day.[213]

211   Michael A. Palmer, *Stoddert's War: Naval Operations during the Quasi-War with France, 1798-1801.* (Annapolis, MD: Naval Institute Press, 2000), 55.

212   Ibid, 54.

213   Irving H. King, *The Coast Guard Under Sail: The U.S. Revenue Cutter Service 1789-1865.* (Annapolis, MD: Naval Institute Press, 1989),

Aside from Cochran's ineptitude, the revenue cutters performed remarkably well during the Quasi-War. From 1798 through 1801, the cutters would account for capturing twenty-six French privateers/pirates in the Caribbean, while recapturing ten American merchant vessels seized by the French.[214] As the Americans would capture some ninety to one hundred French privateer/pirate vessels during the two-and-a-half years of the Quasi-War, the contribution made by the Revenue Cutter Service would prove to be substantial.[215]

Pickering would be particularly active during the campaign, netting five French privateers and providing one of the most brilliantly-fought actions of the war. On November 18, 1799 *Pickering* was patrolling off Pointe-a-Pitre, Guadeloupe, when she sighted the privateer *l'Egypte Conquise* -- one of the "best vessels belonging to the French in the West Indies" -- armed with 14 nine-pound guns and four six-pounders, carrying a crew of 250 men. *Pickering*, armed with only 14 four-pounders and seventy men, engaged the privateer in a running fight which lasted for nine hours. Lt. Benjamin Hillar kept close to the French schooner, peppering the privateer with broadsides and dodging away each time the schooner attempted to board. Despite holding a three-to-one advantage in artillery weight, *l'Egypte Conquise* could barely bring her guns to bear and was forced to strike her colors.[216]

The *Pickering* had been officially transferred to the Navy

24.

214   Michael A. Palmer, *Stoddert's War: Naval Operations during the Quasi-War with France, 1798-1801.* (Annapolis, MD: Naval Institute Press, 2000), 55.

215   Eugene S. Ferguson, *Truxton of the Constellation: The Life of Commodore Thomas Truxton, U.S. Navy, 1755-1822.* (Baltimore: Johns Hopkins University Press, 2000), 214.. Originally published in 1956.

216   Michael A. Palmer, *Stoddert's War: Naval Operations during the Quasi-War with France, 1798-1801.* (Annapolis, MD: Naval Institute Press, 2000), 149-150.

on May 20, 1799. Tragically, while accompanying the store ship *Florida* to meet up with Commodore Truxton's *President* (44), both *Pickering* and *Florida* were lost with all hands in a gale on September 8-9, 1800. Truxton's hard-fought-for French prize, the former *l'Insurgente*, rechristened *Insurgent* after being commissioned into the U.S. Navy, disappeared in the same gale. The two warships and over 400 men sacrificed would constitute America's largest loss during the Quasi-War.[217]

Revenue cutters would continue to catch pirates in the early 1800's and throughout the early third of that century. The cutters would also form part of the U.S. Anti-Piracy Campaign during the 1820's. The New Orleans and Gulf Coast region would witness several captures, many of which were taken by the cutter *Louisiana*. There would be three cutters named *Louisiana*, each stationed at New Orleans beginning

Revenue Cutter *Louisiana*

in 1805, barely a year after the Louisiana Purchase. Each later version of revenue cutter eventually replaced a decommissioned predecessor -- except for the years 1813-1818. As the War of 1812 took precedence above all else until 1815, it is understandable that no replacement was assigned during those years. However, due to the notoriously high rate of smuggling and piracy in the New Orleans area during the years following the war, it is rather puzzling that no replacement cutter was sent to the port until 1819.

The first *Louisiana*, carrying thirty men and ten four-

217   Ibid, 218.

pound guns, was commissioned in 1804 and arrived at New Orleans in early January, 1805. In April, the cutter recaptured the schooner *Felicity* from illegal privateers. In early 1812, Lt. Angus Fraser chased a small pirate vessel into the Mississippi River and captured it. Later that month, *Louisiana* engaged two pirate vessels and "twenty shots were exchanged, but by their superior sailing and night coming on, they made their escape."[218] The following month would bring another victory when Fraser seized the illegal privateer *Two Brothers* in New Orleans.[219] The *Louisiana* would sink during a hurricane in August, 1812, putting her out of commission. After her guns were recovered, she would be sold, raised and used as a merchant schooner.[220]

The second revenue cutter named *Louisiana* was a much smaller topsail-schooner, armed with only one pivot gun. Commissioned and dispatched to New Orleans in 1819, she joined with the revenue cutter *Alabama* -- originally dispatched to the port of Mobile -- to capture the Laffite-owned pirate vessel *Le Brave* after exchanging musketry, roughly 100 miles west of the Florida Keys. Commanding *Le Brave* was long-time Laffite associate Desfarges, captured along with his crew of seventeen men. On November 22, 1819, they would all be found guilty of piracy and then sentenced to death by hanging on December 30.[221]

Still operating in concert, the two cutters would land twen-

218   www.usskidd.com/ships-la-uscg.html.   Unknown author, information attributed to USCG.

219   William C. Davis, *The Pirates Laffite: The Treacherous World of the Corsairs of the Gulf.* (New York: Harcourt, 2005), 84.

220   www.usskidd.com/ships-la-uscg.html.   Unknown author, information attributed to USCG.

221   William C. Davis, *The Pirates Laffite: The Treacherous World of the Corsairs of the Gulf.* (New York: Harcourt, 2005), 404 describes capture, 407-408 trial and sentencing.

ty-five men on Breton Island and destroy a pirate lair in April, 1820.[222] This island had long been involved in smuggling and piracy. The pirates caught at New Orleans by David Porter in 1809 had armed their ships with artillery at this island, the same location where in 1811, ninety illegally-imported slaves were first landed.[223] In July of 1820, *Louisiana* would reportedly capture four pirate vessels off the coast of Belize -- but this is most likely *the Balize*, the customs station off New Orleans located at the mouth of the Mississippi. The cutter *Louisiana* would later team with US sloop-of-war *Peacock* and HM sloop-of-war *Speedwell* off Havana to capture five pirate vessels on November 2, 1822.[224] Ironically, much of Britain's commitment to hunting Caribbean pirates had arrived only that previous summer, after the *Peacock* came to *Speedwell's* aid as she was being attacked by four pirate schooners. The British public was irate that a Royal vessel had been rescued by an American craft, an embarrassment which prompted the British Admiralty to immediately dispatch more ships to patrol off Cuba.[225] In 1824, the second *Louisiana* would be sold at auction.[226]

The third revenue cutter *Louisiana* was commissioned in 1825 and sent to New Orleans to replace her worn-out predecessor. Little about the cutter's size or armament is known, though it is doubtful that she was heavily armed. In late spring, 1827, *Louisiana* captured the Columbian privateer *Bolivia* after she had first fired upon and then pirated an American merchant schooner in the Southwest Pass downriv-

---

222   www.uscg.mil/LouisianaII.html

223   William C. Davis, *The Pirates Laffite: The Treacherous World of the Corsairs of the Gulf.* (New York: Harcourt, 2005), 54 tells of arming pirate ships, 96 the smuggled slaves.

224   www.uscg.mil/LouisianaII.html

225   Peter Earle, *The Pirate Wars.* (New York: St. Martin's, 2003), 241.

226   www.uscg.mil/LouisianaII.html

er from New Orleans. Well-used, the cutter would be sold-off in 1830.[227]

Another notable revenue cutter during the early 1800's is the *Active*, which patrolled Chesapeake Bay and seized a questionable Spanish brig in 1816. In July of the following year, *Active* made port in Baltimore with the brig *India Libra*(10), whose crew had mutinied, put their officers ashore and turned pirate. In August, *Active* fired upon and then seized the ship *Margaret* in the Bay, after word had spread that she was off to Amelia Island to begin a piratical cruise. The next month *Active* seized the privateer schooner *Hornet* in the Patapsco River. However, Lt. Marshall and his prize crew would be overwhelmed by the pirate crew they had captured and dropped ashore at the Virginia Capes. *Hornet* sailed off to continue her piratical cruise. *Active* would make up for the loss by capturing the pirate brig *Irresistable* the very next day, a Spanish warship whose mutineer crew had taken British, French and American vessels. Twenty-two pirates would be captured and clapped in irons. The cutter *Monroe* also cruised the Chesapeake, netting the armed brig *Columbia* in October, 1818. *Columbia* was formerly a warship of the Venezuelan Navy, until she was cut-out from the fleet by several crew members.[228]

Also of interest are the exploits of the cutter *Vigilant*, sailing from Newport, Rhode Island. On October 11, 1817, *Vigilant* took the pirate brig *B* of five guns and forty-six men in Vineyard Sound. Later that same day, the cutter seized the Spanish brig *Bell Corunnes* off Block Island, which ran aground and eventually sank. Twenty-five pirates would be

---

227   www.uscg.mil/Louisiana_1825.html

228   Irving H. King, *The Coast Guard Under Sail: The U.S. Revenue Cutter Service 1789-1865*. (Annapolis, MD: Naval Institute Press, 1989), 73-76.

captured, with another eleven surrendering shortly thereafter. *Bell Corrunes* would be raised by the men who seized her, libeled in prize court and the proceeds spilt, along with that of the libeled *B*. During the summer of 1818, the revenue cutter *Dallas* captured the pirate ship *Young Spartan* and prize *Pastora* off Port Royal, South Carolina. As a result, the pirate captain Ralph Clintock would be convicted of piracy during his trial at Savannah, Georgia in December, 1819.[229]

The American Civil War would prove disastrous to the Revenue Cutter Service, as no fewer than fifteen cutters would be seized or captured by the Confederacy -- two of them burned -- along with the seizure/capture of at least eleven Lightships.[230] The cutter *Aiken* was seized by South Carolina just prior to the Civil War and was sold by the state when she was rejected for government service. She became the commissioned privateer *Petrel* and was sunk on July 28, 1861 on the first morning of her maiden cruise. USS *St. Lawrence*(52) sank her when one of only two shells fired at her smashed through her bow and exploded.[231]

**USS *St. Lawrence* sinks privateer *Petrel*,
former revenue cutter**

229 Ibid, 76-78.
230 www.uscg.mil/history
231 William Morrison Robinson, Jr., *The Confederate Privateers*. (University of South Carolina Press, 1990), 125-126.

The most notable Confederate capture would be the schooner-rigged cutter *Caleb Cushing* in late June, 1863. *Caleb Cushing* was armed much like Jefferson's gunboats, with a twelve-pound swivel and 32-pound main gun. Lt. Read and nineteen Confederate sailors muffled the oars of two long-boats and rowed into the harbor of Portland, Maine during the night and cut-out the *Caleb Cushing* without a shot being fired. Jedediah Jewett, the Port Collector, commandeered the steamer *Forest City* without any authority and loaded aboard two twelve-pound field howitzers and an ad-hoc assembly of civilians, soldiers and members of *Caleb Cushing*'s crew -- on shore leave -- before making steam and giving chase the next morning. Portland's mayor impressed the steamer *Chesapeake*, which eventually joined the chase. Lt. Read opened fire on the steamers, but as the cutter had only five or six cannonballs for the 32-pound long-gun, his cannonade ended by firing any available projectile at his pursuers. Reportedly, his last shot fired a ball of Dutch cheese which splattered across the deck of the *Chesapeake* -- the only shot to do so. Before being caught by the steamers, Lt. Read and his men took to long-boats after setting fire to the *Caleb Cushing*, which exploded after the fire reached her powder magazine. The Confederates were captured, imprisoned and later exchanged just prior to the war's end.[232]

Lt. Read had been given one of CSS *Florida*'s captures, the brig *Clarence*, which he used to begin a very busy twen-ty-one days, during which he captured twenty-two merchant/fishing vessels. For a variety of reasons -- such as flying false colors while capturing vessels, burning neutral cargoes, flying international signs of distress in order to dupe prizes and the murky question regarding the legality of "commissioning"

---

232   Chester G. Hearn, *Gray Raiders of the Sea.* (LSU Press, 1992), 90-93.

a domino-like chain of prizes for "official" use -- Lt. Read's actions are more piratical than many would like to admit.[233]

An act of Congress would merge the Revenue Cutter Service and Life-Saving Service together in 1915, which created the U.S. Coast Guard. The Coast Guard not only pre-dates the U.S. Navy, but has served with distinction in nearly every U.S. war and conflict.[234]

Cutter *Vigilant* fought and captured the British privateer brig *B*

---

233   Ibid, 86-90. Hearn provides the valid information, but the assessment is mine.

234   www.uscg.mil/history/

Toussaint Louverture

Toussaint Louverture

Born Toussaint Breda, as he was born into slavery on the Breda plantation, in 1793 Toussaint would chose the new name of Louverture -- "the opening"-- mostly due to its voodoo connotations; such as being the portal through which revolutionary forces shall spring forth. Mixed together with a slave insurrection after brutal years of oppression, the spirits possessing those involved in the Haitian revolution would foster unheard of butchery and brutality, issuing waves of terror so vivid that the American South would never forget it. What became the Haitian revolution -- which began as a slave uprising in 1791, largely as an effort to abolish the whip as punishment and to gain an extra day off -- would merge with the French revolution in 1793, but would never be proclaimed as a war for Haitian independence for as long as Louverture lived. As if fighting French forces were not enough, Britain and Spain would also land troops on Hispaniola in an effort to pluck France's colonial crown jewel away from her.

Toussaint has been called "a black Spartacus" as well as a "black Napoleon," both of which are apt monikers, although he gained his freedom fifteen years prior to the insurgency and actually owned slaves himself at the time of the uprising. Forever known as a fighter, his skills at diplomacy dwarf his battlefield accomplishments, as he was one of history's shrewdest players at the game of international politics -- until showing a fatal error in judgment by declaring himself ruler for life, which would cost Toussaint his life. Prior to 1801, Toussaint managed to juggle and control the variety of warlord-like factions and enclaves which comprised revolutionary Saint Domingue. In a like fashion, he did much the same concerning relations with France, Spain, Britain and the United States.

The story of the Haitian revolution is rather complicated, as it not only involves a variety of factions on the island of Hispaniola itself, but was further confused by the French Revolution. As a result -- much like many American colonists prior to Bunker Hill -- Toussaint and many rebel leaders claimed loyalty to King Louis XVI. This was due to the belief, wrongly held, that royalty wasn't to blame, but "ministerial forces" which acted without the King's knowledge. For the Americans, a proclamation from King George III set the matter straight, but in Saint Domingue, news of Louis' beheading

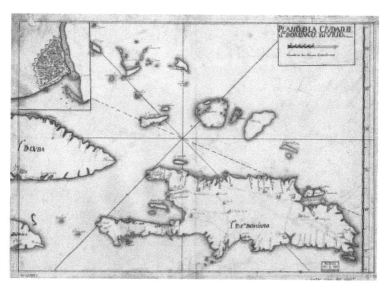

Hispaniola, late 1700s — U.S. National Archives

would lead rebels to fight alongside Spanish forces from the eastern half of the island, Santo Domingo. When the British tried to capitalize on the situation and landed forces in September, 1793, many rebel leaders would then side with Revolutionary France by the following spring, as Toussaint himself did.

Race would prove the most troublesome facet of the fighting on Saint Domigue. In his biography of Toussaint, Madison Smartt Bell does an excellent job at illustrating the difficulties which race added to the fighting. Not only had the revolution begun as a slave uprising, but due to previous French decrees, mulattos (*gens de couleur*) were accorded a great deal more freedom. Many of them greatly resented free blacks, whether this freedom had been granted by France or not. Likewise, as slavery returned to many French colonies, it was only natural that Saint Domingue's former slaves would fight against even the perceived threat of slavery being reinstituted. As a result, the race issue would be an easy way for many of the island's factions to secure power, as black against white turned into black-mulatto against white and then whites and mulattos against former black slaves. While this is only a rudimentary run-down, the issue of race also fed problems with economics. Saint Domingue was considered France's "Jewel of the Antilles" not for its scenery, but for the colony's worth in production. Not only was it France's major sugar producer, but the colony also out-produced any British sugar colony. While coffee was relatively easily grown and harvested for export, Saint Domingue's real money came from plantation-oriented exports, such as indigo and especially sugar. The process for obtaining brown sugar was somewhat technical, but could be mastered. However, as the real money came from white sugar, which took more knowledge to refine, it was necessary for Toussaint to allow white plantation own-ers back into the country, as most had fled -- or been killed -- early in the uprising. Getting former slaves to return to their former masters would continue to spark the race issue, especially when used as a playing card in the regional disputes of warlords. A variety of blood-lettings would result from this, even claiming the life of Toussaint's former master in 1801, Bayon de Libertat. Race would be the issue which helped turn Andre Rigaud against Tous-saint, even after Rigaud's defeat at Jacmel in 1799 -- largely a result of American warships which interdicted his supplies and capped-off the episode with a bombard-ment of Jacmel's forts by the frigate USS *General Greene*.

André Rigaud

France and Spain concluded the Treaty of Basel in 1795, which brought peace between them and awarded Santo Do-mingo to France, although it would not be turned over until Toussaint overran the colony in 1801, against Napoleon's or-ders. This union did not last long, as Santo Domingo would eventually revolt in 1844 and become today's Dominican Republic.

Britain's fight against Toussaint would last for five years. Initially, they would sweep through nearly a third of the territory in eight months, losing a mere fifty men. However, disease would take a disastrous toll. Britain would lose more men on Saint Domingue than Wellington during the Peninsular War, 1808-1814. France would feel the effects of disease as well, after Napoleon sent forces to crush the rebellion in mid-1801. France would lose 50,000 of the 80,000 men sent to Saint Domingue, although they would manage to capture Toussaint in June, 1802. He would be sent back to France, be imprisoned in a remote location near the Alps and die of sickness in 1803.

Battle on Santo Domingo
Painting by January Suchodolski

The Haitian revolution was one of the bloodiest ever fought, as passions aroused from voodoo spirits and years of brutal slavery sparked torture and horrendous acts of violence. Early on, when the rebels were nearly unarmed, men would throw themselves in front of cannon fire to shield their comrades behind them, literally hugging the muzzles in order to absorb the blast. Men were sawn in half, others were ripped apart by dogs. Once begun, no one was beyond such means, as this torturous protocol was practiced by the invading British and French, along with the rebels of Saint Domingue. This violence easily spread out into the surrounding coastal waters as deadly picaroons raided becalmed vessels and generally murdered all they found. Among the most atrocious were men like Jean-Jacques Dessalines, Dieudonne and Jeannot, who killed so many white prisoners that Toussaint had him summarily executed.

When Britain pulled out their forces in August, 1798, Thomas Maitland and Toussaint brokered a trade deal, the key item being that Toussaint was not to export the Saint Domingue slave rebellion to British colonies. Maitland was hoping that the unstable situation would spark a civil war with the remaining French on the island, which would at least become a drain on enemy resources. President John Adams had a similar notion.

After Toussaint sent a delegate carrying dispatches to President Adams, by late April, 1799 a three-way trade agreement was brokered between Toussaint, Britain and the U.S. Britain would provide "manufactures," while vital food stuffs and raw materials would come from the U.S. Due to political reasons, the U.S. would sign no documents in this accord, which allowed trade with Saint Domingue at a limited number of ports in exchange for Toussaint checking piracy and agreeing not to issue privateer commissions or begin any shipbuilding. All trade was one-way, with no vessels from Saint Domingue allowed at American ports, lest the slave rebellion infest the American South. Beginning in 1822 after Denmark Vessey's scripted slave revolt was broken up beforehand, South

Carolina would lock-up all black sailors arriving in port, regardless of nationality. This practice would spread to the entire South, with Nat Turner's 1831 uprising doing much to stiffen the program. As both men were literate -- like many of the rebel leadership in Saint Domingue -- religious gatherings and reading and writing skills would be regulated for both free blacks and slaves in the South. In *What Hath God Wrought*, historian Daniel Walker Howe states, "The fear of slave insurrection haunted the white South." This fear would arrive with the first shiploads of white planters who began fleeing Saint Domingue in 1791 and continued sporadically throughout the next few years. As one in every five sailors of the American merchant and whaling fleets were free blacks, many would feel the repercussions of this fear every time they hit port in a Southern locale. In *Drawn with the Sword*, historian James M. McPherson succinctly illustrates U.S.-Haiti relations: "To placate the South, the U.S. government refused to recognize Haiti until 1862 -- after the South had seceded." Thus, Abraham Lincoln would not only put forth great effort in abolishing slavery in America, but would also acknowledge the fact that former slaves were capable enough to govern.

Toussaint was also given military aid, which President Adams viewed as a way to weaken France. Adams was hoping trade with Toussaint would act as a sort of "indemnity" from the French to counter the cost of plundered American ships. This trade also acted as a serious incentive for Toussaint to play an active role in quelling piracy. His rebel army was constantly short of provisions, attesting to Napoleon's adage that armies "march on their stomach." In the long run, the dollar value of trade to Hispaniola would prove rather paltry for the Americans, as the island's ongoing turmoil greatly affected production and reliable logistics. However, many of

Saint Domingue's shattered cities and towns would get rebuilt as a result of this trade. For Toussaint Louverture, it was the best deal in the world.

Not only would Toussaint receive military supplies from the Americans, especially much-needed gunpowder and some 30,000 muskets, but he also directly benefited from the number of U.S. Navy warships patrolling the area, which President Adams instructed to assist Toussaint. Not only did the frigate *General Greene* bombard Jacmel and pave the way for Toussaint's victory over his rival rebel General Rigaud, but these warships had routinely seized Rigaud's supply ships, which did much to weaken his forces. Toussaint realized the advantage of being on good terms with such a navy and always did his best to accommodate American officers and practically shower them with gifts. For pounding Jacmel with the *General Greene*, Captain Perry was given 10,000 pounds of coffee and lavished with praise by Toussaint. It should be noted that Toussaint played his hand well, especially by courting high favor with the young American commanders. High praise, gifts, gala affairs and first-rate treatment does seem to have played well with American commanders, who often performed "small favors" for Toussaint, such as expediting provisions or protecting coastal shipping lanes. Perry would later face courts-martial and be driven from the service for a variety of reasons. Not surprisingly, one of the charges levied against him can be attributed to Toussaint, who begged him to linger in port, contrary to Navy Secretary Stoddert's orders.

Thomas Truxtun

Commodore Thomas Truxton — Naval History and Heritage Command

Thomas Truxtun's early career, in many ways, began in a similar fashion as countless other sea-faring colonial New Englanders. Growing up on Long Island, he began the life of a sailor at age twelve, and at sixteen was pressed into service by the Royal Navy aboard HMS *Prudent*(64) in 1771. He was fortunate, as the politics behind the British need for an increased navy lasted only as long as Truxtun's impressment, roughly six months. He would later serve aboard the *Nancy* when eighteen boxes of Captain Chambers' tea were dumped into New York harbor by Isaac Sears and the local Sons of Liberty in April, 1774.

Like many other watermen, Truxtun would respond to the need for revolutionary war supplies as the air still reverberated from the shots fired at Lexington and Concord. Recently married, in April, 1775 he became half-owner of a small sloop christened *Charming Polly*, after his wife -- oddly, Polly was a common nickname for Mary at the time. On his second run to the Dutch island of St. Eustatius, located in the Caribbean's Lesser Antilles, *Charming Polly* was seized by HMS *Argo*(28), although the British government would not officially authorize such seizures for a few more months. Released shortly after his capture, Truxtun would make it back to Philadelphia in time to serve as a lieutenant aboard the sloop *Congress*(6) in April, 1776, one of the first privateer vessels to obtain a commission from the Continental Congress. The first prize taken by the *Congress* would be the schooner *Thistle* sailing from Mobile. Her master would call the crew of *Congress*, "Pirates! Worse than pirates and highway robbers."[235]

Truxtun and Isaac Sears became part owners in the privateer sloop *Independence*(10), with which Truxtun took four British merchant vessels before December, 1776, though one of the prizes would be recaptured. He then took command of the privateer *Mars*, armed with twenty-two guns and a dozen swivels, sailed her from Boston to the English Channel and landed five captured prizes in France. As these actions happened in 1777, with the Franco-American alliance still more than a year in the future, the selling of prize goods and vessels in France constituted an act of piracy. Officially, France would complain about such sales, but allow many of them to occur. Benjamin Franklin, the American envoy to France, had full knowledge of maritime law. However, Franklin encouraged such privateer action as a way of furthering friction between England and France, as he hoped to draw France into the war on America's side by practically any means necessary.

By spring, 1779, Truxtun wished to resume smuggling lucrative military supplies and luxury goods from the Caribbean with his newly-purchased ship *Andrew Caldwell*(10). He obtained a privateer commission as well, in case he should happen across an easy British prize. This would prove wise the following summer, when he captured the brig *Clyde* on returning from his third smuggling voyage in the renamed ship *Independence*. However, the *Andrew Caldwell* would be seized by the British outside St. Eustatius on her first run. Released, merchant backers would support Truxtun's ventures

---

235   Eugene S. Ferguson, *Truxton of the Constellation: The Life of Commodore Thomas Truxton, U.S. Navy, 1755-1822.* (Baltimore: Johns Hopkins University Press, 2000), 24. Originally published in 1956.

and provide the ship *Lydia*, which would later become *Independence*.

By October, 1781, Truxtun had yet another new ship, the *St. James*(20). Sailing from Philadelphia with American consul to France Thomas Barclay aboard, the *St. James* fought off a flotilla of Tory picaroons off Reedy Island, Delaware before gaining the open sea. Similar picaroons would capture the privateer schooner *Harlequin* in September, 1782, which Truxtun owned a share of. As it was, as soon as the *St. James* reached open water, she met with the Tory privateer *Goodrich* of some 24 or 26 guns. The ships engaged for a quick action which left both vessels shot-up. Each side suffered few casualties, but *Goodrich* wanted no more and sailed off. Upon delivering Barclay to L'Orient, France, the French were so impressed with the tale that they stopped work on a French warship to copper *St. James'* hull. Truxtun would finish the war running goods from the Caribbean and would fend off two British privateers with the *Commerce* outside the harbor at Tortola in the Virgin Islands. *Commerce* would have only one man killed, while the British suffered 15 dead and 24 wounded. The island merchants would hail Truxtun as a hero and throw a magnificent dinner party.

At war's end, Truxtun would get involved with a terrible business partner and purchase three shiploads of English goods, which would see his business dissolved when no one bought them. It would take him years to pay off this debt and keep him at sea as a merchant captain. As a result, Truxtun would be in France with the *London Packet* in July, 1785 and would take Benjamin Franklin home to Philadelphia after picking him up in England. The voyage would prove instructive, as Franklin took temperature readings several times per day and did much to map the Gulf Stream. Upon returning,

Truxtun would take the *Canton* to China in late 1785, the first Philadelphia ship to engage in that trade. He engaged in several such trading ventures and in 1790 met Lord Cornwallis upon arriving in India. Before arriving home in April, 1791 many of the *Canton's* sailors would succumb to scurvy due to the length of the voyage.

Meanwhile, the early 1790's brought problems with the Barbary Coast, which prompted President Washington to push for the construction of a navy. At the same time, he had to come up with a list of captains for the six proposed vessels and the name of Thomas Truxtun happened to fill the sixth spot. Truxtun had met Washington at a dinner in 1782, and was shocked that the General remembered him bringing in gunpowder to Continental soldiers early in the war. This was certainly not the only reason he was chosen to command, but it did not hurt. As it turned out, there was a clause in the 1794 Congressional naval act which called for the withdrawal of funding should peace be reached with Algiers. That is precisely what happened and all work on the frigates stopped in 1796. Truxtun would have to wait until 1798 and the coming of the Quasi-War to command a warship.

Due to French spoliations of American merchant shipping, which began in 1796 and occurred mostly in the Caribbean -- although some prizes were taken within sight of American shores -- Congress allocated funding in 1797 to finish the one 36-gun and two 44-gun frigates which had been half-built. Under President Adams, funding and a series of legislation would soon arrive which not only finished the other three frigates -- barely started -- but also created the Navy Department, Marine Corps and added a small fleet of converted merchantmen and freshly-built warships to the nascent U.S. Navy. As appointed captains also oversaw a ship's construction, Truxtun had been present for the laying of nearly every timber of the 36-gun *Constellation* -- which actually caused a design flaw, later to be corrected by adding 14″ to her width -- and was literally itching for her "official" launch in June, 1798, so he could "pay my respects" to the French "piratical Junto."[236]

Truxtun is thanked by many for having established both discipline and workable systems in the young Navy, and although some would refer to him as a tyrant, there is little doubt that the crew was well-ordered and skilled by the time *Constellation* engaged the French frigate *l'Insurgente*(36) on February 9, 1799 off Nevis.

American commanders during the Quasi-War had great leeway in deciding what weight of cannon should be placed on their ships. The results were over-gunned warships which were either slowed or handled poorly. Truxtun was guilty of this as well, and when *Constellation* engaged *l'Insurgente*, the wind pushed her top-heavy hull to such an angle that Truxtun had to give up the weather gauge and attack from the lee side in order to use his guns. Less than fifty yards separated the two frigates when *Constellation* opened fire. While cannon weight had caused *Constellation* to heel onto her side, the large 24-pounders now proved lethal to the French, spreading panic throughout the ship. They fired a broadside into *Constellation*'s rigging before attempting to board and received devastating

24-pounder
Naval History and Heritage Command

---

236   Michael A. Palmer, *Stoddert's War: Naval Operations during the Quasi-War with France, 1798-1801.* (Annapolis, MD: Naval Institute Press, 2000), 25. Originally published by South Carolina Press, 1987.

raking fire which ran through the French frigate from stem to stern. The frigates swapped three more broadsides at close range when *Constellation* pulled ahead and raked her again. After an hour of combat, *l'Insurgente* struck her colors, suffer-

ing 29 dead and 41 wounded, her captain utterly shocked. *Constellation* lost only one man, a member of the gun crew who Lt. Sterett ran through for leaving his post.

Truxtun sailed with his prize to nearby St. Kitts, the island which the British let the Americans use as a base of operations while keeping an eye on French Guade-loupe. The *Constellation* was repaired

Lt. Andrew Sterett

there, along with the rechristened USS *Insurgent*, which did not sit entirely well with Navy Secretary Stoddert nor the Adams administration, as the ship had not gone through proper prize court channels. In March, *Constellation* ran down and captured the privateer schooner *l'Union*(6), which was also hauling trade goods, a sure sign that seizing American shipping wasn't as lucrative as before.

As enlistments for U.S. sailors only lasted for one year, Truxtun returned to Norfolk by late May, 1799 with *Constellation* and *Insurgent*. The French frigate would finally go through condemnation in the courts, which would award Truxtun $12,000, while most sailors received $106.80 -- providing they had not sold their prize tickets to speculators, which many seamen did. Truxtun also replaced *Constellation*'s 24-pounders with eighteens, in order to lower her center of gravity so she would not heel over as she had when fighting *l'Insurgente*. H also replaced the quarterdeck long-twelves with 24-pound carronades, which had only recently become available. Truxtun received a hero's welcome not only in Norfolk, but the entire country celebrated the capture of *l'Insurgente*, the first major prize taken by the U.S. Navy. Unfortunately, that summer would also reveal the size of Truxtun's ever-growing ego, as he resigned from the Navy in August. He felt he deserved to be ranked as the first captain on the list and quit in protest when President Adams ranked Truxtun behind Silas Talbot. Adams was correct to do so, as Talbot had a long Revolutionary pedigree, but Truxtun cared little about it and resigned. Only as a result of George Washington's prodding, which repeatedly mentioned "duty to one's country," did Truxtun swallow his pride and obtain another commission -- but only if he was never to serve under Talbot. President Adams agreed and Truxtun set sail for the Caribbean with *Constellation* on Christmas Day, 1799.

Silas Talbot

Fate can be fickle, and the ironies about to face Commodore Thomas Truxtun were largely of his own making. There had been some squabbling over the size of *l'Insurgente* during condemnation, concerning whether or not the frigate was "bigger" than *Constellation*. If the prize was larger, then the entire prize value went to the captain and crew, but the government would claim half if the prize was of equal strength or smaller. She did carry two more guns, but *Constellation* thoroughly out-gunned the French frigate in weight of iron, which Truxtun himself had acknowledged -- in between insisting that *l'Insurgente* was the "bigger" ship. While his prize money reflected a larger ship, the fact was a known technicality. Without a doubt, Truxtun sailed to Guadeloupe with only one thought in mind -- to engage a frigate larger than his own and take her a prize.

Fate appeared to smile on the commodore, for almost immediately upon his arrival, Truxtun sighted a large French frigate which sailed away. He immediately gave chase, but had previously ordered two other American vessels to patrol elsewhere, instead of accompanying *Constellation*. Obviously, he wanted this frigate for himself. On February 1, 1800, Truxtun would get a crack at the only heavy French frigate cruising the Caribbean at that time.

As it happened, *la Vengeance*(40) was not only bigger than *Constellation*, but also carried two French generals, perhaps eighty soldiers, thirty-six American prisoners and was loaded with gold and silver. She was everything Truxtun wanted. Captain Pitot, due to his cargo, had no desire to engage a ship of his own size and continued to flee. The chase continued until nightfall, when Pitot realized he could not outrun the American frigate and turned to fight, firing at his opponent's rigging in standard French form. Truxtun ordered his guns aimed at the French hull, the typical British and American tactic, and for two and a-half hours the frigates battered each other with broadsides. The French attempted to board and at fifty yards were punished by marine sharpshooters and quarterdeck carronades loaded with grapeshot. Unable to board, both ships kept firing broadsides for another two or three hours. Fire from *la Vengeance* stopped around 1:00 A.M., when the frigate struck her colors -- for the second time, but the first had gone unnoticed due to darkness. Truxtun, swelled with pride, prepared to board his prize. Closing to within twenty-five yards, *Constellation*'s mainmast suddenly snapped and collapsed into the sea. All Truxtun could do was watch as his "prize" drifted further and further away, until she was gone from sight.

Both Pitot and Truxtun thought they had sunk each oth-er. *Constellation*, "the most perfect wreck you ever saw," had fifteen dead and twenty-five wounded, while *la Vengeance* suf-fered terribly, with 160 men dead or wounded.[237] While both ships were roughly the same size, the French frigate was more heavily armed and delivered 559 pounds of broadside iron to *Constellation*'s 372. While *la Vengeance* was listed at 516 broadside pounds, this does not account for the fact that the French pound weighed 8.33 percent more than the English or American pound. However, what truly affected the battle was the high rate of American fire, whose gunners out-shot the French roughly two-to-one. The irony, of course, is that Truxtun would have taken another prize had he not gone it alone. He was lucky not be become a prize himself, as he had heard a corvette was consort to the French frigate and wished to take them both by himself. As it was, the engagement would be hailed as a great "victory." The U.S. Congress would have a gold medal struck in honor of Commodore Thomas Truxtun.

The near-defeat would not humble Truxtun, but would expand his growing ego to a ridiculous state, where he would soon take it upon himself to issue sailing orders to the fleet and reap Stoddert's wrath for it, although the Navy Secretary would keep it quiet. As the Navy fell victim to serious budget cuts after the Quasi-War, Truxtun would retire on half-pay, until recalled by President Jefferson during the "war" against Barbary Corsairs. Again, the commodore would resign, being affronted by not having a captain assigned to run his ship, which would leave him free for a commodore's duties.

---

237   Ibid, 187. Quote from ship's surgeon Isaac Henry, who performed six amputations.

Quasi-War French National Piracy:
Birth of the United States Navy and Marine Corps

The actual birth date of the U.S. Navy is a debatable topic. The same could be said for the Marine Corps. While both services like to trace their beginnings back to the Continental Navy of the American Revolution, this is not precisely accurate, for a number of reasons. Oddly, if the Navy should truly be linked back to 1775 -- with its "home" located at Whitehall, in upstate New York -- then it would only be fair to attribute the most notorious traitor in American history as the father of that navy -- Benedict Arnold. It was Arnold, who not only requested the vessels be built at Whitehall, but also oversaw their construction and subsequently commanded the small squadron against the British off Valcour Island in Lake Champlain.

Model of *Bonhomme Richard* — Naval History and Heritage Command

At any rate, that was the *Continental Navy*, which would little resemble the United States' Navy. At the time of the Continental Navy, the United States -- specifically the constitutionally constructed Federal Government -- did not yet exist. The U.S. Navy was officially born on April 30, 1798, when President Adams signed the act creating the Department of the Navy. A permanent Marine Corps was created when Adams signed another act on July 11, 1798. Prior to this, during the revolution, there was no training given to marines and methods of procuring them for Continental ships were rather ad-hoc. Also, there was no integral marine command until the 1798 legislation, which also called for specialized training. Prior to the Quasi-War, there were neither marines nor even Continental sailors, as the last Continental vessel, the *Alliance*, was sold in 1785. Employees of the Revenue Cutter Service, created in 1790 -- also referred to as the Treasury Navy or Revenue Marine -- were often called marines, but this had nothing to do with any job-related similarities, for there really weren't any.

Likewise, attributing one single man as the "Father" of the U.S. Navy -- or even its Continental predecessor -- is a whole different argument entirely. Due to his exploits with the *Ranger* and *Bonhomme Richard* during the American Revolution, there are those who would argue that John Paul Jones should fill that role. Others make the argument that Silas Talbot should hold that title, while Congress itself declared John Barry to be "Father of the U.S. Navy" in 1981. Arguments have also been made which point to Thomas Truxtun, not just for his engagements during the Quasi-War, but mostly because he did much to organize the young Navy and establish

Commodore John Barry, USN — Naval History and Heritage Command

precedents for crew training and vessel operations. John Adams, who had lobbied throughout the revolution for naval power and passed the later acts which established the Navy Department during the Quasi-War, has been long-touted by many as the rightful patriarch. Benjamin Franklin should not be forgotten either, as his exploits during the revolution did much to further American warships -- both public and private -- which would place his name on one of America's first ships-of-the-line. As interesting as many of these arguments are, however, none of them are precisely accurate.

President George Washington
White House

If one single man should be elevated above all others for that of the Navy's "Father," then by all rights the title belongs to George Washington. This is not merely because he is considered to be the "Father of the Country," but for two particular reasons. In 1775, before the Continental Congress had established the Continental Navy, Washington took command of the Continental Army outside Boston. Due to a bit of leeway in the general's commission, he took it upon himself to issue commissions for six schooners, which technically were under Army command. Desperate for munitions, Washington's need for gunpowder specifically directed his actions in commissioning these sloops and schooners, many of which fell into congressional command after the Continental Congress got around to legislating the Continental Navy. Not only did Washington commission these vessels, but he oversaw every aspect of them, from provisioning and manning them to acting as the court of condemnation when it came to judging their prizes -- many of which were found to be illegal captures. While this alone might garner Washington the title as naval "Father," there is a more serious argument to be made. As president, Washington lobbied Congress in 1794 for six frigates in order to engage the Barbary States, who had begun pirating American vessels now that they no longer fell under Royal Navy protection. Peace would come with Algiers in 1796 while the frigates were still being built, but the fact that they were constructed and not simply converted merchant vessels was also Washington's decision, as he knew that a "heavy frigate" design would best suit America's interest. While dormant for a couple years, it would be the frames of these six frigates which John Adams would complete as president and use as America's flagships during the coming Quasi-War. *Constitution*(44) "Old Ironsides" and *Constellation*(36) would become the most famous of these frigates, but *United States*(44), *President*(44), *Congress*(36) and *Chesapeake*(36) would all serve well into and after the War of 1812, which would also prove Washington correct in his decision to construct and not convert. Ironically, the first frigate built by the U.S. government, *Crescent*, would be delivered to the Dey of Algiers as a stipulation in the treaty.

Aside from George Washington, the next-best argument for fatherhood is undoubtedly Benjamin Stoddert, who became the first Secretary of the Navy in 1798. Stoddert is often overlooked, but should not be, for his leadership of the newly-created Navy Department would not only lead to the successful prosecution of the young nation's first conflict, but also set precedents which the Navy would follow for over a hundred years.

Neither a legislator nor a sea captain, Stoddert had the inglorious task of dealing with the day-to-day nuts and bolts problems of putting a naval force together as well as formulating a plan of action. His problems in dealing with merchant conversions and the construction of warships were legion, especially as each of the first six frigates were built in different ports for political reasons. This proved to be much more expensive and more difficult to schedule than if they had been built in even two or three different areas. Due to initial confusion, many captains had to locate their own cannon, which caused the majority of warships to be badly over-gunned, which not only slowed them but affected maneuverability. Stoddert did much to trim these extra guns and also played a firm hand in the development of American arms, as he stood by such outfits as Henry Foxall's Eagle Furnace long enough for them to produce quality weapons. By 1800, such contractors were supplying enough quality carronades, cannons and arms to fill America's needs. Paul Revere would begin rolling copper in 1801, and many of these sheets would find their way fastened to the bottoms of American warships.

Stoddert also played a large role in getting the Washington Navy Yard built, and when authorized $200,000 for the purchase of ship timber, he bought wooded Grover and Blackbeard islands off the coast of Georgia for a mere $22,000 instead. These islands would supply naval needs well into the nineteenth century, including the tough live oak which put much of the strength into "Old Ironsides." Had Stoddert's proposed 74-gun "liners," made of the same material, actually been finished in time for 1812, there is no telling how well they might have performed.

Stoddert also played a direct role in raising the pay for the

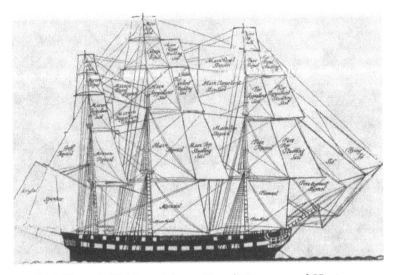

Sail Plan of *Old Ironsides* — Naval History and Heritage Command

naval services -- which equalized the pay and rank structure between the Navy and Revenue Cutter Service -- along with creating a half-pay retirement system, which allowed captains to be called back to duty if it should be required. He created a supply scheme which would become protocol until at least 1900. The practice involved the use of neutral ports for supply depots, and if neutral nations were unwilling to do this, a number of supply ships hovering around the area would be used instead. As problems quickly became evident with sailors serving only one-year enlistments, he lobbied Congress for a change to two-year terms, which was implemented in 1801. Stoddert had to deal with captains who liked to linger in foreign ports -- contrary to his orders -- which caused many sailors to contract disease and die unnecessarily. He also had to deal with the egos of these commanders, famously that of Thomas Truxtun, along with a variety of offenses and incidents which would have led to court-martials which, due to some rather seedy details, might have blackened the Navy's eye during such politically-turbulent times. As such, Stoddert approved of President John Adams' less-visible method of releasing these officers by executive order. While not under Stoddert's complete control, it should be noted that while the Royal Navy lost ten ships due to accidents or weather for each lost in battle from 1793-1815, the American ratio under Stoddert's years of service was only three-to-one.

While fights over fatherhood might still be on-going, there can be no argument concerning why the Navy was created -- which was specifically to fight piracy. Those six frigates would finally get to battle the Barbary Corsairs which they were originally intended to fight, under the Jefferson administration. However, before that opportunity arrived, the frigates would prove instrumental in fighting French national piracy during the Quasi-War. While the Barbary campaigns would prove to be rather ugly affairs, the Quasi-War brought immediate acclaim to the six frigates which Washington originally proposed. As fights over fatherhood might prove entertaining, all of the previously mentioned men combine to form a part of that parentage, as do many others not mentioned. In the same respect, it is easy to credit a ship's commander, but his crew should never be forgotten.

Frigate *Essex*, 1799
(Background: Letter from George Washington
to Earle of Dundonald)

chapter Three

Pax Brittanica Piracy - The Deadliest Period: 1815-1835

Piracy on the Rise

The year 1815 would witness the close of the Napoleonic Wars and the War of 1812. The ensuing peace would contribute to a dramatic rise in piracy levels across the Caribbean, drastically hampering the shipping of all nations while ushering in a level of violence never before subjected to commercial merchant fleets. An array of revolutions occurring in the Spanish colonies of Central and South America would fuel a piratical fire lasting for over twenty years. The eventual backlash of unlicensed privateers and local pirates launched from Cuba and Puerto Rico -- Spain's only remaining loyal colonies -- would not only bear the marks of a colonial Spanish policy of "revenge," but also include the brutality of such a policy. The targeting of American vessels, partly in retribution for perceived or actual wrongs done to Spain and her colonies by privateers and pirates fitted out in American ports, coupled with tension from Andrew Jackson's efforts in West Florida, would cause Congress to expand the United States Navy. Congress also allocated funding for a West Indies Fleet and subsequent two-part Anti-Piracy Campaign, brought to culmination with the dispatch of Commodore Porter's historic "Mosquito Fleet" to the Caribbean in 1823. While much of this writing will focus on Porter's tactics and success, along with his subsequent relief and courts-martial, that would be starting at the end, not the beginning of this tale. The issues involved have deep roots, but a great many of them can be traced to the year 1808.

Revolutionary Profit

The year 1808 bore witness to Napoleon's invasion of Spain. The weakened state of the mother country would cause a rash of revolutions across Central and South America, which in turn, would spark a great deal of investment in the United States by building and equipping not only privateer fleets for these revolutionary governments, but also substantial portions of their state-owned navies. Baltimore would be the leader of such American ports, but New York, Boston, Charleston and New Orleans would also provide their fair share of vessels. 1808 also marked the end of the international slave trade for the United States. This would have great effect on the operations of two French-born brothers -- Pierre and Jean Laffite -- whose smuggling operations surrounding New Orleans and Barataria Bay would become legend after their relocation to that area in 1809.[238] In 1806, President Jefferson established a naval station at New Orleans. Two years later, Captain David Porter would be sent to command this station, specifically to suppress piracy along the coast. However, he would be confounded by inadequate vessels and manpower, along with a local population who decidedly favored cheap pirated or smuggled goods. Concerning pirates, Porter noted, "As they spend their money freely, the local authorities rather

238   William C. Davis, *The Pirates Laffite: The Treacherous World of the Corsairs of the Gulf.* (New York: Harcourt, 2005), 47,30.

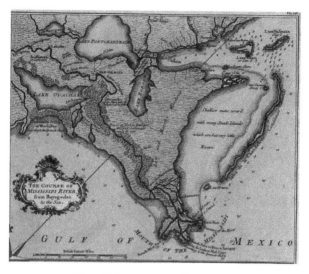

New Orleans area circa 1720

encouraged their presence."[239]   By July, 1810, Porter would
resign his position, as disgusted with the lack of adequate
vessels, men and materials provided by the navy as he was at
the legal situation in New Orleans, which condemned barely
any of the ships he managed to capture, nor successfully pros-
ecuted any pirates.[240]

While the international community was ambivalent in
the case of ships sailing under commissions from revolutionary governments, the law stipulated that these ships had to
be commissioned in a home port of the issuing authority.[241]
When the U.S. severed relations with Spain in 1809, this
helped to ad a "patriotic" flavor to not only American-backed
revolutionary privateers, but also to the upsurge of Ameri-

---

239   Ibid, 42. Jefferson's Embargo Act of December, 1807, helped
smuggling to thrive in this area.
240   Ibid, 54-55. Davis notes the *Duc de Monetebello, L'Epine* and
L'Intrepide, all captured under dubious or blank Republic of Cartagena
commissions, were seized as a result of their intent to illegally fit-out.
241   Ibid, 44.

can-based pirating of Spanish vessels in the Gulf.[242] This Spanish-American strife would only grow in scope, eventually to include the British, whose privateers also sailed under revolutionary flags and whose seamen could be found on a variety of revolutionary vessels. While the coming of the War of 1812 would bring many American-built privateers "home" to the service -- and legal commissions -- of their country, the stage was already set for the surge of piracy that would begin to rise at war's end.

The Pirates

American seaman George Little, who sailed on merchant ships prior to joining six Buenos Aires privateering voyages, eventually lost out on most of his funds and made his way back to the United States just as war broke out in 1812. In Norfolk, Little joined the privateer schooner *George Washington* as a lieutenant. The *George Washington* hosted a twelve-pound pivot, two nine-pounders and a crew of eighty men, who Little describes. "The crew were a motley set indeed, composed of all nations; they appeared to have been scraped together from the lowest dens of wretchedness and vice, and only wanted a leader to induce them to any act of daring and desperation."[243]

Similar sailors would be sought out by many revolutionary nations, especially respected British and American naval officers, or those with previous experience commanding privateers. Peacetime invariably led to a draw-down in warships,

---

242   Ibid, 48.
243   George Little, "Privateering," from *Life Before the Mast: Sailors' eyewitness accounts from the age of fighting ships,* edited by Jon. E. Lewis. (New York, Carroll & Graf, 2002), 398-399.

as many countries tried to lessen expenses no longer necessary. Historically, this generally led to a large pool of unemployed sailors, as it usually took some time before post-war merchant fleets grew large enough to accommodate them. Thus, many of these British and American sailors flocked to South America in search of employment. Without a doubt, the most famous of these men was Thomas Cochrane, Earl of Dundonald. Lord Cochrane's exploits during the Napoleonic Wars are now legendary, and at the time so world-renowned that the revolutionary government of Chile sent their agent to England with an offer for Cochrane to become their Admiral. He sailed from England just prior to the enactment of the British Foreign Enlistment Act of 1819, which was a direct effort to keep men like Cochrane (as the act was much centered on him) from serving in the navies of foreign nations.[244] Word of Cochrane coming to Chile added fuel to the exodus of American and British sailors heading south, especially as he appealed to the revolutionary governments to seek out such sailors. These seamen were only too happy to receive an initial bonus and promises of high pay by these often desperate governments. However, American business ventures would continue to be the largest contributor to these governments.[245]

---

244   Chester G. Hearn, *Gray Raiders of the Sea.* (LSU Press, 1992), 50. This act would have large implications concerning English and Irish sailors manning Confederate raiders during the American Civil War.

245   Gerald S. Graham, editor, *The Navy and South America, 1807-1823: Correspondence of the Commanders-in-Chief on the South American Station.* (London, Navy Records Society, 1962), 371-372, *Hardy to Croker*, August 29, 1823. In this report, Hardy notes that Cochrane's statements to the government of Pernambuco (Cochrane was now commanding Brazil's revolutionary navy) preferring the talents of British seamen were translated and published in the local papers. "The consequence has been...that a great many men had already deserted from the merchant vessels." Earlier letters by Hardy and Bowles note the arrival of a variety of Baltimore-built

American naval involvement concerning Spain's revolting colonies would not be inconsequential, both in terms of the number of ships and arms sold to these revolutionaries along with the sheer volume of sailors and officers that were more than willing to work for them. Britain would also provide men and ships, as the man Chile dispatched to London carried 100,000 pounds in specie for this purpose.[246] The depth of American involvement would be much deeper than merely that of arms supplier and provider of mercenary sailors, for the level of involvement connected to the merchant and legal community -- specifically due to the financial ties of prominent men of both fields in certain port cities -- would often lead to a unique melding of governmental and business interests. In May, 1817, Commodore Bowles, Commander of the Royal Navy's South American Station wrote;

"With respect to the American scheme I only know that the armed ships fitted out at Baltimore ... were consigned to the American consul here, who transacted all their business, procured them their commissions from this government and, in short, appeared to be the person to whom they looked for directions on all occasions."[247]

The involvement of Baltimore in the international arena of privateer ventures cannot be understated. The War of 1812 had brought huge profits to the city, and with the decommissioning of American privateers, switching these vessels over to the flags of insurgent governments -- regardless of how dubious the commissions might be -- was a simple matter of broadening the practice already in place prior to 1812. Perhaps the best overall picture yet presented on the situation

warships to Chile, which would compose much of that country's navy.
246   Ibid, 204, *Bowles to Croker*, June 30, 1817. Don Jose Antonio Alvarez de Condarco was Chile's agent.
247   Ibid, 197-198, *Bowles to Croker*, May 24, 1817.

in Baltimore is given by Jeffrey Orenstein in the spring, 2007 edition of the scholarly law journal *The Green Bag*. Orenstein highlights the career of Joseph Almeida, who first achieved fame sailing from Baltimore as an American privateer during the War of 1812. His success in this war not only brought him a modicum of fame, but also large profits for himself and his investors, many of whom comprised high places in the local law and business community. Approached by an agent in a commercial firm after the war, who happened to have a blank commission, a bargain was struck with Almeida. Sailing from Baltimore in the *Orb*, at a ceremony held at sea two weeks later, the ship was rechristened *Congreso* and the flag of Buenos Aires was hauled up the mast. While Almeida would eventually be shot by Spain for his piracies in 1832, five years after his capture, he would first provide reasons for a rash of litigation in Baltimore concerning piracy. Between 1820-1825, three of Almeida's cases would eventually be decided by John Marshall's Supreme Court. It is a testament to the degree of involvement by Baltimore's trading agents, lawyers and judges -- clearly illustrated by Orenstein -- which not only saved Almeida from an American noose, but would continue to support his piracies long after authorities were on his trail.[248]

While events in Chile do well to offer a snapshot of what was occurring in many parts of the revolutionary Americas, it should be noted that Chilean happenings were also among the most orderly of the era -- especially after the arrival of Lord Cochrane in 1819. By far, the number of commissions coming from Buenos Aires, Carthagena, the United Provinces, Spanish Loyalists and the insurgent government of Mexico

---

248   Jeffrey Orenstein, "Joseph Almeida: Portrait of a Privateer, Pirate & Plantiff, Part I," excerpted from *The Green Bag: An Entertaining Journal of Law* Volume 10, no.2 (Spring, 2007): 314-322.

would be a much greater cause of disturbance, as blank commissions would nearly paper the world in an effort to procure help in the violent revolutions against Spain. Above all else, this is what Jean and Pierre Laffite would excel at -- not so much in actually commanding pirate vessels, but more in the way of enabling the practice by providing commissions from insurgent governments and offering refuges like the establishments at Barataria and Galveston. These islands were not only havens for pirates and borderline-lawful privateers, but also provided the outlaws with the means of disposing their pirated vessels through prize courts of dubious legality while also offering a sophisticated network of smugglers and bootleggers which enabled the quick sale of stolen goods.[249] While the United States would eventually remove the Laffites from both of these islands, the subsequent pardoning of the Baratarian pirates by the Madison administration after their assistance during the Battle of New Orleans would provide the Laffites with six more years of business, largely at the expense of Spanish shipping. Only in 1821 did the U.S. Navy run-off the Laffites from Galveston permanently, although "escorted from" is a closer reality than "run-off" would be.[250] The U.S. government's relative acquiescence in Laffite's Galveston operations would not go unnoticed by the Spanish, who not only suffered as a primary consequence, but also made their political voice heard in Washington, as weak as it was. Spain's

249   William C. Davis, *The Pirates Laffite: The Treacherous World of the Corsairs of the Gulf.* (New York: Harcourt, 2005). Practically Davis' entire work is an account of the smuggling operations of the Laffite brothers. Page 324 tells of Jean taking over the Galveston Island operation from Louis Aury, to better facilitate the commissioning and prize rendering of the insurgent Mexican government.

250   Richard Wheeler, *In Pirate Waters: Captain David Porter, USN, and America's war on piracy in the West Indies.* (New York, Crowell, 1969), 96-98. Also, notes on Laffite commissions, 49,50 and Madison's pardon, 58-62.

A myth heavy portrayal of the Battle of New Orleans
Library of Congress

outcry would finally prove to be the prime motivation for Laffite's removal, but would only be acted on two years after the signing of a new treaty. 1819 would prove to be a watershed year, in both the state of Spanish-American relations and concerning simultaneous international action aimed at reigning in the relatively unchecked scourge of revolutionary privateers.

Mutiny

It would not take long for the actions of American and British-backed revolutionary privateers to plunge into unrestricted piracy, and a very brutal and savage variety at that. Murder, in keeping with the age-old "dead men tell no tales" motif, would spread rampant across the Caribbean as water-borne thieves -- with either dubious commissions or none at all -- were quick to rob any merchant from any nation, as it did not take long for Spanish shipping to practically dry up in the Caribbean after years of being such a popular target.

William Dampier, long considered the pirate's own sage, noted in 1684 that, "…it is generally seen among privateers, that nothing emboldens them sooner to mutiny than want, which we could not well suffer…"[251] Not much would change in this regard from the days of Dampier to those of the post-Napoleonic period. Sometimes, mutinous over-throws of a privateer's leadership -- providing that the officers themselves didn't inspire a "mutiny" only in the technical sense of the word -- could be directly linked with the fall of a revolutionary government. Such was the case with Bolivar's Cathagena, which fell back in Spanish hands for some time, creating chaos among their already dubiously-commissioned fleet of privateers. Joseph Alemida, whose first enterprise after the War of 1812 was a smuggling endeavor to Carthagena, was captured by Spanish forces who continued to fly Bolivar's Patriot flag in order to dupe men such as Almeida, along with any wayward privateers lacking fresh news of the city's fall.[252]

However, the vast majority of privateer mutinies which occurred -- and a great many mutinies did occur, to include even some state-owned ships of the revolutionary navies themselves -- related much closer to Dampier's observance.

---

251   William Dampier, *A New Voyage Round the World.* (Warwick, NY: 1500 Books, 2007), 132. Reprinted from 1717 6th edition, originally published in 1697.

252   Jeffrey Orenstein, "Joseph Almeida: Portrait of a Privateer, Pirate & Plantiff, Part I," excerpted from *The Green Bag: An Entertaining Journal of Law* Volume 10, no.2 (Spring, 2007): 315. Almeida's vessel and cargo were seized and he was forced to march 140 miles to Santa Marta, during which time many other prisoners died. He was later released after a short imprisonment. Undoubtedly, these affairs shaded his future piratical exploits against the Spanish, whose losses to Almeida are estimated at some hundreds of vessels, worth perhaps a million dollars.

The main reason American and British sailors ended up under the flags of these revolutionary governments had everything to do with promises of above-average payment and plentiful prize money. Sometimes events worked out as promised, but most generally they did not, as each of the revolutionary governments had serious financial difficulties. Not only would this be reflected in lack of payment for services, but shipboard conditions themselves would often deteriorate to a dismal degree, as funding for naval stores and money for refitting quickly became scarce to many state-owned navies.

It took relatively little time for these mutinies to spread across the Caribbean. Commodore Bowles wrote of an incident he witnessed in October, 1817 at Valparaiso, Chile, when the crew of the 18-gun *Liberty*, reportedly fitted-out at Buenos Aires, mutinied. After off-loading their officers, Bowles states they "are gone, according to their own declaration, to cruise against all nations."[253] Chile, once again, can be used as a general reference to these mutinies, but in this aspect the Chilean mutinies should be recognized as being located at the low end of the scale. Much of this can be attributed to Lord Cochrane, who seized roughly $285,000 from San Martin's "Peruvian" treasure ship in late 1821 and refused to turn it over to the Chilean government. Instead, Cochrane used the bulk of the money to pay soldiers and sailors who had not received any pay at all for some months, if not longer.[254] This

253   Gerald S. Graham, editor, *The Navy and South America, 1807-1823: Correspondence of the Commanders-in-Chief on the South American Station.* (London, Navy Records Society, 1962), 210, *Bowles to Croker*, October16, 1817. This book is littered with such entries until the book's ending in 1823. A great many of them depict a high degree of British and American seamen involved.

254   Robert Harvey, *Cochrane: The Life and Exploits of a Fighting Captain.* (New York: Carroll and Graf, 2000), 261. Always lured by prize money, Cochrane would take none for himself here, and would leave the Chilean service with their financial debts to him being not inconsiderable.

action, without a doubt, did much to limit Chilean mutinies, for their war for independence was over, and by July, 1822, their fleet was disbanded due to a severe lack of funding and Admiral Cochrane was out of a job. The Chilean brig *Araucano* would be the sole state-ship mutiny at this time, for in the summer of 1822, all officers would be off-loaded on the California coast prior to launching their piratical cruise. Cochrane would not be jobless long, for he would attain the same position with the Brazilian revolutionary navy within two year's time, starting the cycle afresh.[255]

Accompanying the escalation of these privateer and state-ship mutinies was a growing frustration among those loyal to Spain, particularly for the colonies of Cuba and Puerto Rico. This frustration would flaunt the use of commissions at all for many of these pirates, who were mostly local to the shores of these islands. These conditions inspired widespread land-based efforts against the shipping of all nations, but particularly that of the United States and Britain. A policy of ruthless "revenge" would be carried out against many nations, but as an example of the extent of Anglo-Spanish strife, it would be Cuban pirates who would invent the practice of making their victims "walk the plank," which was first documented on July 18, 1822, when the captain of the sloop *Blessing* was subjected to the practice. Oddly, many American pirates ended up in Cuba.[256]

255   Gerald S. Graham, editor, *The Navy and South America, 1807-1823: Correspondence of the Commanders-in-Chief on the South American Station.* (London, Navy Records Society, 1962), 359-360, *Hardy to Croker*, October 29, 1822. Hardy goes on to note Cochrane's arrival in Brazil as their Admiral in April, 1824 on page 366.
256   Peter Earle, *The Pirate Wars.* (New York: St. Martin's, 2003), 222. Earle's list of the period's pirate atrocities are extensively covered.

Changes In Policy

The year 1819 would bring great changes in international attitudes toward the growing problem of shipping depredations caused by renegade privateers, specifically those flying the flags of revolutionary governments in the Americas. In June, 1818, the Royal Navy became empowered to chase pirates of all nations.[257] This helped ease many restraints in chasing pirates, because prior to this, warships were only allowed to chase pirates known to have robbed their nation's shipping. The precedent for this was the long-standing problems of unauthorized British and French seizures of neutral shipping, which had previously led to the Quasi-War and War of 1812. Also, in order to restrain illegally-commissioned privateers, these vessels began to be held in port, while their manifests, cargoes and papers were better scrutinized. The subsequent rise in legal proceedings, which did not generally end in the hanging or jailing of many pirates just yet, did help to scare many of them into more honest lines of work.

By early 1817, Spain had begun to violently protest the obvious collusion of some U.S. ports with pirates preying on Spanish shipping, particularly Baltimore and New Orleans.[258] This, along with the actions of General Andrew Jackson in West Florida, would cement a new contract between the United States and Spain with the Adams-Onis Treaty of 1819. Signed in Washington in February, 1819, the treaty gave all of Florida to the United States, the cost of which was mostly figured around the price of piracy these two nations had

---

257   Ibid, 234.
258   Richard Wheeler, *In Pirate Waters: Captain David Porter, USN, and America's war on piracy in the West Indies.* (New York, Crowell, 1969), 79-80.

shared through the years, with the U.S. promising five million dollars. This freshly-signed treaty would have immediate implications for piracy in the Caribbean, particularly from an American standpoint.

On March 3, 1819, President Monroe signed the U.S. Anti-Piracy Act of 1819, which called for the construction of five schooners built specifically to cruise for pirates in the shallow waters that the majority of Cuban and Puerto Rican pirates operated. The act also created the West India Squadron, whose job it was to check any and all privateer commissions and craft for legality, and specifically, to hunt down pirates and secure safe shipping around the island of Cuba. *Enterprise, Peacock, Hornet* and *John Adams* would be immediately dispatched to the area, bolstered by what few serviceable navy schooners were at hand.[259]

President James Monroe
White House

In order to facilitate cooperation with the various revolutionary governments, who played an essential role in checking the rise of renegade privateers, a diplomatic mission was necessary. In July, 1819, President Monroe dispatched Captain Oliver Hazard Perry in the *John Adams* to visit the governments of Venezuela and Buenos Aires, with the schooner *Nonsuch* to be used for the 300 mile journey up the Orinoco river to Angostura, (today's Ciudad Bolivar), the capital of Venezuela. While the government of Buenos Aires proved too disorganized to deal with, Perry has success with Venezuela, who promised to enforce international regulations regarding their privateers as well as pay indemnities to the United States

259   Ibid, 86.

Oliver Hazard Perry
U.S. Naval Museum

for past piracies.[260] The key here proved to be the lure of formal recognition for the revolutionary governments. As it happened, the United States would be the first nation in the world to offer such recognition, during the spring of 1822, under President Monroe.[261] This was accomplished little more than a year after the Adams-Onis Treaty took effect in February, 1821, to allow time for the occupation of Florida. Had the U.S. acted earlier in recognizing these governments, Spain may not have been so quick to detach Florida from its empire quite so cheaply. As it was, diplomacy came at a cost. Oliver Hazard Perry, hero of Lake Erie during the War of 1812, died of yellow fever on his thirty-fourth birthday,

---

260   Walter R. Borneman, *1812: The War that Forged a Nation.* (New York: Harper Collins, 2004), 135.
261   Ronald P. Formisano, "James Madison," from Brinkley, Dyer, et al, *The American Presidency.* (New York: Houghton-Mifflin, 2004), 65.

August 23, 1819, near Trinidad.[262]

In the announcement of his Anti-Piracy Act, Monroe encouraged merchants to defend themselves and fight for their ships, which is a stark contrast from the arduous debates concerning this very issue merely twenty years prior during the Quasi-War, which was the fledgling nation's original attempt at quelling Caribbean piracy.[263] Monroe had good reason to urge merchants to defend themselves; for listed in their petition to him in December, 1819, insurance companies tallied forty-four U.S. ships as having been pirated in the Caribbean that year.[264] Charles Tyng, who captained his brig *Eight Sons* in the Caribbean and across the world, states off-handedly in his memoir that by 1826, merchants were required to carry arms by their insurers -- both cannons (generally the lighter carronades) as well as muskets. Tyng's brig carried four six-pound carronades, twelve muskets and a variety of pistols, cutlasses and boarding pikes.[265] While some merchants did manage to fight-off pirates, some did not -- which lead to a caustic letter from Commodore Porter in August, 1824 chastising some merchants for not even attempting to defend their property, as in the case of the *Castor,* whose crew gave

262   Richard Wheeler, *In Pirate Waters: Captain David Porter, USN, and America's war on piracy in the West Indies.* (New York, Crowell, 1969), 88-92.

263   Alexander DeConde, *The Quasi-War: The Politics and Diplomacy of the Undeclared War with France, 1797-1801.* (New York: Scribners, 1966), 70, 101.

264   Richard Wheeler, *In Pirate Waters: Captain David Porter, USN, and America's war on piracy in the West Indies.* (New York, Crowell, 1969), 86. Page contains all the above-mentioned elements to the Anti-Piracy Act of 1819. Monroe went on to stipulate that convicted pirates would be hung.

265   Charles Tyng, *Before the Wind: The Memoir of an American Sea Captain, 1808-1833.* (New York: Penguin, 1999), 132-133. This manuscript came from a found, previously unpublished source of Tyng's handwritten memoir.

up the ship to seven pirates in a small boat after making no effort to resist.[266]

British shipping had been taking a similar beating in the Caribbean, but without an Adams-Onis Treaty of their own, the Royal Navy was much slower to seriously implement their commitment to chase pirates, which had been enacted the previous year. There was some talk suggesting that the Royal Navy paid little attention to Caribbean pirates because of the large commissions their captains were paid to haul specie. Requests from merchants for their gold and silver to be hauled by warships always increased in times of instability or piracy.[267] A great part of British attention was being paid to the antics and exploits of their subject, Lord Cochrane, along the coast of South America. Having seized a number of British vessels for violating neutrality laws, Cochrane threw Britain's long-played game back at them, no doubt capturing a great deal of the Royal Navy's attention prior to 1821.[268]

The weight of British public opinion, more than the influence of those in the shipping or insurance industries, would finally toughen the Royal Navy's policy on Caribbean pirates, along with stiffening the number of British warships in the Caribbean. Arguably, as by early 1821, the arrival of the U.S. Navy's five new schooners had much influence on the opinion of the British public. Specifically built to hunt pirates and curtail the illegal slave trade, armed with tenacious names such

---

266   Richard Wheeler, *In Pirate Waters: Captain David Porter, USN, and America's war on piracy in the West Indies.* (New York, Crowell, 1969), 140.
267   Peter Earle, *The Pirate Wars.* (New York: St. Martin's, 2003), 241. *The Times* was quick to bring up this matter.
268   Gerald S. Graham, editor, *The Navy and South America, 1807-1823: Correspondence of the Commanders-in-Chief on the South American Station.* (London, Navy Records Society, 1962), 317, *Hardy to Croker,* Dec 12, 1820.

Loss of the *Peacock*
Naval History and Heritage Command

as *Alligator* and *Grampus*, the U.S. Navy would not only garner much international attention, but would do so specifically by catching pirates. The Americans would get off to a hot start, as vessels like *Enterprise* managed to capture eight pirate vessels in one day. Sometimes the action was comprised of a swift chase and sharp artillery duel, but as more and more vessels became captured -- or rescued, as was often the case with many of the pirated merchant ships -- these chases became more of a race to the shore. Once ashore, the pirates had little trouble in melting into the general population, which mostly consisted of relations and cohorts. Often, they would simply hop on a horse and gallop off. While the Royal Navy began picking up a few piratical vessels in 1821, it would be the following year when a more serious British effort began. During the summer of 1822, HM sloop-of-war *Speedwell* was attacked by four pirate schooners off the northern Cuban coast and "being overwhelmed by numbers would have been taken, had not the U.S. sloop-of-war *Peacock* come to her assistance."[269] The press had a field day, especially *The Times*, which shared many readers' outrage that a royal vessel had to be rescued by an *American* craft! Reaction would be swift. By October, Britain had dispatched five additional ships around Cuba and within three months had managed to capture or destroy nine pirate vessels and kill or capture a total of seventy-seven pirates.

USS Grampus engaging pirates in the West Indies
Hampton Roads Naval Museum

Porter's "Mosquito Fleet"

Originally not willing to help in either the capture of pirates fleeing on land, nor in letting foreign military forces chase them, Cuba began to change this policy in 1822. Some of the initial reluctance had to do with the fear that the United States might be looking for a pretense for invasion, as there had been much talk in the Southern states of desiring such an island, so close to their shores and with a massive population of slaves. As the United States had seemed ambivalent to illegally outfitting privateers and looked the other way as "filibusters" planned the overthrow of other Spanish colonies, such as Mexico, in addition to supporting the efforts of Andrew Jackson, which did result in the eventual attainment of Florida -- it is understandable why authorities in Cuba might at first be a little stand-offish.[270] Of

---

269   Peter Earle, *The Pirate Wars*. (New York: St. Martin's, 2003), 241.
270   Ibid, 240.

course, the fact that some areas of the island were obviously supporting piratical operations did not help matters, but due to increasing pressure from Spain and the fact that many of the pirates driven ashore had become regular bandits who ravaged the countryside, Cuba became more helpful and even caught a few pirates on their own. By the end of the year, the Cuban authorities would cooperate closely -- more or less -- with American and British forces who chased pirates ashore.

It was just such an incident in November, 1822 which would not only offer a snapshot of the changing tactics used in the Anti-Piracy's Campaign to fight land-based pirates, but would also enrage the American people. Lt. Allen of the *Alligator* located a pirate vessel close to the shore and charged in with his ship's boats. Standing in the lead boat, encouraging his men, Lt. Allen was shot twice by the pirates defending their vessel before they leapt into the sea and swam ashore. Allen lived long enough to conduct the rest of the engagement and died some four hours later.[271]

Up until this point, American casualties had been few, and the news of Lt. Allen's death prompted Congress to pass an act on December 20, 1822 which appropriated more funds for the suppression of Caribbean piracy.[272] Commodore David Porter would be dispatched and given a free reign over appropriating vessels and men for the campaign. Given his long history with fighting pirates, this was a wise choice. In regards to this squadron, historian Peter Earle notes, "Porter was supplied with a fleet of vessels specifically tailored to the task in hand, the first time that such a sensible policy had been adopted in pirate-hunting history."[273]

271   Ibid.
272   David D. Porter, *Memoir of Commodore Porter of the United States Navy*. (New York: Kessinger, 2007) Originally published by J. Munsell, Albany, NY, 1875.
273   Peter Earle, *The Pirate Wars*. (New York: St. Martin's, 2003), 242.

Pirate Hunter

As a young lieutenant during the Quasi-War, David Porter served aboard the USS *Experiment*, a small sloop-of-war armed with half a dozen six-pound carronades and equipped with oars. Early on the morning of New Year's Day, 1800, while escorting four U.S. merchantmen along the coast of Haiti, off St. Marc, the vessels were becalmed by a lack of wind and sat motionless not far from shore. At dawn, four to five hundred Haitian picaroons, spread out in eleven large cutters equipped with small swivel guns and armed with muskets, rowed out against the convoy. After a four hour fight, during which the *Experiment* nearly ran out of ammunition, the picaroons were beaten back, losing several boats and men. However, the pirates returned before nightfall and managed to make off with two abandoned vessels, having killed just one man -- the captain of the *Bestsy* who defended his vessel early in the morning -- and wounding only one other, young David Porter. The effect of the *Experiment's* oars in such becalmed conditions, which enabled the vessel to turn about and bring fresh guns to bear, as well as keep a safe distance, would not be lost on the young lieutenant.[274]

Enterprise engaging Tripoli Corsair
Naval History and Heritage Museum

274   Michael A. Palmer, *Stoddert's War: Naval Operations during the Quasi-War with France, 1798-1801.* (Annapolis, MD: Naval Institute Press, 2000), 164-167. Originally published by South Carolina Press, 1987. Palmer does an excellent job here, especially in setting the record straight. David D. Porter's *Memoir* of his father was embellished here, in which he states his father took command from Captain Maley, who supposedly

Porter had just begun to fight pirates, for the following year would see him aboard the *Enterprise*, which captured an Algerian Corsair after a three hour gunfight.[275] He would spend years in the Mediterranean, even taking part in the raid on Tripoli, where he was wounded again.[276] Of all Porter's naval experiences -- either his War of 1812 accomplishments or his aforementioned attempt to quell piracy around New Orleans -- by far, his experience in the *Experiment* and subsequent Quasi-War operations would have tremendous bearing on his upcoming campaign.

By February 1, 1823, Porter had his squadron together and was set to sail. He had purchased ten schooners, most fitted with sweeps and none drawing more than seven feet of water, which would enable work close to shore. However, no doubt inspired by Lord Cochrane, who had invested heavily into the building of the steamer *Rising Star* for use and eventual sale to the Chilean Government[277] -- none of which happened, other than the construction and vessel's eventual appearance at Valparaiso -- Porter also purchased the side-wheeled steamer *Enterprise*, built by the Connecticut Steam Boat Company. Rechristened the *Sea Gull* and mounted with cannon, the ves-

---

wished to surrender. As this area was well-know for murderous picaroons who took no quarter, Palmer does much to clear this up. However, Maley wasn't much of a commander, and Porter did soon replace him in command of the *Experiment*, but not on that day, and certainly not for those reasons. This should be made clear, however, as many historians fall victim to the myth. William M. Fowler, Jr., in his work *Jack Tars and Commodores: The American Navy, 1783-1815*, perpetuates the myth on pages 51-52 by "siding" with David D. Porter's written portrayal.

275   Eugene S. Ferguson, *Truxton of the Constellation: The Life of Commodore Thomas Truxton, U.S. Navy, 1755-1822.* (Baltimore: Johns Hopkins University Press, 2000), 220. Originally published in 1956.

276   William M. Fowler, Jr., *Jack Tars and Commodores: The American Navy, 1783-1815*, (New York: Houghton Mifflin, 1984), 77-79.

277   Robert Harvey, *Cochrane: The Life and Exploits of a Fighting Captain.* (New York: Carroll and Graf, 2000), 225-226.

sel would become the world's first steam-powered warship.[278] Credited with sinking at least one pirate vessel and possibly more, the steamer's primary purpose was to act as tug and mother ship to the five large "barges" Porter bought. More like large, double-banked cutters with room enough for roughly forty men each, these boats would be the primary method used in the following few years to root piracy from the shores of Cuba. In a near-carbon copy of the incident which killed Lt. Allen -- occurring in the same isolated bay -- the barges *Gallinipper* and *Mosquito* would chase pirates onto the very same shore, capturing the pirate leader Dioboleto and killing scores of pirates, many of which were either still swimming or begging to surrender. The battle cry of "Remember Allen!" not only led the day, with no U.S. casualties suffered, but would compose the backbone of Cuban pirate hunting methods. Long weeks spent in open boats, constantly investigating creeks, cays and caves, the work would prove frustrating -- but ultimately successful. By 1822, Cuban officials were more readily helpful in assisting both British and American naval efforts by providing a stiffer resistance to the now-problematic eruption of roving gangs. British-U.S. cooperation grew as a result of these tactics, with boat crews occasionally joining up to defeat pirates in similar engagements, such as when mixed boat crews converged to capture the pirate schooner *Socorro* in March, 1825.[279] In all, these methods would account for the seizure or sinking of 97 pirate vessels and death or capture of roughly 1,741 pirates.[280]

278   Unknown author. www.history.navy.mil\seagull.htm
279   Peter Earle, *The Pirate Wars*. (New York: St. Martin's, 2003), 244-246. The biggest obstacle was disease, as yellow fever killed the majority of those lost during the campaign -- aside from deaths caused by shipwreck. Several of the Mosquito Fleet's vessels would wreck, most notably the active *Alligator*, which crashed into a reef in the Florida Keys. Today, a lighthouse stands on Alligator Island.
280   Ibid, 247.

Power Politics

While Cuba had made great strides in cooperation, Puerto Rico had not. Unfortunately, the sheer success of the U.S. Anti-Piracy Campaign, which would have Caribbean piracy largely wrapped-up by 1825, would be somewhat blackened by events that, to many, would appear to be a replay of Andrew Jackson's actions in West Florida.

Ordered to sail immediately for Puerto Rico, in order to deliver the U.S. policy on piracy surrounding the island and to ask for Puerto Rican assistance, Porter did just that, arriving on March 4, 1823. Shortly thereafter, Lt. Cocke of the *Fox* returned to San Juan for a response and was fired upon by the fort. The fort's second shot killed Lt. Cocke on the spot. While this action in itself may have been cause for serious retribution prior to 1819, it was handled with an exchange of correspondence and lackluster Spanish apologies.[281]

With the improprieties of Lt. Cocke's death simmering in the background, along with the grudging cooperation given to the campaign from Puerto Rican authorities, this issue would lay dormant only until the following year. In October, 1824, pirates from Puerto Rico broke into the store of the U.S. Consul at St. Thomas and stole $5,000 worth of goods before fleeing back to the Puerto Rican town of Foxardo. The following day, Lt. Platt landed with a shore crew at Foxardo to check with local authorities about the stolen property. Platt, in an effort to defuse any possible tension, made the mistake of landing in civilian cloths. As a result, the local authorities jailed him and the shore party, accusing them of being pirates themselves. While ridiculous, as Platt did have his necessary

---

281   Richard Wheeler, *In Pirate Waters: Captain David Porter, USN, and America's war on piracy in the West Indies.* (New York, Crowell, 1969), 116.

papers, it was really just an attempt to move the stolen goods from the town. When enough time had passed to allow this, Platt was released.[282]

Porter was outraged. His instructions clearly stated "In regards to pirates, there is no neutral party ... all nations are parties against them and may be considered as allies."[283] The Commodore weighed this information against the political cautions also levied against him in his instructions, as well as the fact that the Governor of Puerto Rico had previously circulated an order of compliance with U.S. forces. Porter acted swiftly. In early November, Porter landed with a force of sailors and marines at Foxardo, spiking several guns which had been emplaced against just this sort of landing, and with-

President John Quincy Adams
White House

in half an hour was meeting with apologetic local leaders. In less than three hours, after Lt. Platt and all involved had received satisfaction, Porter and his shore party left. Almost immediately, the Commodore would feel the political ramifications of the Foxardo incident, as Spain and Puerto Rico would erupt in a political protest. Porter was relieved of command in December and ordered back to Washington, with Commodore

282   David D. Porter, *Memoir of Commodore Porter of the United States Navy.* (New York: Kessinger, 2007), 298-299. Originally published by J. Munsell, Albany, NY, 1875.
283   Ibid, 300. Quote from Sec. of Navy Thompson's initial order of Feb 1, 1823.

Warrington replacing him. Upon arrival, he was informed that he would face a courts-martial for exceeding his orders at Foxardo, along with the catch-all charge of "conduct unbecoming an officer." Since his trial wouldn't transpire until summer, 1825, the press coverage was substantial. That proved to be Porter's undoing, for he published his view of events, during which he made a solid enemy of President Adams. Even without Porter's media effort, it is unlikely that Adams -- who is credited by many historians as having saved Andrew Jackson from similar (though more egregious) proceedings following his unauthorized encroachments during the West Florida campaign of 1818 -- would not have had much to say in support of Porter, considering that this was the same Adams who had negotiated the Onis treaty as President Monroe's Secretary of State.[284]

An "Andrew Jackson" defense was offered at the courts-martial, which centered around Porter's instructions and Jackson's message to the Spanish Governor at Pensacola in 1818: "The conduct of this banditti, is such as will not be tolerated by our government, and if not put down by Spanish authority will compel us in self-defense to destroy them."[285] This tactic would not be enough to

President Andrew Jackson
White House

---

284   Daniel Walker Howe, *What Hath God Wrought: The Transformation of America, 1815-1848.* (New York: Oxford, 2007), 101-103.
285   H.W. Brands, *Andrew Jackson: His Life and Times.* (New York: Doubleday, 2005), 308.

prevent Porter's conviction and subsequent resignation from the navy. Much like Lord Cochrane, David Porter would also be employed by an insurgent government, as Admiral of the Marine of Mexico for three years, 1826-1829. After the death of two of his sons in this service, along with two attempts on his life, Porter would return to America at the request of President Andrew Jackson and serve as the U.S. Consul to Turkey until his death in 1843.[286]

---

286   David D. Porter, *Memoir of Commodore Porter of the United States Navy*. (New York: Kessinger, 2007), 341, 352, 375, 385-396.

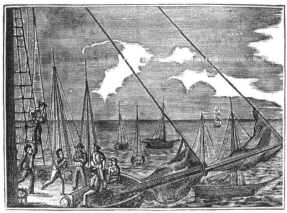

The Pirates flogging the Captain of a sloop. Page 155.

Piracy in the West Indies, woodcut
Naval History and Heritage Command

Pirates and Their Prey

In 1825, Brazil and Argentina escalated their border conflicts and various disputes into all-out war, with a large number of privateers being commissioned by both sides. The country of Uruguay would come into existence largely as a buffer state between these two former enemies. This would not occur until after mutiny spread rampant through the privateer and state-owned fleets of both nations, generally beginning in 1827, which provided a last bloody gasp of wide-spread Caribbean piracy. By 1829, this final flame had mostly flickered out. In April, Captain Wilson of HMS *Tribune* reported, "no privateers or prizes about these islands or anywhere else."[287]

While the number of piracies committed in the "Pax Britannica" period (1815-1835) far surpassed that of the "Golden

---

287   Peter Earle, *The Pirate Wars.* (New York: St. Martin's, 2003), 235, quote on 236.

Age" (1714-1730), the generally recognized "end" occurred in Boston, with the hanging of five pirates from the *Panda* on June 11, 1835. This included pirate captain Don Pedro Gibert, who received notoriety in the press for his crimes as well as his striking features. Notably, mate Bernardo de Soto was pardoned as a result of having aided shipwrecked Americans in the Bahamas, although his piracy was undisputed. The *Panda*'s tale serves well to encapsulate the period.[288]

In August, 1832, the slave schooner *Panda* sailed from Havana for West Africa. On the way, *Panda* met up with the American brig *Mexican*, which the crew of the *Panda* boarded. After robbing $24,000 in gold and everything else of value, the pirates disabled the rigging and hacked down the yardarms. After locking the crew below, the pirates set fire to the *Mexican* and sailed off. The crew escaped without much trouble and extinguished the fire as soon as the *Panda* was out of sight. Patching together the rigging, the *Mexican* managed to sail back to Salem, where the crew was able to offer detailed descriptions of the pirates and their vessel. These reports were rapidly dispatched across the globe.[289]

The *Panda* was found in a West African river and boarded by boat crews from HMS *Curlew*. Many pirates escaped ashore, but Gibert, de Soto, and sixteen others were captured. The pirates were brought back to England, but as it was an American ship they had pirated, the British Admiralty waived jurisdiction and sent them off to Salem. As luck would have it, the *Mexican* happened to be in the harbor, with many of the *Panda*'s former victims still among the crew. Their testimony ensured a speedy trial.[290]

While the atrocities committed by the pirates of the

---

288   Ibid, 236-237.
289   Ibid, 237.
290   Ibid, 238.

period collectively comprise the most horrendous record in all piratical history, it should be noted that large quantities of hard alcohol forms a common thread for the majority of the most ruthless pirates, regardless of the age. The historical record is littered with testimony from such men, a great many of whom attribute their crimes and piracies to a love of strong drink and a lazy life. Certainly, alcohol alone cannot be blamed for their actions, but access to large quantities of drink seems to have been a powerful motivator. Perhaps the best illustration of this can be found in the account of Ned Myers, a U.S. Navy seaman who fought the British on Lake Erie during the War of 1812. Aside from plundering a local store of several gallons of whiskey with his gun crew, Myers also relates the following;

"Among other things we took, was the body of an English officer, preserved in rum, which they said was General Brock's. I saw it hoisted out of the *Duke of Gloucester*, the man-of-war brig we captured, at Sackett's Harbour, and saw the body put in a fresh cask. I am ashamed to say, that some of our men were inclined to drink the old rum."[291]

A feeling of revenge, more than a fill of hard liquor, was the real factor behind the majority of the period's cruelty, murder and torture. This was certainly true in the case of Puerto Rican and Cuban pirates, who had long felt the effects of seized Spanish shipping, both to and from their islands. However, some of the bloodiest pirates of the period were mutinied privateer and state vessels, along with what amounted to slave insurrections among others. Haiti was the general

---

291   Ned Myers, "The War of the Lakes," from *Life Before the Mast: Sailors' eyewitness accounts from the age of fighting ships,* edited by Jon. E. Lewis. (New York, Carroll & Graf, 2002), 356-358. Quote on 358.

destination of this last group.[292]

The Cuban and Puerto Rican pirates were also the last group to fly the Jolly Roger, or at least some derivative of the pirate flag made famous during the previous century. Generally, these pirates flew either red or black flags -- sometimes both -- and there are accounts which describe a few of these flags bearing the white skull and crossbones.[293] Their favorite pastimes centered around heavy drinking, playing music and torturing many of their captives. The torture they found most appealing was to slip a noose around a man's neck, run the rope over a yardarm and dunk him repeatedly into the sea. Many were simply beaten with any weapon or item at hand, or even slashed to pieces.[294] Slow fires, biting insects and gunpowder-related tortures also seemed to be well liked.

However, it is the most famous of all pirate practices which can be attributed to Cuban pirates; that of making their victims "walk the plank." This was first documented by the *Jamaican Royal Gazette* in the summer of 1822, which reported that a captain Smith was made to walk off a plank into the sea, where he was then shot. Within a few years, another report shows that this practice had evolved to the point where a cannonball was fixed to the victim's feet, to

**Walking The Plank
by Howard Pyle**

---

292   Peter Earle, *The Pirate Wars*. (New York: St. Martin's, 2003), 217-218.

293   Ibid, 220.

294   Ibid, 220-221.

ensure a quicker end. According to this later report by *The Times*, the Dutch victim managed to drag one of his killers down along with him, gripping him in a vicious chokehold.[295]

Many merchant crewmen were killed outright or locked below while their ship burnt around them, while others were caged in a similar fashion as their ship was sunk. The captain and mate of the brig *Ann* were murdered as they begged for their lives. In 1822, the USS *Alligator* discovered a drifting sloop, stained with blood, with only a small dog aboard. This was just one of many such discoveries.[296] With pirates like the Cuban leader Cofrecinas claiming to have killed some three or four hundred people, accounts of vacant vessels are not surprising. Nor was the fate of Cofrecinas and his mates, who were not only shot by a Spanish firing squad in Cuba, but also beheaded and quartered. Their parts were sent to various small town ports, posted conspicuously to forewarn others of the true price of piracy.[297]

Some merchants were able to escape similar atrocities by managing to evade capture altogether. In 1826, merchant captain Charles Tyng, with his brig *Eight Sons* empty of cargo and nearly un-ballasted, threw caution to the near hurricane-winds and put out every available scrap of canvas in order to harness storm winds and outrun the pirate schooner *Las Adamantis*. Tyng was fortunate and managed to evade both capture as well as shipwreck. The pirates aboard *Las Adamantis* would not be so lucky, as Tyng gave a description of their vessel to the Royal Navy brig *Douro*, which soon sank the pirate schooner after capturing the crew. Most of these

---

295   Ibid, 222.
296   Ibid, 221.
297   Richard Wheeler, *In Pirate Waters: Captain David Porter, USN, and America's war on piracy in the West Indies.* (New York, Crowell, 1969), 169.

men were later convicted of piracy and hanged.[298]

A few merchants would fight back and stand firm in the defense of their vessel, although as it took less men to crew the common brigs and schooners of the time -- perhaps as little as six or eight men -- many merchants didn't dare to attempt fighting against often overwhelming odds. However, some did. In his memoir, Charles Tyng tells of a German merchant who sank a pirate vessel in self-defense outside of Havana harbor in 1826.[299] In 1822, the American brig *Belvidere* was chased by a pirate schooner with twenty-two men aboard. However, as the *Belvidere*'s captain, Z.G. Lamson, had previously been robbed and beaten by similar Caribbean cutthroats, he had vowed never to suffer such treatment again. The brig was armed with a 24-pound carronade, a brass three-pounder (probably a swivel gun), and a variety of muskets, pistols, pikes and cutlasses. When Lamson ignored the pirates' demand for surrender, they opened up with a volley of musketry. With "as smart a fire as possible," the *Belvidere*'s crew returned fire, giving the pirates "a most terrible cutting up." The pirates disengaged after a short while. The *Belvidere* suffered one loss, a sailor shot through the head.[300]

It should be noted, that by this time frame, a great many more owner/captains were allowing their wives to ship with them. This applied to coastal fisherman along with merchant vessels. The New York brig *Patriot* was such a vessel, with captain Horace Jacobs' wife of three months aboard. As pirate atrocities were well publicized at the time, Jacobs had no desire to surrender to the pirate schooner he met with off

298   Charles Tyng, *Before the Wind: The Memoir of an American Sea Captain, 1808-1833.* (New York: Penguin, 1999), 146-148.
299   Ibid, 148.
300   Richard Wheeler, *In Pirate Waters: Captain David Porter, USN, and America's war on piracy in the West Indies.* (New York, Crowell, 1969), 105.

Cape San Antonio, loaded with fifty men. The *Patriot* had a crew of ten men and a boy, who fought furiously to repulse the pirates, twice beating off attempts to board with muskets and a stern-mounted swivel gun. Having taken some casualties, the pirates sailed off in search of an easier prize. Jacobs' efforts had saved his bride, but in the process, he received a nasty head wound. Five days later, the heroic husband died of "lockjaw and violent convulsive fits."[301]

Shipwreck, the common calamity of all who sailed, was doubly dangerous for merchant sailors during this period. The tale of the brig *Betsey*, sailing from Maine, does well to illustrate this. Passing through the Straits of Florida, the *Betsey* rammed into a rock in the Double Headed Shot Keys during the night of December 20, 1824 and was bashed apart. The seven men onboard were fortunate enough to get off in a longboat and even managed to save the brig's money box. Rigging a sail from a blanket, the men made it to Cruz del Padre Key, roughly fifteen miles from mainland Cuba and inhabited only by a few fishermen. Unfortunately, some of the fishermen were in league with local pirates, who robbed the shipwrecked sailors, tied them up and butchered them. Two sailors managed to escape; one of them, second mate Collins, was freed by an errant blow from a machete which cut his bonds after glancing off his head and shoulder. Collins would eventually swim to Matanzas, using small islands and reefs as resting spots along the way. Word of his story would soon have the schooner USS *Ferret* dispatched to the area in search of the murderous pirates.[302] *Ferret* would find no pirates. Instead, like the *Betsey*, she would wreck -- capsizing in a gale off the Double Headed Shot Keys, losing five men

---

301   Ibid.
302   Ibid, 150-152.

on February 4, 1825.[303]

While the benefits of employing shallow-draft vessels in shoal water can be traced even further back than William Dampier's notations in 1684, this by no means insured their safe passage.[304] David Porter's "Mosquito Fleet" -- specifically organized to chase pirates through shallow coastal water -- would still lose vessels as a result of prowling treacherous island coastlines. Schooners *Ferret*, *Wildcat*, *Alligator* and *Enterprise* would be lost during the campaign. *Alligator* had the reef which wrecked the schooner become its namesake, Alligator Reef. Off the southern tip of Florida, this small rocky outcropping has hosted a lighthouse since 1873 in order to prevent other ships from reaching a similar end. The steamer *Sea Gull*, much the workhorse of the campaign's shore duties, was practically worn out by the summer of 1825 and was ordered back to the U.S. for refitting. *Sea Gull* never returned to the Caribbean, but stayed in service as a naval receiving ship in Philadelphia until 1840.[305]

Alligator Reef Lighthouse

---

303   Unknown author. www.history.navy.mil\ferret.htm

304   William Dampier, *A New Voyage Round the World.* (Warwick, NY: 1500 Books, 2007), 92. Reprinted from 1717 6th edition, originally published in 1697.

305   Unknown author. www.history.navy.mil\ferret\sea gull\alligator. htm

The Laffite Brothers

Jean Laffite
Library of Congress

While Jean Laffite is a name easily recognizable in American history, in truth he is only half of the Laffite story, for without his brother Pierre, it is doubtful that his piratical achievements would have been nearly as successful as they turned out to be. Because both men were generally referred to as "Laffitte," this has done much to cloud the history, especially surrounding tales concerning the Battle of New Orleans and the various reported versions of Jean's death.

Born in the Bordeaux region of France near the Bay of Biscay, both Jean and Pierre moved to Saint Domingue around 1800, which comprised half of the Caribbean island of Hispaniola. It seems likely that Jean was involved with either commanding or crewing French privateers at this early stage, while Pierre was more involved with moving the stolen merchandise. This would prove to be the pattern for the bulk of the brothers' careers. Conditions in Saint Domingue were deteriorating badly, resulting from a slave revolt which would eventually lead to the independence of Haiti in 1805. Due to the island's instability, Jean moved to New Orleans in 1803, shortly before the Louisiana Purchase delivered the city and surrounding area to the United States on December 20, 1803. Pierre would split his time between New Orleans and Spanish

West Florida as he did his utmost to create a trade in smuggled Spanish wares. In 1806, France issued the "Berlin Decree" and Britain issued a series of "Orders in Council," both of which called for the seizure of neutral vessels shipping goods to enemy ports. President Jefferson

Laffite Brothers

countered with his Embargo Act of 1807, which closed practically all American trade. As a result of these acts, the smuggling trade boomed around New Orleans -- accompanied by nearly unrestricted piracy along the Gulf coast -- which led to huge profits and easy money for pirates and smugglers alike. Additionally, the United States abolished the international slave trade on January 1, 1808, which created a large market for smuggled, pirated slaves, sold at a discount.

That same year would bring Jean to New Orleans full-time, along with a great many other former occupants of Saint Domingue, who would be evicted from Cuba in droves during the next two years due to a Spanish edict, sprouting from Napoleon's occupation of Spain. With the British seizing the French islands

President Thomas Jefferson
White House

of Martinique and Guadaloupe in 1809, a great many French privateers would come to the New Orleans area, using islands in Barataria Bay as their new bases. It was at this time that the Laffites would work out a near-perfect business model, with Jean dealing with the pirates and privateers at Grand Isle and Cat Island while Pierre lined up buyers for their stolen goods in New Orleans. Sales would also take place at these islands, with Jean having prospective buyers ferried over, generally through secret swampy shortcuts. The brothers would become so effective in smuggling pirated goods that they would fill this niche for over thirteen years and expand their operations to mythic proportions.

As the plantations surrounding New Orleans mostly grew sugarcane, practically a death sentence for those laboring to grow it, there became quite a market for smuggled slaves. Ingeniously using the law to their advantage, the Laffites soon began to "launder" slaves into legal property. The law at the time rewarded informants with half of all fines levied and half of all proceeds obtained from the sale of imported slaves taken from their captors while attempting to smuggle them into the country. Once the slaves were sold by the government, legal title was given to whoever purchased them at auction. Not surprisingly, often the informant -- or one of his agents -- ended up with the purchased and now legal slaves, having paid less than a quarter of their worth. Conveniently, Pierre Laffite happened to be a deputy marshal in the New Orleans area for some time during 1809-1810. Certainly, this did much to ease the "laundering" of pirated slaves during Pierre's short "service" in law enforcement.

Bolivar's Cartagena declared independence from Spain in November, 1811. While no nation recognized this, the revolution brought many privateers to Barataria and flooded

New Orleans Gulf Shore
Library of Congress

the Caribbean with blank privateer commissions. By international law, these privateers had to be commissioned at a home port, and several of these ships were seized in New Orleans for illegally fitting-out, including one backed by Louis Aury. Due to duplicity within the courts, many of these vessels were later returned, aside from Aury's.

As a result of such increased activity, the revenue cutters and navy gunboats around New Orleans did make some captures at sea during 1811-12, with Lt. Catesby Jones being one of the most active commanders. However, the navy gunboat was generally much slower than the common pirate schooner and often more lightly armed, as a pair of such vessels managed to repel an attempt by Jones at capturing them and forced him to flee. These inadequacies were just some of the reasons why David Porter resigned his command of the New Orleans Naval Station in 1810. Little improved for Porter's successor, as Captain Shaw had only two brigs and eleven sluggish gunboats with which to chase smugglers and pirates in 1812.

The year 1812 would bring heady days to American seaports, especially after war with Britain was declared in June. The U.S. government would issue only eleven privateer commissions for New Orleans between 1812-13, and while Laffite associates like Beluche got one for the *Spy*, the brothers had no desire for a U.S. commission. They preferred dubious commissions issued from revolutionary governments, as it was much easy to skirt the law with them -- especially when it came to condemning vessels at prize courts. While the Laffites would purchase the first of eventually four privateer vessels in October, 1812, their masters -- such as Captain Jannet -- would sail with no commissions at all. With the Americans preoccupied over the war with Britain, the Laffites would greatly expand the scope of their operations -- but would soon suffer the consequences.

Events during the following year would begin to unravel the Laffite brothers, as shoot-outs with revenue officers and soldiers would lead to Pierre's arrest and incarceration while putting a $500 bounty on Jean's head. In retaliation to the bounty posted by Governor Claiborne in November, 1813, Jean circulated a reward for twice that amount should the governor be delivered to Cat Island. His notice ended by suggesting it was all "in jest." However, Claiborne didn't consider it a laughing matter and began pushing hard for the Laffite's removal from Barataria.

Pierre would land in jail in July, 1814, due to assorted shoot-outs which led to a few deaths and injuries the previous year. The original warrant was related to a slave he had sold some years prior, which did not belong to him. As the political atmosphere was beginning to change in New Orleans, Pierre was quickly indicted by a grand jury, with piracy listed among the charges. With help from local sources, Pierre would soon escape from his New Orleans jail. The newspapers ran his $1,000 reward notice until November.

Meanwhile, Jean had his hands full. In July, 1814, Navy Secretary William Jones ordered Commodore Patterson, commander of the New Orleans Naval Station, to attack the pirate lair in Barataria Bay and dispatched the schooner USS *Carolina* to aid him. Before being sunk by a British shell which touched-off the schooner's powder magazine while defending New Orleans in late December, the *Carolina* would amass a very active service record and account for capturing the privateer *General Bolivar* after a brief engagement. The *General Bolivar* would be returned to owner/operator and Laffite associate Beluche in spring, 1815, when he managed to produce a valid commission.

In early September, Captain Nicholas Lockyer arrived off Grand Isle in HMS *Sophie*. While this caused a dramatic stir with the pirates which Jean had to mollify, the point of Lockyer's visit was to offer Jean a commission in the British army in exchange for the pirate's ships, which would then be used to augment the British squadron while it conducted invasion operations against the Americans along the coast. As Jean had no desire to command British militia forces, coupled with the fact that the pirates he commanded -- most of them with a long-held hatred for their age-old English enemy -- would never agree to serving under the Royal Navy's auspices, Jean forwarded the papers to Governor Claiborne. He included his counter-offer to defend Grand Isle against the British, in exchange to what amounted for a piracy pardon for the lot of them. Governor Claiborne would have none of it, however, and gave his approval for the planned naval invasion of Barataria on September 8, 1814.

One week later, Commodore Patterson landed naval forces at Grand Isle, aided by *Carolina*, *Sea Horse* and six gunboats. As luck would have it, the Laffites were conducting a sale at the time, which not only netted the navy some $200,000 in seized goods and thousands in gold and silver, but also captured twenty-seven vessels and burnt several others. Several "privateer" vessels were also captured, along with stacks of incriminating papers which were left by panicked merchants as they hurriedly fled the scene. Not surprisingly, no investigation was followed up concerning these merchants and none were arrested. Many of the pirates were not so fortunate, and although Jean escaped, every structure on the island was put to the torch.

Had the American forces defending New Orleans been well supplied, Jean and Pierre probably would have abandoned the area quickly and sailed to safer shores. Contrary

Andrew Jackson at New Orleans
Library of Congress

to popular belief, General Andrew Jackson wanted nothing to do with such "banditti." However, with the British drawing closer everyday and chronically short of supplies -- especially gun flints and powder, which Jean had large stores of hidden in the area -- on December 17, Jackson agreed to pardons for the pirates should they join the American cause. Roughly 400 of them did, although they would be dispersed throughout the area in many defensive positions and only fifty or so would actually fight the British at New Orleans. The most famous of these was Laffite captain Dominique Youx, who commanded a twenty-four pound cannon which wreaked terrible havoc on the British. Contrary to popular belief, it was not American militia which won the day at New Orleans, it was the devastating grapeshot fired from entrenched American artillery. In fact, many of the militia which arrived shortly before the battle were without arms and practically naked, much to Jackson's disgust.

Some reports place Jean at the Battle of New Orleans, or rather, "Laffite," which many generally suppose was Jean. However, Jean was commanding a shore battery which guarded one of the approaches to the city and was far from the battle. Pierre was present, however. He probably was not in the trenches, but historian William C. Davis clearly shows that he was used to guide forces around the battlefield. Thus, "Laffite" was at the Battle of New Orleans -- sort of.

On February 6, 1815, President Madison granted an official pardon for those pirates who had helped defend New Orleans, provided they had the correct paperwork from Governor Claiborne.

In December, 1815, Cartagena would fall to the Spanish after a siege of 106 days, negating all their privateer commissions. A few months later, many of these vessels headed for Gal-

President James Madison
White House

veston Island, where Louis Aury began to offer them questionable commissions from the insurgent Mexican government. Only a few months later, during a squabble amongst the pirates, Aury was shot and wounded. Just a few days later, he would leave for Matagorda, to be shortly driven off by Spanish frigates. This would lead to a brief stay at Amelia Island off of Florida, before being forced to flee again after U.S. forces occupied the island in September, 1817. Aury would eventually set-up a relative pirate haven on the island of Old Providence in mid-1818. Three years later, the hapless pirate would suffer a fall and die from his injuries.

Almost immediately, Jean Laffite arrived at Galveston and by April, 1817, began once again running smuggling/piracy operations into New Orleans with the aid of his brother and Mexican letters of marque. In July of the following year, Pierre was onboard the ten-gun privateer *Lameson* when it was captured by Lt. Cunningham off New Orleans, later to be condemned in the courts. Merely a passenger, he would face no charges. Not long after, a powerful hurricane struck Galveston Island. By settling near-mutinous conditions, Jean would demonstrate stern leadership qualities that would lead to the rebuilding of a restructured Galveston settlement. However, Andrew Jackson had already begun his unauthorized expedition into Spanish Florida that spring, starting a chain of events which would culminate in the Adams-Onis Treaty of 1819 and seal the fate of Jean's Galveston operation.

1819 would prove to be an active year along the Gulf Coast. Commodore Patterson would capture nine picaroon/smuggling vessels just below New Orleans in July. In September, the Navy would raid Grand Isle again and evict William Mitchell, who was something of a smuggling middle-man. After an exchange of musketry, the Laffite-owned privateer *Le Brave* would be captured by Navy cutters *Alabama* and *Louisiana*. Desfarges, the vessel's Laffite-appointed captain, would be found guilty of piracy and hanged on December 30.

Meanwhile, in an attempt to placate the U.S. government as a result of some Laffite men having robbed a man named Lyons of slaves, Jean had George Brown hanged and banished his three accomplices. Lt. McIntosh of the U.S. Navy would arrive a few days later and return to New Orleans with the three outcast criminals. December would prove a bad month for Gulf Coast pirates, as notorious Laffite captain Vincent

Jean Laffite
Rosenberg Library
Galveston, TX

Gambi would be decapitated by one of his sailors at night while sleeping on deck, after having cheated the crew of prize money.

Realizing his operations on Galveston were at an end, and not wishing to have a repeat of the Grand Isle invasion, Jean offered to abandon the island in exchange for a guarantee of safe passage, which Commodore Patterson agreed to. On May 7, 1820, with the flames of what was left of the establishment at Galveston burning in the background, Jean sailed off with his remaining few ships, under escort from the U.S. Navy.

Almost immediately, Jean would command his own ship and turn pirate. Upon discussing this with his crew, thirty-nine sailors refused to sail without a commission, as the U.S. government no longer spoke of hanging pirates but were now actually doing so. They made their way to New Orleans aboard a crippled prize instead.

Jean would end up working with shore-based Cuban pirates for the next two years. Pierre would have the honor of paying a ransom of $4,000 to reclaim the Laffite vessel *Nancy Eleanor*, in August, 1821, which had been pirated. He could come up with the money because -- perhaps for the first time -- he was commanding his own pirate vessel, a small felucca which took a prize off of Campeche, Mexico, laden with $60,000 in silver. Near Cancun a short while after, Pierre would be captured by Spanish authorities after a prolonged shoot-out which killed a few pirates and wounded others on both sides. In captivity, Pierre died of illness on November 9, 1821 and was buried in a church yard near Santa Clara. Rumors have long abounded that Jean died of yellow fever somewhere along the Central American coast. Again, the old story is close, as "Laffite" did die in a similar fashion in the relative neighborhood.

Meanwhile, Jean had his hands full. In the spring of 1821, his vessel was jumped by two Spanish ships as he brought a prize into a Cuban port in order to collect on the ransom.

He made it to shore with a handful of men and soon found himself wounded in a shoot-out with Spanish officials. Taken prisoner, Jean was hospitalized for some months, until he managed to escape with the aid of others in February, 1822. Within two months, he would pirate U.S. and British shipping in the Old Bahama Channel.

That same month, April, 1822, Jean would be captured by the relentless USS *Alligator*, hounded by boat crews after fleeing into a river. Lt. Stockton handed Jean and his crew over to Cuban authorities, who soon released him. The next month, Laffite's vessel would be chased ashore again by *Alligator*, with help from *Grampus*. After exchanging shots, Jean would successfully elude American capture.

Sailing his remaining schooner to Cartagena, Jean took a Colombian commission and commanded the schooner *General Santander*, his first legal privateer. He reportedly escorted a few American merchant vessels through the treacherous Old Bahama Channel, but this is unclear. Five months into his first legal cruise, the *General Santander* was lured into an artillery duel with a brig and schooner towards nightfall. While the privateer withdrew, it was not without casualties. Jean Laffite was mortally wounded and would be buried at sea shortly thereafter, on February 5, 1823 at the age of forty-one. It is quite possible that the ships he encountered were U.S. Navy vessels, as it was common practice for Porter's "Mosquito Fleet" to use decoy merchantmen in order to bait pirates, which appeared to have happened here. There were several Navy reports of similar, inconclusive nighttime engagements. This account also gives weight to many of the old tales which told of "Laffite" dying in a similar fashion.

While certainly criminals on a variety of levels, it should be recognized that the Laffites were the era's "gentlemen pirates," for they were neither prone to cruelty nor condoned it. While they occasionally ransomed prizes, they never ransomed people. A variety of reports from captured merchants who met Jean -- usually after their ship was brought either to Grand Isle or Galveston -- not only attested to his civility, but spoke of his charm. Charm and civility may have aided in Jean's escapes from jail and with evading law enforcement, but ultimately, it would not spare him from a fate shared by untold numbers of Caribbean cutthroats.

David Porter

Entering the United States Navy at its birth during the Quasi-War with France (1797-1801) as a young midshipman, Porter would serve aboard the *Constellation* under Commodore Truxtun during the engagement and capture of *L'Insurgente* in February, 1799. On New Year's Day, 1800, he would fight Haitian picaroons while serving aboard the schooner *Experiment*. In the Mediterranean the following year, Porter would serve as first lieutenant aboard the sloop *Enterprise* during an engagement which netted a Barbary Corsair of fourteen guns after a sharp action. He would return to fight Barbary pirates during President Jefferson's "war" on Tripoli, serving on the *Philadelphia*, which was run aground, captured, and then later burnt by American forces. Porter would be wounded

Captain David Porter
Naval History and Heritage Museum

during a raid on Tripoli and later captured when the *Philadelphia* ran aground, spending nearly two years as a prisoner of war before his release in June, 1805, after a treaty was signed between the United States and Tripoli.

In 1808, Porter was sent to command the New Orleans Naval Station with specific orders to suppress piracy. However, due to severe naval budget cuts by Jefferson and the Republicans, he had little men, material or proper vessels with which to do so. Coupled with a local population which was either in league with pirates and smugglers, or who just preferred the cheaper goods, Porter was constantly frustrated in his efforts, especially by the courts. At least one attempt on his life was made, and by 1810 he resigned his post in utter disgust.

In August, 1811, Porter was given command of the frigate *Essex*, and on July 2, 1812, was promoted to Captain, just weeks after war was declared with Britain. The *Essex* would be the first American ship to take a Royal Navy vessel during the War of 1812, the warship *Alert* of twenty guns. Dispatched to South America, Porter took two smaller British warships before arriving in the Pacific, where he cruised along the coast of Chile and Peru, capturing over a dozen vessels of the British whaling fleet and several other merchant ships. However, in March, 1814, the *Essex* was taken by the British frigate *Phoebe* and sloop *Cherub* after an intense artillery duel which killed or wounded 154 American sailors. To Porter's credit, his offer to fight the *Phoebe* was repeatedly rejected, and when the British attacked him, he was anchored well within the marine league of neutral Chile, repairing a broken topmast.

Frigate *Essex*, 1799

While this act was against the rules of war at the time, the *Essex*'s true undoing was a lack of long-guns, as she was mostly armed with carronades. This enabled the *Phoebe* and *Cherub* to stand well off and pound the frigate with their long-guns. Even so, British casualties were not insignificant, and while badly outgunned, the crew of the *Essex* managed to put eighteen holes below the *Phoebe*'s waterline.

In the defense of Washington shortly thereafter, Porter commanded shore batteries which engaged British vessels. At war's end in 1815, he was placed on the three-man Board of Naval Commissioners until dispatched to fight Caribbean piracy with the Mosquito Fleet in 1823. Highly effective, Porter's Caribbean campaign was also innovative, utilizing the world's first steam-powered warship to bring the fight against pirates haunting the coasts of Cuba and Puerto Rico. After his courts-martial due to the events surrounding his landing at Foxardo, Puerto Rico, Porter resigned from the Navy in August, 1826 and took Mexico's offer to command their revolutionary navy that same month. Porter served Mexico until 1829, when President Andrew Jackson requested he return to the United States. Due to serious financial trouble with the Mexican government, along with two attempts on his life, Porter returned to the U.S. and was named the U.S. Consul to Turkey, a position he filled until his death in 1843.

Married in 1808, Porter and his wife Evelina would have many children. Of these, two would die during his service in Mexico, one a young boy due to fever, and the other, David H. Porter, was killed in action while commanding the Mexican brig *Guerrero* against a Spanish frigate off the coast of Cuba. Several of his sons would serve in the navy, most famously Admiral David Dixon Porter and his adopted son David Farragut, who would become the U.S. Navy's very first Admiral. Both of these men would achieve fame during the American Civil War. David Dixon Porter would command gunboats on the Mississippi in support of General Grant, become mired during the Red River campaign and then lead a flying squadron which helped defeat Fort Fischer, the gateway to Wilmington, North Carolina. David Farragut will be forever famous for his order, "Damn the torpedoes, full speed ahead!" as he rushed his squadron past the defenses at Mobile Bay, in an action similar to his prior seizure of New Orleans.

Captain David Porter
Naval History and Heritage Museum

Thomas Cochrane

With his uncle Alexander Cochrane pulling some strings, a tall and skinny seventeen-year-old Thomas Cochrane began his service in Britain's Royal Navy as an inexperienced midshipman aboard his uncle Alexander's command, the *Hind*, in 1793. Quick to learn, with an unquenchable curiosity and sharp mind, Thomas swiftly learned the ropes, and after having served on a number of ships, was promoted to lieutenant the following year. By the age of twenty-three, he

Admiral Thomas Lord Cochrane

had served aboard two flagships. In the process, he developed a reputation as being disrespectful to superiors which would form the common thread of his brilliant career in the Royal Navy. His uncle Alexander would eventually command the fleet which burned Washington and shipped troops to fight at New Orleans during the War of 1812.

Thomas Cochrane was an aristocrat, a Lord, the Tenth Earl of Dundonald. However, his family was relatively "poor," and his father spent much while attempting to restore the family fortune. As a result, Thomas was more than a little thirsty for prize money and would forever resent the Admiralty's dishonest distribution of prize money, along with their generally corrupt practices.

In 1799, the flagship Cochrane was serving on came across Lord Nelson's fleet in the Mediterranean, fresh from battle.

Making an impression on Nelson, Cochrane was made prize master of the captured French battleship *Genereux*. This was not much of a favor, for the ship was not only badly damaged, but equipped with a crew of sick and wounded men. Cochrane rose to the occasion, sailed through a storm and made it into Port Mahon without losing the prize. In an effort more to be rid of the uppity lieutenant more than to reward him, he was given command of the brig *Speedy* in 1800 to cruise against the French and Spanish in the Mediterranean.

While armed only with small four-pound guns and manned with barely ninety sailors, the little *Speedy* would become a terror to shipping in the Mediterranean. By July, 1801, Cochrane would capture more than fifty prizes with the tiny vessel, sink roughly a dozen more and take over 500 enemy prisoners. Like the best of pirates, Cochrane would fly false flags and use bluff, misdirection and fear to every advantage throughout his career. Additionally, in order to avoid Admiralty "fees" and percentages, he often buried gold and silver found aboard his prizes and would come back later, dig up the loot and disperse it amongst his crew. When trapped by the Spanish frigate *Gamo*, of 32 guns and 319 men, Cochrane would charge the enemy, getting in close under the enemy's lee side while peppering the frigate's decks with grapeshot and keeping safe from Spanish guns, which merely shot over the smaller *Speedy*, due to the difference in height. With a

Capture of the *Gamo*

crew of only fifty-four men, Cochrane ordered his men to blacken their faces in order to play on Spanish superstitions, hoping to create as much disorder as possible. Due to the death of their captain during the *Speedy's* first broadside, this worked, as Cochrane's British sailors swarmed aboard, fighting fiercely before he ordered a man to lower the Spanish colors. With no captain and a lowered flag, confusion abounded and the Spanish quickly surrendered, losing fifteen dead and forty-one wounded. Amazingly, the crew of the Speedy suffered only three men dead and eighteen wounded. To this day, there are many who consider this to be one of the most spectacular single-ship victories in British naval history -- no small feat.

Captured by three French battleships in July, 1801, Cochrane so impressed his enemies while trying to evade capture that Captain Palliere refused to accept his sword upon surrender and paroled him within a few days. This would be a grave mistake, for Cochrane would continue his exploits against the French and earn the nickname "The Sea Wolf" from Napoleon. He would return to England as a hero celebrated by the people and be promoted to Captain in August, 1801, but would make hardly any prize money off the *Gamo*, as it was practically given away to the Dey of Algeria.

Instead of being given a respectable command after his exploits in the *Speedy*, the Admiralty continued to dislike Cochrane and gave him command of a converted collier which was barely seaworthy. Then, he was sent off the northern English coast to protect nonexistent fishing waters for over a year. Cochrane would be "exiled" in such fashion until 1805, when a change in government placed command of the freshly-built frigate *Pallas* into his lap. Within a few short months, Cochrane captured four rich Spanish prizes off the

Azores and returned to England. He used some of his prize money to build a high-speed galley of eighteen oars capable of carrying 180 men, which would be carried aboard the *Pallas* and enable him to launch commando raids on the French coastline as well as to attack ships becalmed in windless conditions -- both of which were relatively new ways of thinking in the Royal Navy. He also used some of his prize money to run for Parliament, getting elected in 1806, shortly before receiving orders returning him to the coast of France.

Haunting the Aix Roads region, Cochrane began using his galley in raids along the shore, destroying five corvettes over the course of one night. Ever brazen, he sailed the *Pallas* into the harbor at Aix, sinking two brigs and shooting up a heavy frigate before escaping. He also managed to destroy many signal houses along the coast, as well as a few batteries and small forts. For his efforts, by November, 1806, Cochrane was awarded with an even larger, faster frigate, the *Imperieuse*, which held a crew of 300. Among the crew was a 14-year-old midshipman, Frederick Marryat, who would later use Co-

Cochrane's Attach on French at Aix

chrane as a model for his fictional Captain Savage and would be the first of three novelists to pattern their main characters after Cochrane. Home long enough to be reelected to Parliament in 1807, he was sent back to the Mediterranean, raiding along the coast and even "cutting-out" a French munitions ship in the Bay of Almeira. For all his exploits in the *Pallas* and *Imperieuse*, by September of that year, his crew had only one man wounded. Oddly, had he lost more men, he would have gained even more credit, especially with the Admiralty.

Aix Roads

By February, 1809, a fleet of eight French battleships and several frigates "snuck into" the harbor at Aix Roads, reportedly headed for the West Indies. Not wishing the fleet to escape, in April, the Admiralty hatched a plan to attack the ships at anchor, and due to Cochrane's familiarity with the area -- along with the fact that a failure might destroy his reputation -- he was chosen to lead attacking fireships into the harbor. At his own insistence, for the first time ever three of these ships were converted into "explosion ships," packed with 1,500 barrels of gunpowder each. Cochrane led the very first of these "explosion ships" into battle, with the fireships following. The inclusion of these explosion ships was fortunate, for the French had anchored a double-log boom across the mouth of the harbor to protect from a fireship attack. This boom was blown to smithereens by the first explosion ship, allowing the attack to continue. While only four fireships managed to come close to the French warships, the panic created by the two explosion ships -- the third was extinguished before exploding -- created havoc with the French fleet. Panicked into believing all the attacking ships were rigged to explode, the French fleet began to move and almost immediately ran aground.

At dawn, with seven French battleships and several frigates grounded at low tide, Cochrane signaled Admiral Lord Gambier, who received the signal but failed to send in the fleet. After repeated signals brought no ships -- who could now simple punish the grounded fleet with artillery -- Cochrane took matters into his own hands. Weighing anchor, he slid the *Imperieuse* backwards, toward the shoreline, until he was close enough to engage the grounded ships. Then, Cochrane ordered the colors flown upside-down, which was the signal for ship in distress. His trick worked, for at two o'clock, three British warships came to his aid and begin to bombard the grounded vessels. In all, the French lost roughly half their fleet, four battleships, a 56-gun magazine ship and a frigate. Admiral Lord Gambier sent Cochrane back to England the very next day, bearing messages.

Tragically, after seventeen years in the Royal Navy and following his greatest victory, Cochrane would never sail for Britain again. When word spread that Gambier was to receive a vote of thanks from Parliament, Cochrane refused his next command in order to attend Parliament and shed truth on what really happened at Aix Roads -- that Gambier had turned a stupendous victory into half of one. This lead to Gambier's courts-martial, prompt acquittal, and an Admiralty shunning of Cochrane, who soon found himself set-up in the midst of a Stock Exchange fraud in 1814. He would be convicted, dismissed from the navy, ordered to serve a year in prison and, additionally, became the last Englishman ordered to spend time in the stocks at the pillory near the London Exchange. After his brief escape and recapture -- found at Parliament -- this latter punishment was waved when he paid a large fine.

Revolutionary

In 1817, Spain offered Cochrane to lead an expedition to crush the rebellions in their Central and South American colonies, which he declined. Instead, he spread word that his services were available, and soon took an offer to command Chile's navy against Spain. Believing steam-powered vessels to be the future, he invested in the design and building of the *Rising Star*, which he planned to sell to Chile upon its arrival in Valparaiso. As it was still early in the steam era, the *Rising Star* proved to be no grand invention, and when she finally did make it into Valparaiso (mostly under sail), the Chilean government showed no interest in purchasing her.

Cochrane sailed from England in the summer of 1818, shortly before the passing of the Foreign Enlistment Act, which was an attempt at keeping men like him from working for foreign military powers. As it was, when Cochrane arrived in Chile, he not only found many of his seamen to be British and American, but would request that the revolutionary governments try to entice more of them into their service. Even so, Chile's navy was quite small, with the 48-gun *O'Higgins* frigate as flagship, two converted merchantmen acting as "frigates," and four brigs and schooners of eighteen guns of less rounding out the "fleet." After taming his mutinous men aboard the brig *Chacabuco*, Cochrane preyed on Spanish shipping along the coast and earned from them the moniker "El Diablo." Other than that, his first major attacks utterly failed, as he tried three times to take Callao, twice with explosion ships. One explosion ship failed to ignite and was captured by Spanish gunboats, and in the second attempt, a red-hot shot fired from the fort detonated the ship far from shore.

Finally, in February, 1820, Cochrane's luck changed drastically. At Valdivia -- known as the "Gibraltar" of Spanish power -- in a series of land actions which overtook several Spanish forts during the night, Cochrane sailed his damaged and sinking flagship into the harbor the next morning and received the remaining forts' surrender. Already having problems with the Chilean government in the payment of prize money, Cochrane kept the money seized at Valdivia in lieu of unpaid prizes.

Capture of Valdivia
Chilean Naval and Maritime Museum

Cochrane, in some ways a bit strange, harbored a weird desire to concoct a scheme which would free Napoleon from the island of St. Helena, but that scheme died in late 1820 when Napoleon did.

In November of that year, Cochrane would brazenly lead boat crews into the harbor of Callao and "cut-out" two gunboats and the 44-gun Spanish flagship *Esmeralda* in a daring action that ended with Cochrane sailing out of the harbor after raising the lights of a neutral nation to quiet the fort's guns. Cochrane received two wounds in the seizure, with fifteen Chileans killed and fifty wounded. Spanish casualties are reportedly much higher, in addition to having 174 men taken prisoner. As the USS *Macedonian* and HMS *Hyperion* were in the harbor, the guns quit firing and the stolen *Esmeralda* sailed off. Wrongly assuming that the British and Americans had aided the Chileans, an American boat crew was killed in retribution after rowing ashore the next morning, along with several British sailors.

While serving Chile, Cochrane was not above using the old British trick of seizing neutral ships suspected of smuggling, having seized a total of eighteen British merchant vessels. This infuriated many of the British commanders in the area, especially Commodore Hardy, who called the seizures "piratical acts." This made the Royal Navy keep a close eye on their former commander. However, such seizures did not keep them from raving about Cochrane's successes, such as the commander of the *Hyperion*, who had a perfect view of the *Esmeralda* being cut-out.

While Cochrane performed blockade duty on Callao the following year, Chile finally won its independence from Spain due to San Martin's ground forces at Callao. San Martin, wishing to fight now for Peruvian independence, desired

Cochrane's fleet, but offered no money. Outraged, and suffering from crew desertions -- especially valuable British and American seamen -- due to wages unpaid for at least a year, Cochrane acted swiftly and captured San Martin's "Peruvian" treasure ship in November, 1821. Keeping no money for himself this time, Cochrane paid $285,000 to the men of the fleet and thousands of unpaid soldiers. Ironically, Cochrane's one act of indisputable piracy did much to prevent the Chilean navy from beginning a course of mutinies which would enable untold piracies, as unpaid wages and poor living conditions were why most privateer and state ships mutinied and turned to piracy. As it was, only one vessel of the Chilean navy would turn pirate, the brig *Araucano*, in the summer of 1822.

During that summer of 1822, with independence attained and money tight for the Chilean government, it was no surprise to Cochrane when they decommissioned the fleet and, more or less, turned the admiral out of a job. In late 1822, roughly at the same time Cochrane's estate in Chile was being destroyed by an earthquake, he accepted Brazil's offer of $8,000 annually to command their navy. Brazil had declared independence from Portugal earlier in 1822, in a bit of a family squabble, as it was the prince who not only ruled Brazil but also declared independence from his royal bloodline. While Cochrane would hold his position with Brazil for less than two years, his boldest accomplishments to date would occur during a span of three months' time.

Of Brazil's eight ships, two were not seaworthy and two others were only fit for use as fireships. However, the 74-gun *Pedro Primeiro* and frigate *Piranga* were in decent condition. Making the *Pedro Primeiro* his flagship, Cochrane attacked a line of Portuguese warships and was astonished to find no other Brazilian ships had followed him into combat. Breaking off the engagement, Cochrane finally realized how poor the seamen of Brazil were, urged the government to hire British and American sailors, and put all such sailors already in service aboard his flagship. This proved to be wise.

Sailing to Bahia in early July, 1823, Cochrane easily secured the city's surrender, as General Ignacio Madeira feared an Aix Roads-type action, for he felt the fleet was exposed to such an attack. As it was, Cochrane -- with only his flagship -- picked off half of the thirteen-ship Portuguese squadron as they retreated and also beat the remaining fleet to Maranhao. There, Cochrane delivered one of the greatest bluffs in naval history, as he stated that the *Pedro Primeiro* was only the advance guard of a huge Brazilian fleet, which had already completely destroyed the Portuguese fleet. That was enough for Governor Dom Agostinho Antonio de Fama, who promptly surrendered the city to Cochrane's single warship. With the city of Para's capitulation the following month, Cochrane managed to secure northern Brazil for the revolutionary prince in less than three months.

With the situation in Brazil quickly melting into factious civil war, and once again feeling shorted on prize money from yet another cash-strapped revolutionary government, Cochrane took the now-rotting frigate *Piranga* to England in May, 1825. Unsure about how he would be received, due to the provisions of the Foreign Enlistment Act, the salutes fired off at his arrival at Spithead were a warm welcome indeed. He would later receive a bill for 25,000 pounds for the hi-jacked *Piranga*, which he never paid.

Through with his Brazilian service but still looking to increase his fortune, Cochrane was soon contacted by Greece in 1826 and agreed to become their admiral for 37,000 pounds, with an additional 20,000 due upon Greek indepen-dence from Turkey. Forced to sneak out of England to avoid possible legal problems with the Foreign Enlistment Act, Cochrane spent time in Europe while awaiting the arrival of the six steam frigates he had ordered built in England and America on behalf of the Greek government. One year later, the U.S.-built frigate *Hellas* was finally delivered, which Co-chrane made his flagship and sailed to Greece in 1827. Upon his arrival, he found the military situation quite different, as warfare between the Greeks and Turks was extremely brutal and savage, causing him to witness more deaths in his few short months of Greek service than he had seen in all his prior years of warfare combined. His own sailors were the worst he had yet to deal with, and so untrustworthy that he was forced to carry a loaded pistol at all times. A fireship attack on Alexandria utterly failed, and Cochrane's only bright spot in the campaign is to be found during an engagement with the Turkish fleet, which proved the power of steam vessels, as the one commanded by Captain Frank Hastings sank nine ships

and made another a prize. An armistice was signed in summer, 1827, but the Turks quickly violated it, which prompted the "Allied" fleet of Britain, France and Russia to sail into the Bay of Navarino on October 20, 1827 and completely destroy the Turkish fleet, sinking 53 ships and killing 7,000 sailors. By early 1828, his services no lon-ger required, Cochrane traveled back to England and refused

**Thomas Cochrane
10th Earl of Dundonald**

the 20,000 pounds promised him by Greece, insisting it be paid to injured veterans and widows instead. Shortly after, he would again be offered to command the Brazilian squadron -- now at war with Argentina -- but would decline.

While largely lost in history books, Cochrane would be redeemed in England before his death, being reinstated as a retired rear-admiral in May, 1832, after a royal pardon. In 1846, at the age of 70, he would also be reinstated in the prestigious Order of the Bath, which was originally conferred upon him for his exploits against France and stripped during his entanglement in the Stock Exchange "fraud."

Larger than life even in death, Cochrane would be reborn on the silver screen in 2004, with the release of the motion picture *Master and Commander - the Far Side of the World*. Taken from the novels of Patrick O'Brian, the character of "Lucky" Jack Aubrey would be based on Lord Cochrane. Horatio Hornblower, the classic fictional creation of C.S. Forester, was a character also molded from this legendary naval figure.

Photo: Capture of the *Harriett Lane*
Background: American Coast - Civil War Era
U. S. National Archives

Chapter Four

American Civil War Piracy

The American Civil War is not generally featured in studies on piracy, as the vast majority of historians end their piracy timelines in 1835 with the hanging of the *Panda's* crew in Boston. However, these four bloody years need to be addressed, for not only did the North consider all Southern privateers and sailors to be pirates, but actual piracies were committed. Besides which, it was the last war to issue letters of marque and reprisal in any real number and the last war featuring American privateers. As the Civil War is still a bone of contention for many Americans, piracy historians have largely steered clear of it. This is mostly due to years of effective propaganda which has portrayed the fight as a "rights" issue somehow separate from the once Constitutionally-protected right to own slaves, coupled with the aftereffects of a war which shattered the South and forever altered the nation.[306] As a result, the American Civil War is not generally portrayed as a preemptive strike to protect the institution of slavery, and so the kettle continues to boil. This is unfortunate, for if nothing else, the Civil War provides an excellent illustration

---

306   William C. Davis, *The Cause Lost: Myths and Realities of the Confederacy*. (University of Kansas Press, 1996), 180. Davis notes that the "states' rights" argument appeared only after 1865, as part of the "Lost Cause" myth.

**President Abraham Lincoln
White House**

of the laws pertaining to piracy.

Setting The Stage

The bombardment and capitulation of Ft. Sumter on April 12-13, 1861 sparked the American Civil War. On April 17, Confederate President Jefferson Davis released a statement declaring that privateer commissions would be made available. Two days later, President Abraham Lincoln announced a naval blockade of the South and promised;

"… if any person, under the pretended authority of the said States, or under any pretense, shall molest a vessel of the United States, or the persons or cargo on board of her, such person will be held amenable to the laws of the United States for the prevention and punishment of piracy."[307]

The legal basis for Lincoln's statement can be found in a 1790 act of congress which was aimed at deterring Americans from serving aboard enemy vessels and provided execution for those who did so.[308] However, as the Confederate States of America had already been formed and had even adopted a constitution and government nearly identical to the Federal

---

307   William Morrison Robinson, Jr., *The Confederate Privateers.* (University of South Carolina Press, 1990), 14. Originally published by Yale University Press, 1928.
308   Ibid, 140.

system, the citizenship aspect of the 1790 act no longer applied. Regardless of that particular argument, Lincoln had bestowed belligerent status upon the Confederacy by instituting a blockade, in accordance to international law. Certainly, Lincoln's statement was an effort to keep the war a "family affair," but his own actions made this impossible. A blockade meant belligerent status -- soon recognized by Britain and most of Europe, who also declared neutrality -- and this status allowed for commissioned privateers and a state-run navy.[309] On May 6, 1861 Jefferson Davis signed into law the act offering Confederate letters of marque and reprisal.[310] Shortly before the Battle of Bull Run (Manassas), Davis would also release a statement declaring that for every Confederate hung as a pirate, a Union prisoner would be hung in reprisal. In his July 6, 1861 dispatch to Lincoln, Davis states, "…painful as will be the necessity, this Government will deal out to prisoners held by it the same treatment and the same fate as shall be experienced by those captured …"[311] This soon ended all piracy trials and ensured that no Confederate privateers were hung, as early Confederate victories gave them a large pool of Union prisoners for use as leverage. There is a rather large

JEFF DAVIS, ON HIS OWN PLATFORM,
or the last act of secession

Political cartoon passing sentence on Jefferson Davis

309   James M. McPherson, *Abraham Lincoln and the Second American Revolution.* (New York: Oxford, 1991), 76.
310   William Morrison Robinson, Jr., *The Confederate Privateers.* (University of South Carolina Press, 1990), 17.
311   Ibid, 133.

irony to be found in the matter of Civil War privateers, for the 1856 Declaration of Paris abolished the practice for all signatories, such as England, France, Russia and most of Europe. The United States did not sign, however, as it was felt that privateers might be needed to augment naval strength should a future war occur with an enemy of superior naval

THE CONSCRIPT BILL!

HOW TO AVOID IT!!

U. S. NAVY.

1,000 MEN WANTED, FOR 12 MONTHS!

Seamen's Pay,	$18.00	per month.
Ordinary Seamen's Pay,	14.00	" "
Landsmen's Pay,	12.00	" "

$1.50 extra per month to all, Grog Money.

$50,000,000 PRIZES!

Already captured, a large share of which is awarded to Ships Crews. The laws for the distributing of Prize money carefully protects the rights of all the captors.

PETTY OFFICERS,—PROMOTION.—Seamen have a chance for promotion to the offices of Master at Arms, Boatswain's Mates, Quarter Gunners, Captain of Tops, Forecastle, Holds, After-Guard, &c.
Landsmen may be advanced to Armorers, Armorers' Mates, Carpenter's Mates, Sailmakers' Mates, Painters, Coopers, &c.
PAY OF PETTY OFFICERS,—From $20.00 to $45.00 per month.
CHANCES FOR WARRANTS, BOUNTIES AND MEDALS OF HONOR.—All those who distinguish themselves in battle or by extraordinary heroism, may be promoted to forward Warrant Officers or Acting Masters' Mates,—and upon their promotion receive a guaranty of $100, with a medal of honor from their country.
All who wish may leave HALF PAY with their families, to commence from date of enlistment.
Minors must have a written consent, sworn to before a Justice of the Peace.

For further information apply to U. S. NAVAL RENDEZVOUS,

E. Y. BUTLER, U. S. N. Recruiting Officer,
No. 14 FRONT STREET, SALEM, MASS.

Civil War U.S. Navy Recruiting Poster
Naval History and Heritage Command

power. Even by the beginning of the Civil War, the U.S. Navy only tallied roughly ninety vessels. Of this number, only twenty-four were steam-powered, another twenty or so ships would be deemed unfit for service and many of the remainder were spread across the globe.[312] Thus, what appeared to be wise in 1856 would haunt the Union five years later, for had the United States signed the Declaration of Paris and outlawed privateers -- which also would have required an amended Constitution -- then it would have been much harder for the Confederacy to argue the legality of offering letters of marque and reprisal, especially in the international arena.

A great many historians continue to make a living by comparing the American Civil War to the American Revolution. Indeed, many have argued that it was the "Second American Revolution," an interesting position which offers a wide range of comparison. However, perhaps the largest difference is that the Confederate States of America began the war with a central government, while the American Revolution began as a loosely-associated collection of states, all of which claimed their own sovereignty -- meaning each thought they were a nation unto themselves -- which is a more accurate description of the term confederacy. As a result, some states during the early days of the revolution took it upon their own authority to issue privateer commissions and establish prize courts. This did not happen during the Civil War because the power to offer such commissions resided with the Confederate government, as that portion of the Confederate Constitution was identical to the Federal model. The power to declare war and issue letters of marque and reprisal can be found at the same location in both documents, Article I, Section 8, listed

---

312   Alexander DeConde, *A History of American Foreign Policy*. (New York: Scribner's, 1963), 255.

**Confederate President
Jefferson Davis
Library of Congress**

at number eleven.[313]

The Confederacy moved quickly to establish prize courts and ensure that proper standards were met for the commissioning of private warships. While the 1856 Declaration of Paris had slightly altered some of the requirements pertaining to neutral nations and legal blockades, the basic rules really weren't much different than they had been for over a century. A privateer must be commissioned in a home port and consist of crewmen largely native to the belligerent nation, as only roughly thirty percent of the crew could be foreign nationals. No blank commissions were to be issued or considered legal, flags were not transferable -- as the ship was commissioned, not the person -- and the usual bond was necessary. The very reason for the bond was to ensure that any unlawful seizures would be compensated and was an age-old standard concerning commissioned privateers. Additionally, all recognized rules for international combat must also be followed, such as making captures only on the high seas and respecting the "marine league" -- a three mile buffer extending from the coasts of all countries.[314] The marine league had

313   Both documents state, "To declare War, grant Letters of Marque and Reprisal, and make Rules concerning Captures on Land and Water;"
314   William Morrison Robinson, Jr., *The Confederate Privateers.* (University of South Carolina Press, 1990), 19-24 outlines many of the rules for Confederate commissions.

long been an international hallmark, especially regarding neutral nations. Another important international restriction affecting Confederate vessels was the stipulation which limited coaling at the same neutral port to once every ninety days.

The Confederate government was actually quite strict in policing most privateers early in the war. Some prizes were ordered to be released by prize courts after several vessels in the Gulf were taken in violation of the marine league. Such attention was put forth in an effort to limit the cases of piracy -- always a risk with privateers -- in order to smooth international relations. While no nation ever formally recognized the Confederacy or allowed them to bring prizes into neutral ports, attaining such recognition -- and if possible, armed intervention -- was always a goal of the Confederate government, who wisely realized that many nations might become soured by overt acts of piracy.[315]

Perhaps the best chance the Confederates had at attaining official recognition and an intervening ally also best illustrates the proper procedures for seizing ships and the importance of prize courts. The "*Trent* Affair," as it has come to be known, is still an item of debate. In August, 1861, Jefferson Davis named James Mason envoy to Britain and John Slidell his counterpart to France. Slidell -- a life-long Louisiana politico who spent years serving as Congressman or Senator -- had also been President Polk's plenipotentiary to Mexico shortly before the Mexican War. Indeed, Slidell's instructions did much to bring on the war, as Polk had anticipated, even though Slidell would not be officially received by Mexico and would soon leave.[316] On November 8, 1861 the British

315　William C. Davis, *The Cause Lost: Myths and Realities of the Confederacy*. (University of Kansas Press, 1996), 179, notes that no nation recognized the Confederacy or exchanged ambassadors.
316　Daniel Walker Howe, *What Hath God Wrought: The Transformation of America, 1815-1848*. (New York: Oxford, 2007), 734-738.

steam packet *Trent*, carrying both Southern diplomats who had boarded at Nassau, was stopped by the steam-frigate USS *San Jacinto*, which had been dispatched to the Bahamas to search for the CSS *Sumter*. Captain Wilkes of the *San Jacinto* sent a boarding party aboard the *Trent* after sending a shot across her bow and another which exploded nearby. Without incident, both Mason and Slidell were removed and locked in irons aboard *San Jacinto* and the *Trent* was allowed to go on her way. Oddly enough, the mailbag containing official Confederate correspondence was not taken, although such items had long been considered contraband of war.

Both the Confederacy and Britain were irate, although there was much hope among Southerners that such an outrage might propel the British to declare war on the Union. Indeed, the British government was not pleased and almost immediately ordered additional troops mustered for service in Canada and the Royal Navy readied for action. Ironically, the act smacked of impressment, a long-held American complaint against the British which served as one of the reasons for fighting the War of 1812. Not surprisingly, the Civil War would witness a variety of role-reversals concerning Federal positions in several areas of maritime law. The *Trent* drama would end with a British ultimatum -- release the Confederate emissaries and apologize to Her Majesty's government or suffer the consequences. On New Year's Day, 1862, Mason and Slidell were released from their Boston prison and put aboard the British sloop *Rinaldo*, shortly after Secretary of State Seward offered a confused and legally-incorrect apology/justification to the British, who let the matter drop.[317]

317   John M. Taylor, "The Overblown *Trent* Affair," excerpted from Still, Taylor and Delaney's *Raiders and Blockaders: The American Civil War Afloat*. (Washington, D.C.: Brassey's, 1998), 100-108. Also, Alexander DeConde, *A History of American Foreign Policy*. (New York: Scribner's, 1963), 245-247.

As offered by historian John M. Taylor;

"… neither Wilkes nor Fairfax [who led the boarding party] appears to have remembered to seize the Confederate dispatch box, the one item of baggage that might have been regarded as contraband. Nor was the *Trent*, in being allowed to proceed to England, treated in accordance with international law."[318]

To sum up the incident, Taylor refers to the historian Allen Nevins;

"[Wilkes] had a perfect right to search any suspected ship for…contraband of war, and to take a vessel carrying contraband into port to await the verdict of a prize court. But he had no right to decide the question of a violation of neutrality by fiat on the spot, without judicial process. Moreover, it was extremely doubtful whether persons, as distinguished from goods, could ever be deemed contraband."[319]

While the crux of the "*Trent* Affair" focused on removing individuals from neutral vessels, the proper procedure for the disposition of naval seizures has been made clear. This holds true for any commissioned vessel, public or private. In essence, the whole process is akin to police powers. Officers are empowered to arrest suspects -- even by the use of necessary/ deadly force or by placing suspects in irons or a short-term holding cell -- but police officers are not empowered to pass judgment and subsequently sentence suspects to years of imprisonment or death. Just like a prize court, there must be a trial, even for the obvious.

---

318   John M. Taylor, "The Overblown *Trent* Affair," excerpted from Still, Taylor and Delaney's *Raiders and Blockaders: The American Civil War Afloat.* (Washington, D.C.: Brassey's, 1998), 104-105.
319   Ibid, 105.

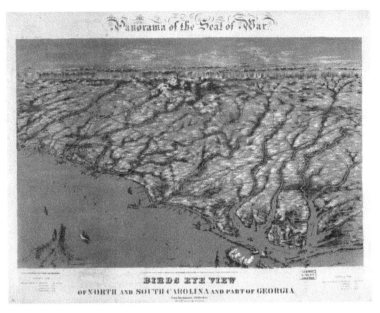

**Aerial depiction of North and South Carolina,
which shows the gaps the Union forces tried to fill.**

The Union Blockade

Careers have been made discussing the variety of ironies which can be found in the annals of the Civil War. Another such irony is the blockade of Southern shores, for the very item which gave legal life to Confederate letters of marque and reprisal would also become the prime obstacle which ended Confederate privateering. Originally knick-named the "Anaconda Plan" in an effort to deride General Winfield Scott, who proposed the idea, the blockade would certainly evolve into such a description. At first the South called it a "paper blockade," as with few Union ships, it didn't seem to exist in many areas. However, the blockade would tighten dramatically, especially concerning vessels under sail.

A large portion of Union efforts to blockade the South focused on seizing key coastal positions -- such as Hatteras Inlet and Pamlico Sound, North Carolina, Roanoke Island, Virginia and Port Royal Sound, South Carolina -- all of which fell by late January, 1862 and commanded various approaches into the Confederacy.[320] Once such positions fell, an "inside" blockade could be implemented by a relative handful of vessels, supported by shore batteries and river obstructions. Closing the ports by taking them in force is by far the most dramatic of these examples, such as with Admiral Farragut's charges into New Orleans in 1862 and Mobile Bay in 1864. Other ports fell by logistics, such as Mosquito Inlet, Florida which became obsolete when the fall of Jacksonville severed the vital railway link.[321] Positions that could not be seized would be cordoned-off by a line of blockading ships, such as Wilmington, North Carolina which was firmly protected by forts and did not fall until late in the war. Charleston would also experience a similar "outside" blockade, as a result of shallow, sandy conditions. This type of blockade required more ships, as a much wider area was covered. Consequently, they were not as effective and literally ate away at supply stocks -- especially coal. Coal would prove to be one of the Civil War's most valuable commodities.[322]

Arguments concerning the overall effectiveness of the

---

320   Charles P. Roland, *An American Iliad: The Story of the Civil War.* (New York: McGraw-Hill, 2002), 66-67.

321   Stephen R. Wise, *Lifeline of the Confederacy: Blockade Running During the Civil War.* (University of South Carolina Press, 1988), 60.

322   William N. Still, Jr., "Technology Afloat." Excerpted from *Raiders and Blockaders: The American Civil War Afloat.* (Brassey's, 1998), 39, description of "inside" and "outside" blockades along with a notation on coal use by the Union Navy, which required 3,000 tons per week to fuel the blockading force. Originally published in 1975 by *Historical Times.*

blockade and its true effect on the Confederacy will forever abound and never be fully reckoned. Historian William N. Still, Jr. boils it down with, "It was not a major factor in the collapse of the Confederacy."[323] The title of Still's work -- "A Naval Sieve: The Union Blockade in the Civil War," uses not only an apt title but an alternate illustration just prior to his conclusion. "It would be an oversimplification to say that it was either effective or not effective. It was both. In general, its effectiveness increased as the war progressed."[324]

Still's "Naval Sieve" comparison does much to explain the effect the blockade had on sailing vessels. During the war's early months, a swift privateer schooner with a bold captain, experienced pilot and a stiff wind might be able to run past a light blockading force comprised of inadequate vessels. Many got to sea without incident. The main problem was in getting prizes back to port. In this, the steam-powered Union Navy was decisive. The ad-hoc expansion of the U.S. Navy by hiring/buying or being lent a variety of steamships early in the war did have an immediate effect -- although these vessels were nowhere near as capable as many of their freshly-produced replacements would be.[325] The final numbers are telling. Growing to over 700 vessels, the Union Navy captured 1,129 prizes, of which 210 were steamers. Another 355 were burned, sunk or driven ashore; of which 85 were steamers. In short, a vessel reliant upon wind was not likely to pass through the sieve.[326]

---

323   William N. Still, Jr., "A Naval Sieve: The Union Blockade in the Civil War." Excerpted from *Raiders and Blockaders: The American Civil War Afloat*. (Brassey's, 1998), 138.

324   Ibid.

325   William Morrison Robinson, Jr., *The Confederate Privateers*. (University of South Carolina Press, 1990), 305-317. *Quaker City* and *Vanderbilt* are but two of many examples.

326   William N. Still, Jr., "A Naval Sieve: The Union Blockade in the

Since no other nation allowed Confederate vessels to bring prizes into port -- let alone set up prize courts -- and as the odds of returning with a prize under sail were no longer appealing, privateering dried up almost entirely. The private money which had backed such ships was instead invested in generally British-built steam-powered blockade runners, the famed "Clyde Steamers." Many Confederate commerce raiders would be converted from blockade runners or become a runner after having served as a warship. The runner *Edith* would become CSS *Chickamauga* in late 1864, while the blockaded CSS *Sumter* would be sold to a British concern and after escaping from Gibraltar, be sold back to the Confederacy as the runner *Gibraltar*. Perhaps the best example is the runner *Atalanta*, which would become CSS *Tallahassee*, be rechristened CSS *Olustee* in 1864 and shortly thereafter became the blockade runner *Chameleon*.[327]

The Confederate government's need for state-owned blockade runners would elevate the small port of St. George, Bermuda to great importance. However, Bermuda was a much farther distance to Southern ports than was the Bahamas, which would turn Nassau into an overnight boom-town.[328] Due to the tremendous profits made by blockade running, historian J.H. Stark notes, "Not since the days of the buccaneers and pirates had there been such times in the Bahamas."[329] John Fraser & Co. of Charleston would prove

---

Civil War." Excerpted from *Raiders and Blockaders: The American Civil War Afloat.* (Brassey's, 1998), 133.

327   Stephen R. Wise, *Lifeline of the Confederacy: Blockade Running During the Civil War.* (University of South Carolina Press, 1988), 119 illustrates *Sumter/Gibraltar*, 199-202 *Chickamauga* and *Tallahassee*.

328   Ibid, 95. Roughly 100 miles further to Wilmington, 150 to Charleston.

329   Michael Craton, *A History of the Bahamas.* (San Salvador Press, 1999, first printed 1962), 217.

Blockade Runner *Advance* - 1863

to be an important financial tie to England and would account for much blockade running, as would other elements of the former Fraser, Trenholm & Co. Many English firms would act in a similar manner and directly finance a number of smuggling operations.[330] Some round-trips from Nassau to Charleston or Wilmington might bring $300,000. New steamers generally paid for themselves in less than three runs through the blockade. The steamers themselves are reminiscent of classic smuggling craft -- shallow draft, long and lean in form, with the capability of high speeds. Usually, these side-wheelers were painted slate gray in an effective attempt at camouflage and like Confederate commerce raiders, burned near-smokeless anthracite coal, which made them even harder to spot.[331]

One of the most notable "cargos" brought into Wilmington was a dreaded case of yellow fever, which arrived aboard

330   Stephen R. Wise, *Lifeline of the Confederacy: Blockade Running During the Civil War.* (University of South Carolina Press, 1988), 46-47.
331   Michael Craton, *A History of the Bahamas.* (San Salvador Press, 1999, first printed 1962), 213.

the blockade runner *Kate* in the summer of 1862. Over 1,500 cases of yellow fever broke out, killing roughly 800 people.[332]

British-backed blockade runners would prove the actual worth of the "*Trent* Affair," as the event gave an unofficial sanction for British smugglers. The Union often violated the marine league while chasing ships in the Bahamas -- such as when USS *Rhode Island* shot at the fleeing British *Margaret and Jessie* within a mile of Eleuthera in May, 1863 -- but Britain did not complain much, as their captured subjects were generally released within a couple weeks. Due to the huge rates of pay awarded these sailors, such a short inconvenience did not deter many from crewing blockade runners.[333]

Piracy

As stated earlier, nearly as soon as some private vessels were commissioned, more than a few unlawful captures were brought into Southern ports and subsequently ordered released by Confederate prize courts. The former packet steamer *Music*, armed with two six-pounders and fifty men, had prizes released, as did the tow steamer *V.H. Ivy*, armed with a fifteen-pounder. Both privateers had taken vessels within the marine league while hunting in the Gulf during the summer of 1861. A variety of other privateers would make similar violations, but this is hardly pure piracy.[334]

However, many other cases are much more blatant. On April 25, 1861 approximately fifty armed citizens seized the brig *Belle of the Bay* and the schooner *Daniel Townsend* during

332   Stephen R. Wise, *Lifeline of the Confederacy: Blockade Running During the Civil War.* (University of South Carolina Press, 1988), 126-127.
333   Michael Craton, *A History of the Bahamas.* (San Salvador Press, 1999, first printed 1962), 215-216.
334   William Morrison Robinson, Jr., *The Confederate Privateers.* (University of South Carolina Press, 1990), 38-42.

Chesapeake and Delaware Bays, 1861
U.S. National Archives

a night "raid" in Mobile Bay. Two days later, an artillery organization called the "Continentals" hired the steamer *Gunnison* and took the bark *R.H. Gamble*, also in Mobile Bay. All of these prizes were released by prize courts.[335] While similar cases can be found along the Confederate coast, even these early, impromptu actions might be written-off to over-zealous emotions gone awry.

Certainly, other examples are harder to wriggle away from. In yet another early action, former U.S. Navy Captain Hollins hatched a scheme to seize a packet steamer in Chesapeake Bay and used it to take more prizes in June, 1861. What is notable about this particular case is that those involved first thought of consulting Confederate Naval Secretary Stephen R. Mallory about the scheme, but decided against it when they

335   Ibid, 189-190.

didn't think he would approve. The governor of Virginia did grant his approval, however, and even financed the operation with $1,000. In an act which would often be copied, Hollins -- who already had been commissioned a captain in the CSN -- boarded the steamer *St. Nicholas* at Point Pleasant, Maryland in civilian clothes with several other men, including some of his sons. Before long, all the men emerged wearing the rather outlandish zouave uniforms; consisting of fez-like hats, Garibaldi shirts and rather puffy pantaloons. Their brandished pistols gave them command of the ship, which was then used to round-up a brig and two schooners before herding the prizes into Fredricksburg. Oddly enough, the brig was the only vessel to be released after adjudication in prize court. The *St. Nicholas* would be purchased by the Confederacy and become the gunboat CSS *Rappahannock*, while sale proceeds from the schooners was split between Hollins and his men.[336]

Richard Thomas was quickly given a colonel's commission by Virginia and tried an identical caper involving the *St. Nicholas'* sister-ship, the *Mary Washington*. Thomas wouldn't be nearly as fortunate, getting captured with fifteen of his men during the attempt. Imprisoned, they would all be tried as pirates, but since the trials were halted due to threats of reprisal, they would eventually be exchanged for Union prisoners of war.[337]

Thomas Hogg and five "Irishmen" booked passage on the schooner *Joseph L. Gerrity*, and after seizing her, sailed to Belize and sold the schooner under false papers.[338]

Then there were those who took their piracy seriously. Utilizing parties of horsemen and small boat crews, several east Florida men took the towboat *George M. Bird* and a cargo of

---

336   Ibid, 180-184.
337   Ibid, 185.
338   Ibid, 206-209.

timbers during the summer of 1861.[339]   Such picaroon action
would prove common along the Gulf shore, on the coasts of
Florida and would be a constant affliction for vessels on Chesapeake Bay — much as it was during the American Revolution.
Even the old standard of sometimes-smuggler, part-time pirate
can be witnessed. In June, 1863 James Duke -- who had previously piloted a few blockade runners -- led eighteen men in a
launch and boarded the tug *Boston* below New Orleans, using
her to take two barks in the Gulf. One bark was torched and the
other set adrift after it was plundered. Duke would be involved
in several such escapades.[340]   Often, the leaders of the various
picaroon bands were given a commission in the Confederate
"naval reserve" and were frequently depicted as members of the
"volunteer coastguard." Surely, these commissions -- generally
handed out just prior to the first performance -- were often to
give the operations an attempt at legality, but they hardly compare to such actual naval "commando" raids which had been
conducted by Lord Cochrane during the Napoleonic Wars and
fight for Chilean independence. Nor are they comparable to
the actions of the Confederate John Taylor Wood, who would
achieve legendary naval/river exploits before being awarded
command of the commerce raider CSS *Tallahassee*.[341]

An interesting comparison between these piratical, pseu-
do-commissioned "sailors" can be found in the war which was
waged in Missouri and the surrounding countryside, along
with similar actions in Kentucky and parts of Virginia. As
noted by historian Emory M. Thomas;

"Not all Southerners with piratical tendencies served

---

339   Ibid, 193.
340   Ibid, 202-203.
341   John M. Taylor, "John Taylor Wood: Confederate Commando."
Excerpted from *Raiders and Blockaders: The American Civil War Afloat*.
(Brassey's, 1998), 243-246. Originally published in *America's Civil War*,
March, 1997 issue.

in the navy. The Confederate Congress offered landlocked partisan groups the same prize rules which governed captures at sea: partisans shared in the sale of captured enemy supplies, wagons, and weapons."[342]

The common thread here is that guerilla cavalry "captains" were officially recognized as holding such titles from the Confederacy. While this included men of renowned action -- such as John. S. Mosby and John Hunt Morgan -- it also included notorious "bushwhackers" such as Bloody Bill Anderson. A great many outlaws of the "wild west" had previously been members of militia cavalry units, such as Jesse and Frank James. What is truly notable in this comparison is that when such partisans were caught by Union troops, they were routinely ordered for summary execution, which was often immediately carried out.[343] Perhaps a similar outcry did not come from the Confederate government because they were already participating in the tit-for-tat violent reprisals covering the areas of guerrilla operation -- for such activity certainly went both ways, and had since the pre-war "Bleeding Kansas" days -- but because this problem of outlaw cavalry was also recognized by a variety of high-ranking Confederates. Confederate Brigadier General Henry McCulloch stated that such partisans were "but one shade better than highwaymen."[344] Ironically, the men committing actual piracies were tame by comparison, as few of their victims were killed or wounded.

One Southern pirate would actually be hung by the Union, although not for his piracies. John Y. Beall was yet

---

342   Emory M. Thomas, *The Confederacy as a Revolutionary Experience.* (University of South Carolina Press, 1991), 53. Originally published in 1971 by Prentice-Hall.

343   William C. Davis, *The Cause Lost: Myths and Realities of the Confederacy.* (University of Kansas Press, 1996), 81, 87, 91.

344   Albert Castel & Tom Goodrich, *Bloody Bill Anderson: The Short, Savage Life of a Civil War Guerilla.* (University of Kansas Press, 1998.), 33.

another "naval reservist," commissioned with the dubious rank of master-not-in-line-for-promotion. He became the leader of a band of picaroons in the spring of 1863 and got quite serious about raiding Chesapeake Bay by summer's end. His band captured six or seven sloops and fishing scows, with a large "sutler's sloop" probably being his best catch, as such vessels sold a variety of goods to Union sailors manning the blockade. In October, Beall took a sloop at Tangier Inlet and was captured. Paroled, Beall would relocate to Canada and take part in the ill-faited "Buffalo-Dunkirk" scheme which tried to free captured Confederate generals who were being transported to Fort Lafayette in New York harbor. Beall was tried by the military and hung on February 18, 1865.[345]

A number of prospective privateers were fitted-out for cruising and seem not to have received commissions at all, but decided to sail anyway. The schooner *Gallatin* and brig *Hallie Jackson* certainly set sail from Savannah, as the *Hallie Jackson* was captured by USS *Union* when attempting to run into Savannah harbor after obtaining a cargo of arms from Cuba. Whether or not she had taken any vessels is unclear. A reported five schooners were also commissioned in the vicinity of the Bahamas in 1864. Their legality would certainly be questionable. Reports of this sort are not uncommon.[346]

Contrary to Confederate regulations regarding the validity of blank letters of marque and reprisal, a number of them were circulated. An appeal by a Southern delegate sent to Europe seems to have fallen on deaf ears, but in September, 1861 the Confederate agent to Mexico issued five blank privateer commissions to Don Mateo Ramirez, the Mexican official for lower California. When Confederate General Wil-

---

345   William Morrison Robinson, Jr., *The Confederate Privateers.* (University of South Carolina Press, 1990), 222-228.
346   Ibid, 241-247.

liam Preston arrived in Mexico as the new CSA envoy in early 1864, he arrived with ten blank commissions.[347] Whether or not any of these commissions were put to use is hard to tell for certain. However, captain Greathouse in the "privateer" schooner *J.M. Chapman* -- armed with two rifled brass twelve-pounders (probably pivot guns) -- was seized in port by a Union warship while attempting to leave San Francisco Bay on March 14, 1863. The *J.M. Chapman* was found to be sailing under a blank Confederate commission.[348]

The tale of the schooner *Retribution* makes for a classic telling. The vessel had formally been the steam tug *Uncle Ben* and had been part of the flotilla which was to re-supply Fort Sumter in early April, 1861. Bad weather blew the tug close enough to the North Carolina shore to allow for capture by the Confederates. She was fashioned into a gunboat and later stripped of her engine in late 1862, which was used in building the ironclad *North Carolina*. Sold to a private concern, her hull was patched and she was rigged as the schooner *Retribution*. Loaded with cotton, she ran off to St. Thomas and arrived on December 7, 1862. After selling her wares, she met up with the Danish schooner *Dixie*. Both vessels left St. Thomas in mid-December and rendezvoused at a small island off the coast of Venezuela where a twenty-pound rifled cannon and two twelve-pound smoothbores where transferred from the *Dixie* to the *Retribution*. Now "commissioned" as a Confederate privateer, *Retribution* reappeared off St. Thomas on January 3, 1863 and promptly harried all Union shipping lying off the harbor.[349]

Retribution's first prize, the brig *J.P. Ellicott*, was manned with a prize crew and sent off, but they were overpowered by

---

347   Ibid, 261-262.
348   Ibid, 279-289.
349   Ibid, 291-292.

the brig's sailors, who sailed her back to St. Thomas. *Retribution* took the schooner *Hanover* on January 31 and sailed her to Fortune Island in the Crooked Island Pass where her cargo was shipped for sale at Nassau. The *Hanover* was then loaded with salt and sent off to Wilmington, where she ran aground under the protection of Confederate guns. After taking her last prize in mid-February, the brig *Emily Fisher*, *Retribution* seems to have been in poor shape and was sold at Nassau.[350]

Now the story gets interesting. The crew of the *Retribution* -- many of which appear to have been British -- split up and proceeded to hi-jack a steamer from New York and another from Havana in the usual method after boarding as passengers. The New York steamer, *Chesapeake*, would be quickly seized by a Union warship in Nova Scotia and then turned over to the Canadian government for adjudication. The Havana scheme was launched in late September, 1864, as apparently this crime took a bit longer to plan. The U.S. mail steamer *Roanoke* was then taken in the usual manner by a man named Braine and ten compatriots who boarded at Havana, wounding an engineer and killing the ship's carpenter in the process. The *Roanoke* made Bermuda on October 4 and after recruiting some locals as crewmen, Braine decided to burn the *Roanoke* and make his way back to the Confederacy. By March, 1865 Braine was leading a band of picaroons in the Chesapeake Bay and took the schooner *St. Mary's*, which Braine decided to command in search of more prizes. *St. Mary's* soon took the schooner *J.B. Spofford*, which was found unsuitable as a prize and released after having transferred all prisoners aboard her. Apparently unable to make anymore captures without having any cannon, Braine set sail for Jamaica, abandoned his pirated schooner and faded from history.[351]

---

350   Ibid, 292-293.
351   Ibid, 296-301.

The Confederate Cruisers

Often the national cruisers of the Confederacy are called "privateers," but this is the wrong usage, for there was nothing private about them since they were purchased by the Confederate government and commanded by officers of the Confederate Navy. However, with only small exception, these ships were bound by the same international maritime laws that regulated privateers. From CSS *Sumter* to CSS *Shenandoah*, these vessels regularly broke a number of maritime laws, which can allow them to be easily branded as "pirates," even to the present day. Historian Emory M. Thomas called these ships, "…a navy composed for the most part of patriotic pirates and smugglers."[352] This is true for the vast majority of revolutionary navies, with the American Revolution providing an excellent illustration. Thomas goes on to conclude, "…the Confederacy sent forth uniformed pirates to do their worst."[353] Not only is this a bit harsh, but it is not altogether correct.

Had the Confederacy truly wished to unleash a tide of desperate cutthroats upon the high seas, the government would have practically given away letters of marque and reprisal from the start of the war and cared not a hoot about subsequent illegal captures. As the South wished to be recognized as a legitimate nation, they realized that such action would not win them favor, so they were generally strict about protocol early in the war. The outright piracies which did occur were

---

352   Emory M. Thomas, *The Confederacy as a Revolutionary Experience.* (University of South Carolina Press, 1991), 52.
353   Ibid, 53.

relatively small in nature and in no way comparable to the mass murders and thefts committed by the former revolutionaries of the Spanish colonies. There was no ransoming of captives, barely any murder and little torture committed by the vast majority of pirates during this period -- excepting for much of the coastal picaroon action, largely undocumented, but even this historically ugly aspect was relatively "clean" by comparison to other eras.

Of course, the Union blockade and West Indies squadron did much to limit the appeal to both privateering and serious piracy; the effects of which were greatly compounded by the number of steam-powered Union warships and also because no foreign port allowed for the sale or even entrance of Confederate prizes. The American Civil War is often credited with having birthed the principals and practice of "total war," as is illustrated with Sherman's "march to the sea" and occasionally spoken of about the Emancipation Proclamation.[354] Closed and blockaded ports allowed for "total war" to spill over into the world's oceans as Confederate cruisers chose to burn the majority of their prizes rather than take the rather bad risk of running them through the blockade. It is one thing to burn an enemy warship, but as burning a privately-owned vessel circumvents prize court procedures -- thus condemning the accused without proper trial -- it is not a legal act and can be construed as piracy. A few neutral vessels and cargos burned as a result, as did numerous captures made after the war's end. The switch from commerce raiding to commerce destruction

---

354   James M. McPherson, *Abraham Lincoln and the Second American Revolution.* (New York: Oxford, 1991), 35-36. Also, Charles P. Roland, *An American Iliad: The Story of the Civil War.* (New York: McGraw-Hill, 2002), 98-100. Perhaps the best encapsulation of the "total war" concept can be found in James M. McPherson, *Drawn with the Sword: Reflections on the American Civil War.* (New York: Oxford, 1996), 65-86, which comprise Chapter 5, "From Limited to Total War, 1861-1865."

CSS Alabama
Painting by Rear Admiral J. W. Schmidt
Naval History and Heritage Command

heralded a marked change and set the modern maritime standard for submarine warfare -- with the exception that the Confederate cruisers spared the lives of those found aboard potential prizes. While burning ships did much to turn-off many European nations as the war progressed, no insurance company paid out a penny in pirate coverage for any vessel burnt by the likes of CSS *Alabama* -- a position upheld by a variety of court decisions.[355] Ironically, these decisions were a sharp contrast to the official Federal position, which never wavered in proclaiming all Confederate vessels to be pirate craft, even long after the trials had stopped.

Aside from burning prizes, there were a number of international infractions routinely disregarded by the Confederate commerce raiders. Neither *Alabama, Florida* or *Shenandoah* were commissioned in a home port. *Florida* might as well be stricken from the list as she was forced by a lack of crewmen to run into Mobile Bay on September 4, 1862, within three weeks of her commissioning off of Green Cay in the Bahamas. In a daring run past Union blockaders, *Florida* was hit repeatedly by Union artillery, which killed one man and wounded nine others. Union naval operations are often highly criticized during the Civil War, and in many respects this is deserved. While a lack of station ships patrolling vital travel routes certainly hindered the odds of running into Confeder-

---

355   Chester G. Hearn, *Gray Raiders of the Sea*. (LSU Press, 1992), 16, refers to the case of Semmes' first capture, the *Golden Rocket*.

ate vessels, Union warships often nipped at the Confederate's heels and managed to blockade them in a variety of ports. *Florida* would escape such ports on three occasions.[356]

Many Confederate cruisers were dependent on foreign sailors to crew the ships, a proportion much higher than allowed by international standards. The majority of these men were English or Irish and bound by the British Foreign Enlistment Act of 1819 not to serve aboard a foreign warship or privateer, although untold scores of them did, generally with twice the pay given regular sailors.[357] These wages, usually paid in gold, would make foreign sailors among the highest paid men in Confederate service. Considering most infantrymen were paid eleven dollars monthly in Confederate currency, a medium as worthless by war's end as the paper "Continentals" had been for Washington's army, these wages were indeed high. Promised "lots of prize money,"[358] this would not occur, as a lack of open ports for selling prizes forced the Confederates to "bond" ships carrying neutral cargos, with the value payable only after the Confederacy won the war.[359] Just one prize would be sold, the *Sea Bride*. Desperate for gold to pay his foreign sailors -- which were prone to desertion -- Raphael Semmes sold an additional cargo with the prize for $16, 940

---

356   Ibid, 59-65. *Alabama* was forced to escape in a similar fashion, while *Sumter* was successfully blockaded in Gibraltar, although she would be sold to Britain, run the blockade to England and then be bought back by the Confederacy as the blockade runner *Gibraltar*.

357   Ibid, 75. Refers to the British Foreign Enlistment Act of 1819.

358   Ibid, 161, covers Semmes' enticements for British subjects to crew CSS *Alabama*, but this was standard fare for the majority of Confederate cruiser commanders.

359   William N. Still, Jr., "The Confederate Tar." Excerpted from *Raiders and Blockaders: The American Civil War Afloat.* (Brassey's, 1998), 85. The *Shenandoah*'s crew proved the exception, due to a lack of funds which couldn't cover wages for the ship's 13 month cruise.

near Cape Town, South Africa.[360] As most Confederate cruisers were not shy about flying false flags and even taking prizes under foreign colors -- strictly prohibited -- many of these foreign sailors were used as boarding crews to further the deception. The rule limiting Confederate vessels from coaling at neutral ports to once every ninety days was routinely violated, although on a few occasions port access was denied them.[361]

One interesting aspect concerned the state of Maryland, which early in the war the Confederates hoped would join their cause. As a result, the state attained a sort of "neutral" status, with many Maryland vessels released or bonded by privateers and CSA cruisers alike.[362]

Several prizes were "commissioned" into service as armed tenders for some of the cruisers, such as *Alabama* and *Florida*. This was not historically uncommon, although it was not historically legal, either. Commissioning vessels for naval operations before they had been adjudicated in prize court had been a problem for U.S. leaders in Washington during the Quasi-War, as captures like *l'Insurgente* and *l'Amphitheatre* were fitted out as U.S. warships and tenders.[363] This practice continued into the War of 1812, as illustrated by Captain Da-

360   Chester G. Hearn, *Gray Raiders of the Sea*. (LSU Press, 1992), 203.
361   Ibid, 27, illustrates how Semmes was denied entrance at Curacao. Both Maffitt and Semmes were notorious for taking prizes under foreign flags.
362   William Morrison Robinson, Jr., *The Confederate Privateers*. (University of South Carolina Press, 1990), 18.
363   Michael A. Palmer, *Stoddert's War: Naval Operations during the Quasi-War with France, 1798-1801*. (Annapolis, MD: Naval Institute Press, 2000), 173-181. David Porter commanded the prize-turned-tender *l'Amphitheatre*, which was worn-out and sold at the end of the Quasi-War. However, after the sale a court decision would find her to be a wrongful capture, with a fine of $7,040.55 being levied against William Maley, former commander of USS *Experiment*, which had captured the vessel.

Rear Admiral Raphael Semmes, CSN portrait by Maliby Sykes

vid Porter's use of the prize *Essex Jr.*[364] However, none of these vessels performed actions like the brig *Clarence*, initially taken as a prize by *Florida* and commanded by Lt. Read, whose "flag" would be transferred to subsequent captures. Armed with a six-pounder and a collection of wooden "quaker guns" -- which proved as convincing as they had during the American Revolution -- Read went on a rampage, taking twenty-two prizes in twenty-one days and burning most of them. His foulest feat came in 1863, when having made a fresh capture, he flew the U.S. flag upside-down -- the international distress call -- and proceeded to torch three additional vessels which came to the rescue of the burning bark. After taking a passenger packet loaded with 750 immigrants, Read amused himself by setting a prize schooner ablaze specifically to terrify the spectators, who undoubtedly felt they were witnessing their future fate, although their ship was spared.[365] Read would be captured after cutting out and burning the revenue cutter *Caleb Cushing* from the harbor at Portland, Maine, but

364   David D. Porter, *Memoir of Commodore Porter of the United States Navy.* (New York: Kessinger, 2007), 151-152. Originally published by J. Munsell, Albany, NY, 1875. The *Essex Jr.* was the former *Georgianna*, a British prize which was used to take at least three British vessels.

365   Chester G. Hearn, *Gray Raiders of the Sea.* (LSU Press, 1992), 79-93, tale of Lt. Read.

would be exchanged in time to command the privateer *Webb*, which he ran out of New Orleans in April, 1864 -- only to ground and burn her when he was unable to break through the Union blockade of the Gulf.[366]

The tale of Raphael Semmes, who racked-up an impressive sixty-four prizes with the *Alabama* and another seventeen with the *Sumter*, yields many strange truths which do much to illustrate the mindset of those commanding Confederate commerce raiders. Semmes commanded a brig during the Mexican War, which capsized in a gale while on blockade duty. He was cleared of the matter, but as the U.S. Navy was still small, there was no replacement for the young lieutenant to command. His next command -- besides a short stint with a mail steamer in 1856 -- would be CSS *Sumter*, and undoubtedly during the years, the matter must have haunted him. As a result, what probably would have pleased

***USS Kearsage* sinks *CSS Alabama*, June 19, 1864**
Naval History and Heritage Command

---

366   William Morrison Robinson, Jr., *The Confederate Privateers*. (University of South Carolina Press, 1990), 244-5.

Raphael Semmes more than anything else would have been to command a steam-frigate, crewed by the Confederacy's best sailors and equipped with ample guns, and be able to fight more traditional or Napoleonic-type engagements. While the *Alabama*'s sinking of the side-wheel steamer USS *Hatteras* in 1863 gives some indication to this mindset, a closer truth might be found when *Alabama* faced and was sunk by USS *Kearsarge* off of Cherbourg, France in 1864, a move Semmes did not have to make. As the sort of navy Semmes might have preferred was not possible for the South, he had to settle for the role of commerce raider.

This does not mean Semmes first set out to burn Yankee prizes, for he didn't. Having gathered a large number of captures, Semmes took them to Havana, where he thought they might be sold, as Spain's official position was not yet clear. He would find out soon enough, as his prizes would be released.[367] In six months with the *Sumter*, Semmes burned seven of his seventeen captures. With *Alabama*, Semmes torched fifty-four prizes, bonding only ten. Historian Chester G. Hearn makes an apt notation, "By the time he returned to sea as the captain of the *Alabama*, Semmes had become a hardened realist, and he ruthlessly used the torch."[368] None of the Confederate commanders burned indiscriminately, as time was usually taken to examine paperwork, with neutrals generally being released. However, many papers were forged in an effort to cover their Northern ownership and some neutral cargos and ships were burned in the process.[369] Closed or blockaded ports and Union diplomacy had taken a toll.

Shenandoah, which decimated the Union Arctic whaling

367   Chester G. Hearn, *Gray Raiders of the Sea*. (LSU Press, 1992), 17-19.

368   Ibid, 41.

369   Ibid, 72. Maffitt with *Florida* would burn the brig *Estelle*, even though she hauled a neutral cargo -- just one of many examples.

fleet, provides the perfect example of the need to bring prizes to adjudication. A great many of *Shenandoah's* captures came after the war had ended, which in itself was not unusual.[370] Due to extremely slow communications, this had been commonplace months after many wars ended, but the matter would eventually be straightened out at prize court. USS *Boston* provides an excellent example, for when she took a French corvette after a hard engagement outside Guadeloupe in October, 1800, the battle happened to occur after the signing of the Convention of Mortefontaine, which brought the Quasi-War to a close. The U.S. government not only returned the French warship, but also paid to repair her.[371] Such is the importance of prize courts.

The British Involvement

The British had much to gain from the American Civil War. As usual, they had played a deft political hand, especially in allowing for the building and sale of Confederate commerce raiders, most notably the dreaded *Alabama* -- although that ship escaped port mere days before it was to be seized. Not only would Britain sell vast supplies of arms and war materials

---

370   Tom Chaffin, *Sea Of Gray: The Around-the-World Odyssey of the Confederate Raider Shenandoah.* (New York: Hill and Wang, 2006), 3-8. Just as one example, ten whalers were taken by *Shenandoah* on June 28, 1865, with eight of them getting torched. While the official day that the war ended is certainly not set in stone, the blockade was officially lifted on June 23, 1865.

371   Michael A. Palmer, *Stoddert's War: Naval Operations during the Quasi-War with France, 1798-1801.* (Annapolis, MD: Naval Institute Press, 2000), 219-220. The *Boston's* crew robbed the French sailors and treated them badly enough for Captain Little to be court-martialed, cleared and soon after dismissed from service due to naval downsizing.

to both sides of the conflict, but they would also walk away from the war with the majority of American merchant shipping literally in their hands, as untold numbers of Northern ships were sold, lest they fall victim to the Confederacy. Over two hundred-fifty merchants and whalers of the Union fleet would be burnt or sunk by the Confederate cruisers alone, which would place the vast majority of the world's shipping into British ownership until this fleet faced similar destruction at the hands of German U-Boats during WWII.[372]

The historian Alexander DeConde provides a succinct note concerning the historic change wrought by this war;

"Although the maritime questions were old ones, the Civil War reversed the traditional positions of the United States and Britain. For the first time, the United States held the position of the big navy power and its opponent that of the

CSS Florida, photograph taken at Brest, France, c 1863-1864

---

372   Alexander DeConde, *A History of American Foreign Policy.* (New York: Scribner's, 1963), 257, 260.

small navy belligerent."[373]

Assuming the historically British role, the United States would play it to the hilt. The old British standard of "continuous voyage" would by practiced by the Union, who regularly stopped and checked neutral shipping, confiscating any goods bound for the Confederacy -- even if the ship was not directly headed there. The Supreme Court would back such actions with three different decisions. Britain, for the most part, was not troubled by such seizures, for they were pleased that the Americans were now playing by their rules, which Britain would apply again in The Great War, WWI.[374]

Many examples illustrate the change in Federal practices when dealing with both neutral vessels and nations. Perhaps the seizure of CSS *Florida* while docked in Bahia, Brazil in October, 1864 offers the best example. Having located *Florida* -- in need of repairs -- a scheme was hatched to send in USS *Wachusett*, sink the raider and simply sail back out of the harbor again. As Brazil's navy had no steamships to give chase, it seemed the perfect plan. However, the action was confused, Union guns overshot the *Florida*, and during the course of a general melee she was towed from the harbor and eventually sunk at her moorings in Newport News, probably not by accident. Brazil officially complained and was richly rewarded.[375] Not surprisingly, Britain was famous for such actions, from the sinking of the "League of Armed Neutrality" at Copenhagen in 1801 to a nearly identical comparison in 1683 concerning the pirate frigate *Trompeuse*, docked at St. Thomas.[376] On July 30, 1683 Captain Carlyle of HMS

---

373   Ibid, 243.
374   Ibid, 256.
375   Chester G. Hearn, *Gray Raiders of the Sea*. (LSU Press, 1992), 144-148.
376   Bernard Ireland, *Naval Warfare in the Age of Sail: War at Sea 1756-1815*. (New York: HarperCollins, 2000), 156-159, describes Nelson's

Francis sailed into the harbor at St. Thomas, set fire to *Trompeuse* and another privateer tied to the wharf and promptly sailed back out. The Danes were outraged over such events occurring in their harbor, as was France, who decried the loss of a Royal frigate, even if she had turned pirate. Britain was happy, however, and rebuked the Danes for protecting a pirate ship. Sir William stated, "This is the ship that took seventeen ships on the coast of Guinea … yet she is protected by the Government of St. Thomas, which is worse than the pirates themselves."[377]

Not surprisingly, the Union stance was quite similar. Secretary of State Seward's statement would proclaim that *Florida* belonged to "…no nation or lawful belligerent, and therefore that the harboring and supplying of these piratical ships and their crews in Brazilian ports were wrongs and injuries for which Brazil justly owes reparations to the United States…"[378]

After having violated Spanish neutrality in 1862 when USS *Montgomery* chased the British blockade runner *Blanche* aground on a reef in the shallows lying off Cuba, the U.S. government would pay a fine of $200,000 to Spain for the intrusion. *Blanche* had Spanish officials come aboard her, who raised the Spanish flag over the English banner. Two Union boat crews ignored this and began preparations to seize the ship when trouble with the boilers set the runner ablaze.[379]

The Union's ability to send representatives to practically every port on the globe -- especially the small Caribbean ones which had historically favored shady dealings with pirates and

---

victory at Copenhagen.

377   Peter Earle, *The Pirate Wars.* (New York: St. Martin's, 2003), 143-144. Quote on 144.

378   Chester G. Hearn, *Gray Raiders of the Sea.* (LSU Press, 1992), 149.

379   Stephen R. Wise, *Lifeline of the Confederacy: Blockade Running During the Civil War.* (University of South Carolina Press, 1988), 84.

smugglers -- would certainly pay big dividends in hindering Confederate operations. Both financial rewards and the possibility of naval action kept many neutral ports firmly in Union hands. St. Thomas makes for a chief example, as it was used by the Union for coaling and as a supply depot. The Confederacy would consider St. Thomas to be "simply a Yankee port."[380] The need for such a Union port was obvious during the Civil War -- as it had been in each previous U.S. naval campaign in the Caribbean -- which would lead Secretary of State Seward to begin the long process of purchasing St. Thomas.[381] The sale would get bound-up in a variety of red-tape for years, with the Virgin Islands finally being acquired by the U.S. in 1917. At that point, a naval station was no longer needed, as Puerto Rico had been acquired in the 1898 Spanish-American War. However, the islands were bought due to fears that Germany might purchase them as bases for submarines during WWI.[382]

Historically, the Royal Navy would usually find itself to be short-handed and undermanned whenever Britain was at war, which had called for centuries of press gangs and forced service. While no press gangs roved American ports, sailor shortages would form a close similarity between the Union and Britain during the Civil War, as the Union navy would suffer chronic manpower problems due to the fleet's rapid expansion.[383] However, regardless of similarities, the Union

380   Ibid, 134.
381   Isaac Dookhan, *A History of the Virgin Islands of the United States.* (Kingston, Jamaica: Canoe Press, 2005, originally published in 1974 by Caribbean Universities Press), 248, description of U.S. use of St. Thomas during Civil War, 251, tells of Seward's January, 1865 advances to purchase the island.
382   Ibid, 258-259.
383   William N. Still, Jr., "The Yankee Bluejacket." Excerpted from *Raiders and Blockaders: The American Civil War Afloat.* (Brassey's, 1998), 54. Originally published in 1985 by *Historical Times.*

navy generally looked on British sailors as though they were the enemy, due to Britain's various dealings with the Confederacy, especially the sale of commerce raiders. As a result, when USS *Powhatan* pulled into St. Thomas and saw a British squadron at anchor, tempers immediately flared. Shore leave was granted without hesitation, with the *Powhatan*'s starboard watch allowed ashore for twenty-four hour liberty, later to be followed by the port-side watch. After a couple of hours went by, a letter arrived from the British admiral, describing a near-riot between Union and British sailors. In response, Union Admiral James Lardner ordered the rest of the crew ashore. Not long after, the Danish garrison was turned out to quell the riot and was promptly driven back into their forts. *Powhatan*'s crew would be rounded up and put back aboard by midnight, with three sailors killed and a variety of wounded. The Royal Navy would suffer similar casualties.[384]

Relations between Britain, the Union and the reconstituted United States would reflect much of the animosity shown by their sailors. By mid-1863, it was becoming obvious to Britain that the Union would win the war. As a result, the British government took a firmer stance on their neutrality obligations and seized two ironclad rams, along with *Alabama*'s sister-ship.[385] This would not be enough for the United States, however, who not only lost millions of dollars in destroyed merchant ships and cargos due to English-built Confederate cruisers, but also the merchant carrying trade itself. Many blamed England for the length of the war, due to British blockade runners carrying British arms and powder, sailing from British ports. After the war was over, U.S. diplo-

---

384   Ibid, 71-72.
385   Alexander DeConde, *A History of American Foreign Policy*. (New York: Scribner's, 1963), 258-259. *Alexandra* was *Alabama*'s "sister-ship," seized on April 5, 1863.

mats constantly harried their British counterparts in order to gain restitution for damages wrought by Confederate cruisers. Britain would show no interest until CSS *Shenandoah* came home to roost in Liverpool on November 6, 1865, months after the war was over. Even so, what truly made arbitration and finally restitution possible was the arrival of a U.S. Navy squadron in 1866, which toured several English ports. The double-turreted monitor USS *Miantonomoh* caused quite a stir, due to a lack of Royal Navy ironclads. The London *Times* stated, "In fact, the wolf was in the fold, and the whole flock was at its mercy."[386] A few months later, Britain agreed to arbitration, which would take six years to bring to fruition. The "*Alabama* Claims" were settled in 1872, with Britain paying the United States $15,500,000 for damages inflicted by British-built cruisers, but not all claims were paid. For example, *Shenandoah*'s first few prizes were not included, only those

CSS Shenandoah
Naval History and Heritage Command

which had occurred after the ship docked at Melbourne, Australia, at which time it was deemed that she should have been seized. Some damages to neutral shipping was also paid out by the United States, resulting from several seizures made during the war.[387]

While it is not difficult to argue that the Union played the British role on the high seas to a near-mirror image, the situation would be back to "normal" by the next large war

---

386   Chester G. Hearn, *Gray Raiders of the Sea.* (LSU Press, 1992), 303. *Shenandoah* note on 298-299.
387   Ibid, 307-308.

**German U-Boat Pirates
World War I
Library of Congress**

-- World War I. Once more, seized American shipping would cause a problem. Historian Robert H. Ferrell notes, "American relations with Britain in 1916 became almost as taut as those with Germany."[388] However, the uncompromising destruction of the German U-Boat and subsequent "unrestricted" campaign of submarine warfare launched by Germany in February, 1917 would lead the U.S. to a declaration of war two months later. Ferrell sums it up nicely. "It was Germany's submarine measures, above anything else, that brought the United States into the First World War in 1917."[389]

Certainly, it is hard not to note the comparisons with American Civil War commerce raiding. New brands of destruction are often abhorred. Especially notable here is that the Confederates also built the submarine CSS *Hunley*, the first submarine ever to sink a ship, the blockader USS *Housatonic*.[390] While modern warships and a lack of large-scale revolutions did much to erase the age-old need for privateers, it would be the submarine which truly replaced them.

---

388   Robert H. Ferrell, *American Diplomacy: The Twentieth Century.* (New York: Norton, 1988), 131-132.
389   Ibid, 131-134, quote on 128. 390 William N. Still, Jr., "Technology Afloat." Excerpted from *Raiders and Blockaders: The American Civil War Afloat.* (Brassey's, 1998), 49. Originally published in 1975 by *Historical Times.*
390   William N. Still, Jr., "Technology Afloat." Excerpted from *Raiders and Blockaders: The American Civil War Afloat.* (Brassey's, 1998), 49. Originally published in 1975 by *Historical Times.*

World War I Navy Recruiting Poster by W. A. Allen
Library of Congress

Practical Piracy

While the commerce raiders of the Confederacy were pirates by technicality, there are a variety of parallels which can be drawn between their crews and those of the pirates of old. This is especially notable regarding the habits of the cruiser commanders. While drawing comparisons to the likes of Blackbeard might be a stretch, the hallmark of any successful pirate captain was how he handled his crew.

Raphael Semmes, for having spent the majority of his naval career on land prior to the Civil War, appears to have been the perfect choice for commanding commerce raiders. Not long after running CSS *Sumter* past the Union blockade out of New Orleans, Semmes entered port at Cienfuegos, Cuba and received small arms fire from Spanish soldiers. Never having seen a Confederate banner before, they didn't know what to make of it and mistook the *Sumter* for a pirate ship. Later, when entrance into Curacao was at first denied, Semmes stood his ship a short distance off the harbor and "worked his guns," firing several exploding shells toward shore. Nearly as soon as the last shot was fired, *Sumter* was permitted in port.[391]

An interesting aspect of the *Sumter*'s crew was that it was comprised almost exclusively of foreigners, which is almost ironic, as the ship was commissioned in New Orleans and first sailed from that port.[392] This is not very surprising, however, as during the age of sail -- especially post-1815 -- a sailor was bound to a merchant ship until he desired a change.

---

391   Chester G. Hearn, *Gray Raiders of the Sea.* (LSU Press, 1992), 17 Cuba notation, 20 Curacao.
392   William N. Still, Jr., "The Confederate Tar." Excerpted from *Raiders and Blockaders: The American Civil War Afloat.* (Brassey's, 1998), 84.

Frequently changing berths was a standard among most sea-men. This could mean a one-way trip, or perhaps round-trip, depending upon the initial agreement. Since the rate of pay was an international standard, it was only natural that a great many foreign sailors found themselves at New Orleans during the outbreak of the American Civil War. Many of these sailors signed-on not only for a higher rate of pay, but also for the chance at lucrative prize money. However, their "enlistments" lasted for a longer duration that what many were accustomed to -- at least six month terms -- and when it became apparent that no prize money would be forthcoming from burnt prizes, many "jumped ship" at the first opportunity. *Sumter* left port with ninety-six sailors and was left with half that number when she found herself blockaded in Gibraltar six months later. Of the eighteen vessels the ship captured, only $1,100 in hard currency was found aboard them.[393] The standard for

Cpt. Semmes and Lt. Kell aboard the *CSS Alabama*
Naval History and Heritage Command

---

393 Chester G. Hearn, *Gray Raiders of the Sea.* (LSU Press, 1992), 37.

desertion aboard Confederate raiders was set when Semmes pulled into Martinique, as noted by historian Chester G. Hearn; "The crew was given shore leave, but this soon deteriorated into a drunken binge, fights, and desertions." While liberty would be rarely granted for many cruisers as a result, Semmes gladly allowed the governor of Bahia, Brazil to jail his drunken sailors, as they were easier to collect.[394]

Easily, Semmes' mark on history will be forever linked with that of CSS *Alabama*, a rightful recognition on both counts. His first nine months witnessed thirty-eight captures, the vast majority of which became floating bonfires. The names *Alabama* and Semmes spread terror across the Atlantic as few others had -- notoriety akin to that received by Lord Cochrane and a handful of pirates from the Golden Age. Before falling victim to *Alabama*, captain Jabez H. Snow of the *Highlander* supposedly had nightmares for three years concerning such a meeting. "The fact is, I have had constant visions of the *Alabama* by night and by day; she has been chasing me in my sleep, and riding me like a night-mare..."[395] Semmes would even catch the same ship twice, one belonging to

"The Approach of the British Pirate *Alabama*"
Naval History and Heritage Museum

---

394   Ibid, 29 quote, 198 Brazil jailing.
395   Chester G. Hearn, *Gray Raiders of the Sea.* (LSU Press, 1992), 217.

the Wales family, who had already suffered one ship burnt. The ship caught twice was carrying neutral cargos and was released each time after bonding.[396]

There are several differences between Semmes' cruises aboard the *Sumter* and *Alabama*, one of which being there were twenty marines aboard *Sumter* and none on *Alabama*.[397] The primary reason marines are found aboard warships is to keep order. This seemingly small item is actually of large importance, especially if a possible mutiny should erupt. Truly, the sixty-four vessels captured can be owed not primarily to the advanced technology aboard *Alabama* -- for she was one of the most technologically advanced ships in the world at the time -- but can be credited to the actions Semmes took as captain of a crew comprised mainly of foreign mercenary seamen.

Lt. Arthur Sinclair wrote a memoir of his time aboard *Alabama* and listed what inducements were used to attract foreign crewmembers; "most alluring -- double pay, *in gold*, generous tobacco *ad libitum*, grog twice a day and in gernerous quantity, prospective prize money..."[398] The seamen were also allowed to purchase monkeys and parrots to keep as pets. Mindful of a sailor's historical penchant for music and song, Semmes made sure to always have a variety of musical instruments on board.[399] Captain (Lt. in actual rank) Waddell did not share such foresight, as it appeared the only musical instrument aboard *Shenandoah* for thirteen months was a badly played accordion.[400]

---

396   Ibid, 192.

397   Ibid, 181 *Alabama* note, 11 *Sumter*.

398   William N. Still, Jr., "The Confederate Tar." Excerpted from *Raiders and Blockaders: The American Civil War Afloat*. (Brassey's, 1998), 85.

399   Ibid, 91.

400   Tom Chaffin, *Sea Of Gray: The Around-the-World Odyssey of the*

Writing of his crew, Semmes states; "The fact is, I have a precious set of rascals onboard -- faithless in the matter of abiding by their contracts, liars, thieves, and drunkards."[401] Certainly, he was not exaggerating, although it should be noted that even without marines to keep the peace, no one was murdered aboard *Alabama*. Many Union warships -- some of which were often full of foreign crewmen -- could not boast such a record, especially USS *Powhatten*, whose decks witnessed a few murders and even more fights and stabbings quite some time before brawling with English sailors after hitting port at St. Thomas.[402] Semmes was merely noting common attributes of the average sailor. Such stereotyping was undoubtedly magnified by the sort of seaman who might be attracted to serving on a foreign warship strictly for pay -- the very same attributes which held true for those who sailed during piracy's Golden Age. No better example can be found but for the many foreign sailors who served aboard the Confederacy's home water vessels. The crew of CSS *Morgan* has been described by one of her officers as "a set of desperate cutthroats." However, the many foreign seamen in the Charleston Squadron proved to be polar opposites, with Lt. William H. Parker of CSS *Beaufort* swearing that such men comprised the best crew he ever had.[403]

Charles Tyng "worked his way up" to owning and operating two brigs, having made his start on a merchantman as

Confederate Raider Shenandoah. (New York: Hill and Wang, 2006), 309.
401   Chester G. Hearn, *Gray Raiders of the Sea.* (LSU Press, 1992), 203.
402   William N. Still, Jr., "The Yankee Bluejacket." Excerpted from *Raiders and Blockaders: The American Civil War Afloat.* (Brassey's, 1998), 71.
403   William N. Still, Jr., "The Confederate Tar." Excerpted from *Raiders and Blockaders: The American Civil War Afloat.* (Brassey's, 1998), 86-87, quote on 86.

a boy in 1815 after the War of 1812. According to Tyng, most sailors had to be treated as though they were children. As mate aboard the brig *Cadet* in 1822, the new crew arrived just before the vessel's departure, and most of them were still drunk. One of them refused to work the capstan correctly, which Tyng knew to be an attempt to try him. Grabbing a bar for the capstan, Tyng told the sailor to do the job the right way, and then smacked him with the capstan bar when the sailor got mouthy. One of the sailor's mates made a rush at Tyng, who sent the man sprawling with another swing. After that, Tyng states the crew worked out just fine. Years later a similar incident happened at sea under his command, which led to Tyng beating several men with a boat tiller. Afterwards, he states; "...they proved as good a set of men as I ever had. All they required was to be impressed that they had somebody to govern them."[404]

Commander James Iredell Waddell
Captain of *CSS Shenandoah*
Naval History and Heritage Museum

Both *Shenandoah* and *Alabama* also obtained crewmen from captured ships, although most of them had to be "persuaded." Semmes would often have the captured crews placed in irons, chained to the deck.[405] After a couple days of weather

---

404   Charles Tyng, *Before the Wind: The Memoir of an American Sea Captain, 1808-1833*. (New York: Penguin, 1999), 88-889 capstan incident, 151-152 tiller incident, quote on 152. This manuscript came from a found, previously unpublished source of Tyng's handwritten memoir.
405   Chester G. Hearn, *Gray Raiders of the Sea*. (LSU Press, 1992), 173.

and waves, some men would eventually sign-on. Of course, not only would these sailors have tired of their bonds, but by then all pertinent information would have been gleaned from passing crewmembers; such as how many men have been killed (none) and all of the details pertaining to pay and benefits. Things were done differently aboard *Shenandoah*, as along with being clapped in irons and made to share space where the animals were housed, many of these men were "triced-up" -- hung from a beam with their thumbs tied together, standing on tip-toes -- until joining the Confederates became more appealing. Lt. Whittle noted the effectiveness of this tactic; "The tricing up had the most wonderful effect -- in two hours the man begged to be let down, as he desired to ship."[406]

"Tricing" saw use as a punishment aboard naval vessels after the U.S. Navy abolished flogging in 1850, although it was not uniformly practiced, nor was it the only form of punishment.[407] Flogging was not reinstituted in either navy during the war, although it was still used by the Union Army. However, the age-old grog ration ended for Union sailors on July 14, 1862 when President Lincoln signed the act abolishing the dispensation of alcohol on warships, except for medicinal purposes. Sailors were paid an extra five cents per day as compensation, although whiskey was still available from sutlers and was one of the first items searched for aboard

---

406   Tom Chaffin, *Sea Of Gray: The Around-the-World Odyssey of the Confederate Raider Shenandoah*. (New York: Hill and Wang, 2006), 107. The book is littered with such examples, which seems to have been an easily-earned punishment. Rear Admiral John Dahlgren -- designer of the "Dahlgren" naval guns -- was chastised by Welles.

407   Claude G. Berube and John A. Rodgaard, *A Call to the Sea: Captain Charles Stewart of the USS Constitution*. (Washington: Potomac Books, 2005), 238-239. President Millard Fillmore signed the act into law September 2, 1850.

prizes. Not all captains agreed with the grog restriction, however, and one commander earned the wrath of Navy Secretary Welles for having appropriated six barrels of whiskey for use "under medical direction."[408]

Confederate cruisers had a grog ration twice a day, which was increased to three times per day aboard *Shenandoah* by the end of her cruise. The Confederate home navy did not generally have a grog ration, however.[409] The reason for this is not precisely clear, but perhaps the various Confederate state laws which banned using grains to distill spirits had something to do with it.[410] Regardless, both *Shenandoah* and *Alabama* would suffer drunken "mutinies" after finding liquor aboard prizes, even though Semmes torched one prize full of various spirits in order to keep it from his crew.[411] Such drunken binges have generally proven to be the moments when real mutinies occurred and real trouble brewed. Even in 1684, William Dampier made a variety of notes pertaining to the turbulence involved in such unchecked drunkenness.[412] Many a pirate captain lost his command during such events, along with suffering even worse fates. While a lack of marines on either

408   William N. Still, Jr., "The Yankee Bluejacket." Excerpted from *Raiders and Blockaders: The American Civil War Afloat.* (Brassey's, 1998), 72, went into effect September 1, 1862. Act was pressured by temperance movement.

409   William N. Still, Jr., "The Confederate Tar." Excerpted from *Raiders and Blockaders: The American Civil War Afloat.* (Brassey's, 1998), 93.

410   Emory M. Thomas, *The Confederacy as a Revolutionary Experience.* (University of South Carolina Press, 1991), 71. Generally the same laws also forbade the sale of such alcohol.

411   William N. Still, Jr., "The Confedcrate Tar." Excerpted from *Raiders and Blockaders: The American Civil War Afloat.* (Brassey's, 1998), 93.

412   William Dampier, *A New Voyage Round the World.* (Warwick, NY: 1500 Books, 2007), 60. Reprinted from 1717 6th edition, originally published in 1697.

Confederate ship certainly must have made for a nervous few days, neither event developed into anything serious. A few men aboard *Shenandoah* were clapped in irons, along with some from *Alabama*. However, on *Alabama*, George Forrest was found guilty of inciting mutiny and then put ashore on a whaling island off Venezuela -- an action reminiscent of the old pirate favorite of marooning guilty crewmen on a desert isle[413]. Forrest had served aboard *Sumter*, deserted, and was later allowed to sign-on when he was found crewing a prize the *Alabama* captured. Had he been an actual Confederate sailor, the punishment would have been hanging.[414] However, under the circumstances -- especially those which held potential international political problems -- Semmes did not hang Forrest, as the crew probably would have deemed it "too harsh." Jean Laffite had faced similar circumstances concerning a few of his associates who had stolen slaves, robbing a well-placed man named Lyons. Laffite only hung one of the thieves and banished the others, as something stiffer wouldn't have sat well with the rest of the men.[415] In this regard, Semmes was a natural commander. While sailors on both vessels pulled a few capers, in the end, those aboard *Alabama* chose to follow Semmes into battle against USS *Kearsarge*. However, with tensions high, the officers aboard *Shenandoah* carried pistols during the last few weeks of their cruise as actual mutiny still appeared to be a distinct possibility.[416] Of course, many of the

413   Peter Earle, *The Pirate Wars*. (New York: St. Martin's, 2003), 174. Pirates marooned during the Golden Age were generally given a pistol, a bottle of powder, another of shot and one filled with water. As it was with Forrest, he found employment on a whaler almost immediately.

414   Chester G. Hearn, *Gray Raiders of the Sea*. (LSU Press, 1992), 182-183.

415   William C. Davis, *The Pirates Laffite: The Treacherous World of the Corsairs of the Gulf*. (New York: Harcourt, 2005), 415.

416   Tom Chaffin, *Sea Of Gray: The Around-the-World Odyssey of the Confederate Raider Shenandoah*. (New York: Hill and Wang, 2006), 351.

USS *Kearsarge*
Naval History and Heritage Command

officers aboard *Shenandoah* exasperated various issues, as there were a host of young men who were on their first cruise and others with little actual experience, which led to unrealistic expectations.[417] Semmes was a bit more fortunate in this area and had more experienced officers, some of whom had previously served under him aboard *Sumter*. As both ships were reported to be rather dirty and unkempt, along with their crews, this goes a long way to illustrate the Confederate need for foreign crewmen and the subsequent power these men wielded.[418]

There are other practices shared by both Semmes and the pirates of old, but again, these are not sure signs of pure piracy

---

417   Ibid, 314-315, among a host of other examples.
418   Chester G. Hearn, *Gray Raiders of the Sea*. (LSU Press, 1992), 213 details on *Alabama*. Also, Tom Chaffin, *Sea Of Gray: The Around-the-World Odyssey of the Confederate Raider Shenandoah*. (New York: Hill and Wang, 2006), 142 for *Shenandoah*. Retired Royal Navy Captain Charles B. Payne noted; "The state of the vessel…both slovenly and dirty." Similar thoughts on crew.

as much as they are indications of how bending the rules of war was practiced by nearly every successful captain -- be he pirate, privateer or an officer of the state. Semmes changed *Alabama's* appearance frequently, as noted by historian Chester G. Hearn; "Semmes took great pains to disguise his ship's appearance: At times the *Alabama* had the look of a peaceful merchant sailing vessel laden with cargo; at other times she appeared to be a swift British man-of-war..."[419]

Upgrading vessels and changing their appearance was a long-held pirate practice, although one not limited only to outlaws. Lord Cochrane tried repeatedly to up-gun the little brig *Speedy*, and took the effort not only to paint her like a similar Danish brig which roamed the Mediterranean, but also to obtain a Dane, complete with officer's uniform. When cornered by a Spanish frigate in late 1800 -- most likely the *Gamo*, which would later become Cochrane's most famous prize -- Cochrane raised the quarantine flag and had his Dane warn-off a boatload of Spaniards who rowed over to investigate. Results were as expected:

"On the boat coming within hail -- for the yellow flag effectually repressed the enemy's desire to board us -- our mock officer informed the Spaniards that we were two days from Algiers, where at the time the plague was violently raging. This was enough. The boat returned to the frigate, which, wishing us a good voyage, filled, and made sail, whilst we did the same."[420]

Semmes would utilize his British crewmen in a similar role, sending them out to board and inspect potential prizes,

---

419   Chester G. Hearn, *Gray Raiders of the Sea.* (LSU Press, 1992), 173.

420   Lord Thomas Cochrane, "The Cruise of the *Speedy*." Excerpted from *Life Before the Mast: Sailors' eyewitness accounts from the age of fighting ships,* edited by Jon. E. Lewis. (New York, Carroll & Graf, 2002), 97-99, quote on 98. Taken from a portion of Cochrane's memoir.

many of which never suspected that they had encountered a Confederate warship. Such practices made it even harder to track down the raider.[421]

By far, the majority of people captured aboard prize vessels were treated fairly well, the degree of difference often relating to available space. Certainly, captured and thus potential crewmen aboard *Shenandoah* suffered recruiting practices that the other Confederate raiders did not use. However, most others were treated as well as possible, given the circumstances. Most of these stories are more poignant than piratical; such as the husbands and wives forced to watch their fishing schooners burst into flames, or the Arctic whaler forced to set fire to his own ship. *Shenandoah* became so crowded that she ended up towing twelve longboats loaded with captives through the icy Bering Sea. Ebenezer Nye, captain/owner of the burnt whaler *Abigail* managed to escape while aboard a prize, slipping off with some of his men in two whaleboats which traveled some 187 miles before they were picked up by the bark *Mercury*. Several potential prizes received fair warning as a result.[422] One whaler made a show at defending himself by brandishing "bomb guns" loaded with ad-hoc grapeshot, but quickly reconsidered and

SJ Waring retaken by Tilghman
Naval History and Heritage
Command

---

421   Chester G. Hearn, *Gray Raiders of the Sea.* (LSU Press, 1992), 173-174.
422   Ibid, 287-289.

THE ATTACK ON THE SECOND MATE.

William Tilghman and his axe
Naval History and Heritage Command

gave up his ship. Captain James M. Clark would have the misfortune of commanding one ship which was sunk by *Alabama*, and another which was burnt by *Shenandoah*.[423]

One of the most noteworthy Confederate merchant captures concerns the schooner *S.J. Waring*, taken prize by the privateer *Jefferson Davis* during the summer of 1861. Nearing Charleston ten days after her capture, *S.J. Waring*'s five-man prize crew was overwhelmed during the night by a freeman cook named Tillman, armed with an axe. Tillman bashed in the heads of three of the prize crew while they slept and sailed to New York with the help of others on board. The two

---

423   Tom Chaffin, *Sea Of Gray: The Around-the-World Odyssey of the Confederate Raider Shenandoah*. (New York: Hill and Wang, 2006), 275-276. Captain of the whaler *Favorite* prepared to fight. A "bomb gun" was similar in appearance to a blunderbuss and was used to launch harpoons. James M. Clark note on 268.

remaining Confederates were put on trial for piracy and later interned as prisoners of war when all Union piracy trials were stopped due to the threat of Confederate reprisals. Tillman was awarded $7,000 in salvage money from the prize court after adjudication. For a short period of time soon after, P.T. Barnum put Tillman in his show, along with his axe.[424]

---

424   William Morrison Robinson, Jr., *The Confederate Privateers.* (University of South Carolina Press, 1990), 84-88.

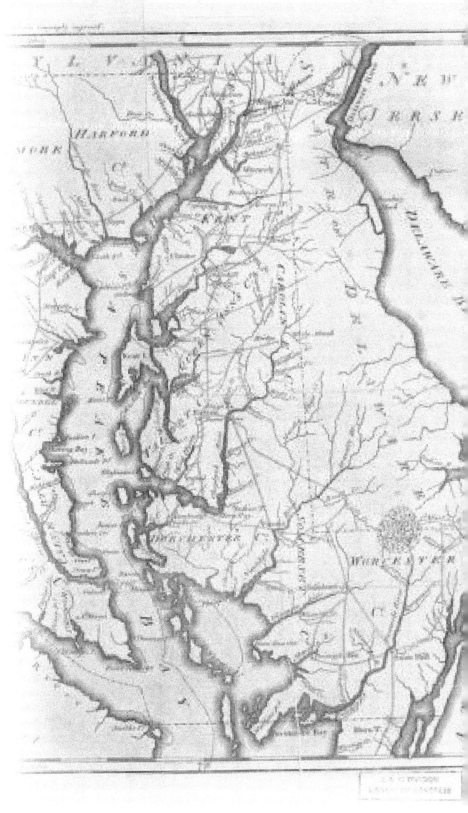

Bibliography

Bell, Madison Smartt, *Toussaint Louverture: A Biography*. (New York: Random House, 2007).

Berkin, Carol, *A Brilliant Solution: Inventing the American Constitution*. (New York: Harcourt, 2003).

Berube, Claude G. and Rodgaard, John A., *A Call to the Sea: Captain Charles Stewart of the USS Constitution*. (Washington: Potomac Books, 2005).

Bobrick, Benson, *Angel in the Whirlwind: The Triumph of the American Revolution*. (New York: Penguin, 1998).

Borneman, Walter R., *1812: The War that Forged a Nation*. (New York: Harper Collins, 2004).

Brands, H.W., *Andrew Jackson: His Life and Times*. (New York: Doubleday, 2005).

Castel, Albert & Goodrich, Tom, *Bloody Bill Anderson: The Short, Savage Life of a Civil War Guerilla*. (University of Kansas Press, 1998.).

Chaffin, Tom, *Sea Of Gray: The Around-the-World Odyssey of the Confederate Raider Shenandoah*. (New York: Hill and Wang, 2006).

Chatterton, E. Keble, *King's Cutters and Smugglers*. (London: BiblioBazaar, 2007). Originally published in 1912.

Cochrane, Lord Thomas, "The Cruise of the *Speedy*." Excerpted from *Life Before the Mast: Sailors' eyewitness accounts from the age of fighting ships,* edited by Jon. E. Lewis. (New York, Carroll & Graf, 2002).

Craton, Michael, *A History of the Bahamas.* (San Salvador Press, 1999, first printed 1962).

Dampier, William, *A New Voyage Round the World.* (Warwick, NY: 1500 Books, 2007). Reprinted from 1717 6th edition, originally published in 1697.

Davis, William C., *The Cause Lost: Myths and Realities of the Confederacy.* (University of Kansas Press, 1996).

Davis, William C., *The Pirates Laffite: The Treacherous World of the Corsairs of the Gulf.* (New York: Harcourt, 2005).

DeConde, Alexander, *A History of American Foreign Policy.* (New York: Scribner's, 1963).

DeConde, Alexander, *The Quasi-War: The Politics and Diplomacy of the Undeclared War with France, 1797-1801.* (New York: Scribners, 1966).

Dookhan, Isaac, *A History of the Virgin Islands of the United States.* (Kingston, Jamaica: Canoe Press, 2005, originally published in 1974 by Caribbean Universities Press).

Earle, Peter, *The Pirate Wars.* (New York: St. Martin's, 2003).

Ellis, Joseph J., *American Creation: Triumphs and Tragedies at the Founding of the Republic.* (New York: Knopf, 2007).

Ferguson, Eugene S., *Truxton of the Constellation: The Life of Commodore Thomas Truxton, U.S. Navy, 1755-1822.* (Baltimore: Johns Hopkins University Press, 2000). Originally published in 1956.

Ferrell, Robert H., *American Diplomacy: The Twentieth Century.* (New York: Norton, 1988).

Formisano, Ronald P.,"James Madison," edited by Brinkley, Dyer, et al, *The American Presidency.* (New York: Houghton-Mifflin, 2004).

Fowler, William M., Jr., *Jack Tars and Commodores: The American Navy, 1783-1815,* (New York: Houghton Mifflin, 1984).

Graham, Gerald S., editor, *The Navy and South America, 1807-1823: Correspondence of the Commanders-in-Chief on the South American Station.* (London, Navy Records Society, 1962).

Harvey, Robert, *A Few Bloody Noses: The Realities and Mythologies of the American Revolution.* (New York: Overlook Press, 2001).

Harvey, Robert, *Cochrane: The Life and Exploits of a Fighting Captain.* (New York: Carroll and Graf, 2000).

Hearn, Chester G., *Gray Raiders of the Sea.* (LSU Press, 1992).

Hoffecker, Carol E., *Delaware: A Bicentennial History.* (New York: W.W. Norton, 1977).

Horwood, Harold and Butts, Ed, *Bandits and Privateers: Canada in the Age of Gunpowder*. (Halifax: Doubleday, 1988).

Howe, Daniel Walker, *What Hath God Wrought: The Transformation of America, 1815-1848*. (New York: Oxford, 2007).

Ireland, Bernard, *Naval Warfare in the Age of Sail: War at Sea 1756-1815*. (New York: HarperCollins, 2000).

King, Irving H., *The Coast Guard Under Sail: The U.S. Revenue Cutter Service 1789-1865*. (Annapolis, MD: Naval Institute Press, 1989).

Lender, Mark E., "The Mind of the Rank and File: Patriotism and Motivation in the Continental Line," from William C. Wright, ed, *New Jersey in the American Revolution*, vol.3, 1976. Excerpted from *Major Problems in American Military History*. (New York: Houghton Mifflin, 1999).

Liell, Scott, *46 Pages: Thomas Paine, Common Sense, and the Turning Point to Independence*. (Philadelphia: Running Press, 2003).

Little, George, "Privateering," from *Life Before the Mast: Sailors' eyewitness accounts from the age of fighting ships*, edited by Jon. E. Lewis. (New York, Carroll & Graf, 2002).

Maier, Pauline, *American Scripture*. (New York: Knopf, 1997).

McLoughlin, William G., *Rhode Island: A History*. (New York: W.W. Norton, 1978, 1986).

McPherson, James M., *Abraham Lincoln and the Second American Revolution.* (New York: Oxford, 1991).

McPherson, James M., *Drawn with the Sword: Reflections on the American Civil War.* (New York: Oxford, 1996).

Morgan, Michael, *Pirates and Patriots: Tales of the Delaware Coast.* (New York: Algora: 2005).

Morison, Samuel Eliot, *John Paul Jones: A Sailor's Biography.* (New York: Little, Brown and Co., 1959).

Morrissey, Charles T., *Vermont: A History.* (New York: W.W. Norton, 1984).

Nelson, James L., *George Washington's Secret Navy.* (New York: McGraw-Hill, 2008).

Orenstein, Jeffrey, "Joseph Almeida: Portrait of a Privateer, Pirate & Plantiff, Part I," excerpted from *The Green Bag: An Entertaining Journal of Law* Volume 10, no.2 (Spring, 2007).

Palmer, Michael A., *Stoddert's War: Naval Operations during the Quasi-War with France, 1798-1801.* (Annapolis, MD: Naval Institute Press, 2000). Originally published by South Carolina University Press, 1987.

Patton, Robert H., *Patriot Pirates.* (New York: Random House, 2008).

Porter, David D., *Memoir of Commodore Porter of the United*

States Navy. (New York: Kessinger, 2007). Originally published by J. Munsell, Albany, NY, 1875.

Robinson, William Morrison Jr, *The Confederate Privateers.* (University of South Carolina Press, 1990). Originally published 1928 by Yale University Press.

Roland, Charles P., *An American Iliad: The Story of the Civil War.* (New York: McGraw-Hill, 2002).

Royster, Charles, *A Revolutionary People at War: The Continental Army and American Character, 1775-1783.* Published by the Institute of Early American History and Culture. (University of North Carolina Press, 1980). Excerpted from *Major Problems in American Military History.* (New York: Houghton Mifflin, 1999).

Sherburne, Andrew, *The Memoirs of Andrew Sherburne.* (Connecticut: Linnet Books, 1993). First published in 1824.

Shomette, Donald G., *Pirates on the Chesapeake.* (Centreville, MD: Tidewater, 1985).

Still, William N. Jr., "The Confederate Tar," "The Yankee Bluejacket," "Technology Afloat," "A Naval Sieve: The Union Blockade in the Civil War." Excerpted from *Raiders and Blockaders: The American Civil War Afloat.* (Brassey's, 1998). Most pieces originally published in *Civil War Times.*

Sugden, John, *Nelson: A Dream of Glory, 1758-1797.* (New York: Henry Holt, 2004).

Syrett, David, *The Royal Navy in European Waters during the American Revolutionary War.* (University of South Carolina Press: 1998).

Taylor, John M., "The Overblown *Trent* Affair," "John Taylor Wood: Confederate Commando." Originally published in *America's Civil War.* Excerpted from Still, Taylor and Delaney's *Raiders and Blockaders: The American Civil War Afloat.* (Washington, D.C.: Brassey's, 1998).

Thomas, Emory M., *The Confederacy as a Revolutionary Experience.* (University of South Carolina Press, 1991).

Tilley, John A., *The British Navy and the American Revolution.* (University of South Carolina Press, 1987).

Tyng, Charles, *Before the Wind: The Memoir of an American Sea Captain, 1808-1833.* (New York: Penguin, 1999).

Volo, James M., *Blue Water Patriots: The American Revolution Afloat.* (New York : Rowman & Littlefield, 2006).

Wheeler, Richard, *In Pirate Waters: Captain David Porter, USN, and America's war on piracy in the West Indies.* (New York, Crowell, 1969).

Wise, Stephen R., *Lifeline of the Confederacy: Blockade Running During the Civil War.* (University of South Carolina Press, 1988).

Websites

www.history.navy.mil\seagull.htm. Unknown Author.

www.uscg.mil/history/first10cutters/LouisianaII.html/Louisiana_1825.html. Unknown Author

www.usskidd.com/ships-la-uscg.html. Unknown author, information attributed to USCG.

CPSIA information can be obtained
at www.ICGtesting.com
Printed in the USA
LVHW070841250323
742592LV00018B/1512

9 781628 060706